Y0-BSA-500

Criminal Justice Research and Practice

The Northeastern Series on Gender, Crime, and Law

Edited by Claire Renzetti

For a complete list of books in this series, please visit
www.upne.com and www.upne.com/series/NGCL.html

Criminal Justice Research and Practice

Diverse Voices from the Field

Edited by Susan L. Miller

Northeastern University Press
Boston
Published by University Press of New England
Hanover and London

Published by University Press of New England,
One Court Street, Lebanon, NH 03766
www.upne.com

© 2007 by Northeastern University Press
Printed in the United States of America
5 4 3 2 1

All rights reserved. No part of this book may be reproduced in any form or by any
electronic or mechanical means, including storage and retrieval systems, without
permission in writing from the publisher, except by a reviewer, who may quote
brief passages in a review. Members of educational institutions and organizations
wishing to photocopy any of the work for classroom use, or authors and publishers
who would like to obtain permission for any of the material in the work, should contact
Permissions, University Press of New England, One Court Street, Lebanon, NH 03766.

Library of Congress Cataloging-in-Publication Data
Criminal justice research and practice : diverse voices from the field / edited
by Susan L. Miller.
   p.   cm. — (Northeastern series on gender, crime, and law)
Includes bibliographical references and index.
ISBN-13: 978-1-55553-684-8 (cloth : alk. paper)
ISBN-10: 1-55553-684-0 (cloth : alk. paper)
ISBN-13: 978-1-55553-685-5 (pbk. : alk. paper)
ISBN-10: 1-55553-685-9 (pbk. : alk. paper)
1. Criminology—Study and teaching.
2. Criminal justice, Administration of.
I. Miller, Susan L.
HV6025.C735 2007
364.072—dc22   2007025457

 University Press of New England is a member of the Green Press Initiative.
The paper used in this book meets their minimum requirement for recycled paper.

For my son Connor, and for my students,
all who present different challenges and joys

Contents

III Sites of Inquiry: Topics and Samples

Foreword

When I read *Criminal Justice Research and Practice: Diverse Voices from the Field*, the feminist slogan, "the personal is political" immediately came to mind. Susan Miller and the authors she has brought together in this volume connect their biographies with the research and practice of criminology and criminal justice. If you are a student reading this book, the people whose work you have likely read in your criminal justice and sociology courses will become more "real" to you, less distant as individuals. At the same time, you will also get a sense of the wide range of career possibilities that criminology and criminal justice hold for you. Many of the students who come to speak with me about graduate school or careers convey a sense of personal inadequacy mixed with a substantial measure of impatience. They seem to feel that they should know, at that moment, their precise career path and how to navigate it flawlessly. That they do not know these things clearly perplexes and disturbs them. I hope that in reading this book students will take some comfort in learning that many successful researchers and practitioners have struggled—and continue to struggle—with the same questions and doubts: What do I *want* to do? What would I *love* to do? What stands in my way, and how can I overcome these barriers? Who are my allies and guides? What if I change my mind?

This book gives students a sense of possibilities and shows how career paths often are not narrow and linear, but rather circuitous, with lots of detours and bends in the road. Some of the detours and bends are chosen and desirable, while some are imposed because of inequalities such as sexism, racism, and heterosexism. Indeed, one of the strengths of this book is that it is not filled with "happily ever after" tales. Authors such as Daniel Atkins and Eliza Patten, Jill McCorkel, Angela Moore Parmley and Jocelyn Fontaine, Walter DeKeseredy, and Michelle Meloy discuss how various elements of their individual identities—sex, race/ethnicity, social class, sexual orientation—have influenced their career choices and paths, affected their relationships with those with whom they work, and helped shape their perspectives of justice and the criminal legal system. They relate as well how these inequalities impact the lives of victims and offenders, and their sense of sadness and outrage at the unfairness that results comes across clearly in their writing. As some of the authors in this volume remind us, many of the people with whom many criminologists and criminal justice practitioners interact have had horrendous things happen to them and have themselves done horrendous things. But neither of these negates their humanity nor their right to be treated fairly, particularly in a system that is supposedly predicated on fairness. Although the authors in this volume are very different from one another, a common characteristic that unifies them is their commitment to justice; even when things do not turn out the way they would like, their commitment to justice remains a primary motivator to carry on. I hope that students reading this book will find the authors' passion for justice inspiring and motivating—so much so that they will incorporate it into their own reflections on what motivates them toward a career in criminology or criminal justice.

If you are a teacher, researcher, or practitioner reading this book, it will likely lead you to reflect on your motivations and experiences in the field, too. In reading the chapter by Joanne Belknap and Hillary Potter, I was taken back to my childhood, when I would use my Barbie dolls in staged crime scenes, implicating the neighbors in the offenses I conjured up in my head. My crime-fighting heroines predated *Charlie's Angels* by a number of years and included Emma Peale from *The Avengers* (the television show, not the movie). Emma was strong and independent and always got the bad guys—and that is how I wanted to be. But like Joanne Belknap, I wanted to get the bad guys not because I had a passion to punish, but because I wanted to "make things better," as I used to tell my parents. I do not know where it came from, but I always remember growing angry at anything I perceived as an injustice. My parents, who hardly could be described as liberal, tolerantly endured what they called my "speeches" and, instead of arguing with me or trying to dissuade me, encouraged me to follow my ideals. They often did not understand or like the views I espoused on specific issues or the causes I supported, but they always let me know they respected my choices, which was important to me.

Susan Caringella and Drew Humphries's chapter made me wish a book like this existed when I was in college and graduate school. Like most undergraduates, I had no idea how one becomes a professor—nor could I picture myself in that role—and I understood even less about the academic job structure. In graduate school, I thought I would end up taking a research position somewhere, although I did not know much about the kinds of positions Angela Moore Parmley and Jocelyn Fontaine describe in their chapter. I knew that I enjoyed doing research, but I was trained in traditional positivist methods and did not learn about feminist methodology, discussed in the chapter by Shana Maier and Brian Monahan, until much later. Fortunately, early in my graduate school career I was given the opportunity to teach, and I discovered I enjoyed it. I became active in department and university committees, thus getting a better sense of institutional service. Upon graduation, I became an assistant professor of sociology at St. Joseph's University, where I remained on the faculty for twenty-five years until joining the faculty at the University of Dayton in 2006. I must agree with Caringella and Humphries that an academic career is incredibly rewarding. The autonomy of an academic position affords one innumerable opportunities to connect teaching, research, and social activism.

As many of the authors in this volume imply, learning does not end after graduate school or just because one becomes a teacher. Among the benefits of teaching and researching is the opportunity—in fact, the *need*—to continue to learn. And we learn not just from listening to paper presentations at conferences or reading others' work but also by doing. I have found that the act of researching is one of the most enriching learning processes. In conducting research, one learns not only about what is being studied, but so much more, including, if one is open enough, insights into oneself. I have studied violence against women, especially marginalized groups of women, for about thirty years. In doing this work, I was usually, like many of the authors in this book, an "outsider": a white, middle-class woman interviewing poor African American women and Latinas in public housing developments; a white middle-class American interviewing Guinean women about female genital mutilation and women's economic empowerment in West Africa, or Aboriginal women at public health centers and women's shelters in Australia; a straight woman interviewing lesbians victimized by their partners. In doing this work, I quickly found, as Saundra Westervelt and Kim Cook describe in their chapter, that feminist participatory research methods that advocate the nurturing of a reciprocal relationship between the researcher and the researched made far more sense than the traditional positivist methodologies I had learned as an undergraduate and graduate student. And I will always be grateful to the women who spoke with me for generously sharing their stories, for welcoming me into their lives, and for patiently correcting my misperceptions and the biases that spring from the privileges of my social class, race, nationality, and sexual orientation. I remain in touch with many of these women years after the research has been completed, and I am grateful to count them among my friends. These relationships and experiences have led me to become increasingly involved in locally based community service and justice projects, again demonstrating the connectedness of teaching, research, and social activism.

Regardless of where you are now in your career, as read this book you will undoubtedly consider where you have been and where you may be headed. Susan Miller and the contributors to this volume have given readers at all career stages valuable gifts: inspiration, reassurance, and encouragement. You will undoubtedly see yourself in one or more chapters in this book, but better yet, you may see your potential. Bon voyage!

—Claire M. Renzetti

Editor's Preface and Acknowledgments

I began my university teaching career as a graduate student at the University of Maryland, where my first teaching assignment was "Introduction to the Criminal Justice System," a popular course with more than 120 students enrolled. About 25 percent of the class consisted of criminology or criminal justice majors, and the rest of the students' majors covered a wide spectrum of social and physical sciences, humanities, and the arts. Their interest in the subject matter was strong because popular culture presentations of crime, law, and justice saturate our lives—available virtually any time we turn on the television, open a newspaper, or frequent the local movie theater. As the semester unfolded, a growing number of students were "converted" and changed their major to criminology and criminal justice, given their keen interest in the subject and, perhaps (as I always hope), by my enthusiastic teaching! However, seldom did the students have a clue about what they wanted to do with a degree when they graduated beyond general statements like "I think I want to go to law school" or "I want to be a police officer."

Today, a number of years later and ensconced at another public university, I come into contact regularly with many students who are still undecided about what kind of career path to pursue. This is where my secret career as a sleuth gets nurtured, because I get to ask them many questions intended to assist them in figuring out their passions, opening them up to possibilities they never knew about or had not dreamed of considering, and encouraging them to follow their interests and curiosity. What consistently comes to light in my conversations with them is that students are neither offered much insight into the career options their degree may provide, nor is there a forum for finding the answers to their questions, or sometimes, for even figuring out the kinds of things to ask. The questions I am asked, over and over, are as follows:

- What is graduate school? (Often followed by: what do you mean, teaching and research?)
- What is law school like?
- How do you do research? Why would people (i.e., gang bangers, drug dealers, victims, and so forth) talk to a researcher about their lives?
- How can I integrate my activism with a career?
- (My favorite one!) How do I know what I want to do?

Finally, there is the common refrain, "I want to help people," or other variations on this statement, such as "I think I want to work with juveniles/victims/ courts, but not as a lawyer."

This book tries to answer questions like these for students who are entertaining the idea of a career related to criminal justice or social problems. But its goal is to accomplish more than this. It is to demonstrate, using multiple examples, how it is possible to integrate passions with a fulfilling career and to imbue an occupational pursuit with a sense that what one does in the areas of criminal justice, criminology, or sociology contributes to the quality of justice as well as human relations and connections. Understanding differences between people across a range of positions—race/ethnicity, gender, social class, sexual orientation—enhances people's efforts to succeed in their work toward making their world a more "just" place.

Bringing together a wide range of established and up-and-coming scholars who address difference and diversity, and asking them to share their perceptions and experiences, has been a joy. Their contributions reflect real achievements as well as the challenges of some intractable obstacles blocking clear success. My hope is that in our post-9/11 life, visions of social justice and a commitment to improving our organizations that deal with justice issues will continue to include both hearing from and working with diverse individuals who can only enhance our understanding of our social world.

Overview of the Book

Despite the growing awareness that not all police officers are male and not all judges are white, it is still not standard university practice to expose students to the faces and stories of criminal justice practitioners, professionals, victims, and offenders—in terms of research articles about these people and subjects—that reveal a wider range of race, class, gender, and sexual diversity. Yet, our social world necessitates interactions with people from diverse cultural and demographic backgrounds. Typically, an approach to learning about diversity across research methods, practitioner experiences, and theory is missing in the criminal justice literature. This anthology fills this void and showcases diversity issues across a range of essays about the criminal justice field.

Presentations of social science research, the fare of university classrooms, often fail to motivate undergraduate students to pursue an academic career. Their excitement for criminal justice is much more likely to be ignited by participating in an internship opportunity or by watching a favorite "law and order" TV crime show. Moreover, although many students are captivated by the subject matter presented in criminology, deviance, social problems, or criminal justice courses, it is often difficult for them to make the leap into imagining a career as a researcher who investigates similar topics. Even within criminal justice professions that students find desirable, such as law enforcement or the legal or corrections fields, students are not typically exposed to the various specializations within these professions, nor do they know how to formulate the kinds of questions important to explore when studying these organizations. Students also do not understand how their intellectual passions can inspire a position as an activist or policymaker. Thus, while highlighting diversity, this book exposes students to a greater understanding of the range of opportunities that a career in criminal justice and criminology offers: as researchers, as professionals such as lawyers or police officers, as activists, or as practitioners.

Both contemporary justice practices and criminal justice research projects are shaped by the kinds of questions asked and analyzed by researchers as well as the kinds of people who are asked these questions. Though often unacknowledged, the political landscape and social norms interact with race/ethnicity, class, gender, and sexual orientation positions; multiple perspectives about crime and criminal justice can either flourish or be stifled. The two dimensions of research and practice can be explicated, first, by exposing the variety of ways that researchers approach a topic and carry out the research, and second, by exploring how one's identity helps to shape research questions and choice of topic. Thus, diverse perspectives are reflected in every aspect of research, advocacy, and professional work.

Exposing students to a wider range of research topics and methodological issues as well as professional diversity and bringing these to the center stage of inquiry is the first step in figuring out how multiple identities affect the research process and ultimately the research results. The essays contained here challenge narrow conceptions of what research is, and who works in the justice field, and what range of topics these people cover. They address the ways in which different approaches to work conducted by criminal justice professionals, the type of questions asked, and the kinds of topics explored are shaped by race, ethnicity, sexual orientation, and gender. In this way, the chapters feature diversity as the central issue in methods, theory, practice, and experience. To that end, the book explores a range of research topics and methodologies, and diversity in professional practice, in three ways.

First, the chapters assembled in part I, "Ways to Inquire: Research Methods," highlight why alternative ways of thinking about crime and conducting this kind of research is important within the criminal justice system and explore how different kinds and qualities of research are conducted (Joanne Belknap and Hillary Potter; Saundra Westervelt and Kimberly Cook; Shana Maier and Brian Monahan). All of these authors discuss ways to integrate the voices and experiences of people who have been marginalized, as well as introduce innovative and creative methodological approaches to aid in this endeavor. Although some of the investigative tools seem to align with "feminist" research methods, one must ask, to paraphrase Loraine Gelsthorpe (1990), is this feminist research, or just good research? I hope that by reading these chapters, students will be eager to embrace a "researcher spirit" that will help them think about crime, justice, deviance, and related social problems from a research perspective while giving greater consideration to the role of difference and diversity in their research.

Second, the chapters contained in part 2, "Inquirers: Professionals, Activists, and Researchers," explore the perceptions and experiences of researchers, practitioners, and advocates and how these affect their view of the profession; in other words, how are people able to "do diversity" within a profession that has been traditionally masculine and white-centered (lawyers: Daniel Atkins and Eliza Patten; activists/advocates: Jill McCorkel; academia: Susan Caringella and Drew Humphries; nonacademic research/government agency: Angela Moore Parmley and Jocelyn Fontaine). As academic and professional settings are challenged to better reflect and address the students and constituents they serve, it is important to envision how "insiders" can use their positions to better secure representation and justice for "outsiders" who have fewer opportunities and resources.

Third, the chapters placed in part 3, "Sites of Inquiry: Topics and Samples," examine diversity across topics and among respondents and the kinds of approaches used to access these areas (Walter DeKeseredy's work on violence against women; Michelle Meloy's work on female probation officers and male sex offenders; my work with colleagues Kay Forest and Nancy Jurik on gay and lesbian police officers; and Dana Britton and Andrea Button's work on "prison pups" and rehabilitation). They promote the importance of having flexibility in approaching social issues across diverse populations, reminiscent of what Sandra Bem (1974) argued two decades ago about how "rigid sex-role differentiation may have outlived its utility in a society in which human flexibility is increasingly associated with higher standards of psychological health, not to mention professional performance." Understanding the ways that race, ethnicity, social class, and sexual orientation intersect with gender can only enhance our collective efforts to do the hard work that tackling social problems and injustice entails. Both men and women need to join in these efforts, as illustrated clearly in Walter DeKeseredy's chapter on the role that men can play in the movement that seeks to end violence committed by (mostly) men against (mostly) girls and women. Finally, the insightful comments in the epilogue by Meda Chesney-Lind tie together the three components of the book.

I look forward to a day when a specific book like this is not necessary and when the issues related to difference and diversity across race/ethnicity, gender, class, and sexual orientation are not highlighted, and are also considered second nature in both research and practice. Until then, the essays in this book contribute to these goals as they both sensitize students to these issues and also provide student career guidance.

Acknowledgments

When I was pregnant with my now almost six-year-old son Connor, I remember leafing through a catalog that sold buttons and bumper stickers, and buying two buttons. One says: "A man of quality is not threatened by a woman for equality," and the other: "No child is born a racist." These little slogans epitomize the spirit of what invigorates my teaching and research pursuits as well as the kinds of messages of social justice that I want to teach my child. The women and men who have contributed to this collection of essays share this vision of a world that is open to, even celebrative of, the ways that difference and diversity can enhance our individual and collective endeavors as teachers, practitioners, activists, and scholars.

It was a joy to work with longtime friends as well as new ones on this volume. We share a common vision of social justice, and I admire the contributors for their tireless quests for equity, their inspirational teaching, their compassion, their advocacy for disenfranchised people, and their commitment to eradicating inequalities. They inspire me in my own work, and I thank them for their belief in the importance of this project.

Finally, it is no small achievement to coordinate an edited volume that addresses such a range of issues. The series editor, Claire Renzetti, continues to be not only one of the best sounding boards for academic concerns but also one of the most thoughtful scholars and mentor-to-millions that I know. Working with Claire is always a pleasure. I also always benefit from my dear friend and colleague-in-crime, LeeAnn Iovanni, for her sound feedback and editing. The phone calls I have with both Claire and LeeAnn invariably consist of one-part work and one-part laughter. Phyllis Deutsch, editor in chief at University Press of New England, offered sage advice throughout the project's development and saw it through to completion with great enthusiasm. I also appreciate the help from my production editor at UPNE and the wonderful copy editing of Beth Gianfagna. My thanks also go to Mona Danner, whose insight and attention to detail made her an ideal external reviewer. Our wonderful secretary, Nancy Quillen, at the Department of Sociology and Criminal Justice at the University of Delaware, was my crucial behind-the-scenes organizer of paper and mailings, all the while retaining her good humor. I appreciate my department colleagues, particularly Maggie Andersen's wordsmithing help with the book's title, and Ronet Bachman and Frank Scarpitti's support and friendship. As always, I thank my family for their understanding of my mountains of paper and my book-related chatter, and I especially thank my son Connor who facilitated many and necessary play breaks.

References

Bem, Sandra L. 1974. The measurement of psychological androgyny. *Journal of Consulting and Clinical Psychology* 42(2): 155–62.

———. 1993. *The lenses of gender: Transforming the debate on sexual inequality.* New Haven, Conn.: Yale University Press.

Gelsthorpe, L. 1990. Feminist methodologies in criminology. In *Feminist perspectives in criminology*, ed. L. Gelsthorpe and A. Morris, 89–106. Philadelphia: Open University Press.

I

Ways to Inquire

Research Methods

Introduction

From Passion to Practice

How does anyone pick her or his passion? Or is the process more one of discovering our passions? The purpose of this chapter is to examine how criminologists choose careers in criminal justice or criminology. In particular, why do we want to study crime and/or work in the criminal legal system? What is it about crime that piques our interest, our passion? If we are working toward a college degree in justice studies, criminal justice, or criminology, what do we want to do with our degree when we are done? And, equally important, how does one's gender and/or race/ethnicity, affect these decisions?

Many factors influence why individuals study crime and the criminal legal system and eventually find themselves in a related profession. While some students fall into their crime-related majors by circumstance or convenience, others are propelled by personal encounters with the criminal legal system and its workers. These experiences are further influenced by one's gender and race/ethnicity. Our lived experiences are, in general, strongly affected by our gender and racial/ethnic identities; therefore, these identities shape how we think about crime and the criminal legal system. And the way we think about crime (our passion) impacts the paths we travel in additional study of and work in the criminal legal system (our practice).

A recent study of criminal justice undergraduate majors asked students to list, in their own words, the top two or three reasons why they chose to major in criminal justice (Tontodonato 2006). Half of the students (50 percent) reported that they selected criminal justice because they thought it was interesting, about a third (30 percent) because it fit their career plans, about a quarter (23 percent) because they were interested in the law/law school, about a fifth (18 percent) because they were interested in policing, and an eighth (12 percent) because they wanted to "help others." (Because students were asked to list more than one, these add up to more than 100 percent.) This study also found that criminal justice undergraduate majors were most likely to report that after graduating they planned to work in the criminal justice field (51 percent), followed by going to graduate school (20 percent) and law school (16 percent), respectively. About 13 percent wanted to work in a different field or had other plans (Tontodonato, 2006).

Another study of criminal justice majors found that the students were most likely to report they wanted their first career to be in law enforcement (44 percent), followed by the corrections field (15 percent), and the judiciary (12 percent) (Kelley 2004). When asked about their long-term career goals, more than one-third (38 percent) reported law enforcement jobs, almost one-quarter (23 percent) reported the judiciary, and only 6 percent reported corrections (Kelley 2004). One-fifth (19 percent) of the students reported non–criminal justice jobs as their long-term career goals (Kelley 2004). Similarly, Krimmel and Tartaro's (1999) study of criminal justice students at fourteen colleges in the United States found that the largest proportion wished to become police officers (45 percent), 14 percent wanted to become lawyers, and 10 percent wanted to work in corrections (31 percent reported no career goal). Surprisingly, the criminal justice students in this study "reported no influence from family, friends, or high school relationships in their decision to study criminal justice in college"; rather, "they thought the subject matter was interesting and relevant to the real world" and expected to find jobs that were "exciting and offered opportunities for promotion" (Krimmel and Tartaro 1999: 294). Notably, women were more interested than men in going to law school, and men were more interested than women in becoming police officers (ibid.). Students of color in this study had less interest in law enforcement than white students and were more drawn by juvenile justice and corrections than white students, while white students were more interested than students of color in "wearing uniforms, apprehending criminals, or protecting the Constitution" (ibid.: 288).

A Passion for Justice or a Passion for Punishment?

In the process of understanding one's interest in criminology, it is useful to ask: "Do I want to be a police officer because I want to wear a gun and have power and control?" or "Do I want to be a police officer because I want to help people?" Both reasons sound trite and more than somewhat childlike. However, these questions are important. A recent study of more than six hundred students at five universities and colleges in the northeastern United States found that criminal justice majors scored significantly lower (average score of 33.2) than students in other majors (average score of 51.7) on an empathy scale (Courtright, Mackey, and Packard 2005). Notably, the non–criminal justice majors tended to have the same average empathy score over time (from freshman to sophomore, and so forth), whereas the criminal justice majors appeared to became more empathetic over the same time period. In a (multivariate) model with many variables, gender was a "clearly strong and significant predictor of empathy, followed by major (CJ and other) and class (grade) level" (ibid.: 137). Women students were more empathetic than men, criminal justice majors were less empathetic than non–criminal justice majors, and "as one increases grade or class level empathy also increases" (ibid.).

Geoff K. Ward (2006) considers three dimensions in his "hypothetical division of justice-related labor" to depict the hierarchical and numerical allotment of occupations in the criminal legal system. His consideration of the power, prestige, and risk of the various positions in the system demonstrate the combined significance and reputation of each of these jobs. As portrayed in Ward's diagram (see figure 1), the number of corrections officers

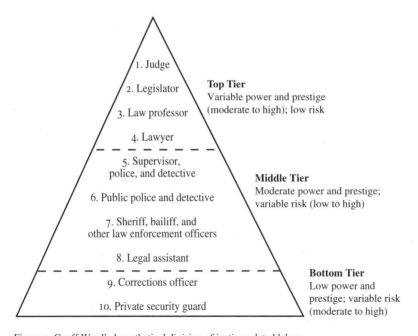

Figure 1. Geoff Ward's hypothetical division of justice-related labor
G. K. Ward, Race and the justice workforce: Toward a system perspective.
Pp. 67-87 in *The Many Colors of Crime: Inequalities of Race, Ethnicity, and Crime in America.*
R. D. Peterson, L. J. Krivo, and J. Hagan (eds.). New York: New York University Press.

and private security guards is quite large, and the risk can range between moderate to high, but these positions are less prestigious. Meanwhile, judges and lawyers have higher prestige and power with low risk, but there are fewer of these coveted positions. The middle-tier consists of jobs with a wide range of risk and moderate levels of power and prestige. Middle-tier jobs include police officers, sheriffs, and probation/parole officers. The study by Courtright and his colleagues on student empathy examined how students rated the appeal of various criminal legal system jobs and how their self-reported empathy levels were related to the perceived job attractiveness of criminal justice-related occupations (Courtright, Mackey, and Packard 2005). First, they found a clear ranking of most attractive criminal legal jobs: almost half of the student sample (44 percent) reported law enforcement as a highly attractive occupation, followed by 30 percent for corrections counselor, 22 percent for probation/parole officer, and 17 percent for prison warden (students could rank more than one of these jobs as attractive, thus the sum of the percents exceed 100 percent). Second, Courtright and his colleagues found that students' levels of empathy were related to their ranking of the appeal of various criminal legal jobs: students favoring law enforcement jobs tended to have lower empathy levels, and the same relationship was found for students attracted to the occupation of prison warden. Not surprisingly, the opposite was found true of the relationship between empathy level and the attractiveness of a corrections counselor job. There was a strong positive relationship; the greater the empathy of the student, the more likely the student reported the attractiveness of counseling offenders. There was no relationship between a student's self-reported empathy level and his/her evaluation of the attractiveness of an occupation as a probation officer.

Courtright, Mackey, and Packard (2005: 139) conclude that the study suggests criminal justice majors, as a group, are lower in empathy than other students, sometimes "remarkably low," and are "more punitive in their attitudes toward crime, criminals, and the CJ system." The researchers were concerned about these findings and support efforts to change the curriculum to include bringing in offenders as guest speakers to the classroom; conducting tours of prisons, jails, and delinquent institutions; incorporating restorative justice philosophies in the classroom; and promoting service-learning opportunities (discussed in the next section). Furthermore, Courtright and his colleagues are concerned that the current state of many criminal justice majors is one in which they are assuming their occupations in the field more as "reactors" to crime than "problem solvers" (ibid.: 140). They also worry that inadequate empathy by criminal legal system employees likely has a negative impact on community relations and respect. Finally, the authors consider whether individuals select themselves for studying criminal justice owing to lowered empathy levels, or if instead the process of the criminal justice education make one less empathetic. The findings on increased empathy of CJ majors over the course of education suggest that less empathetic individuals choose criminal justice as a major but that the college/university experience has the potential to make these individuals more empathetic.

Using Internships, Service-Learning, Paid, and Volunteer Work to Find and Test Your Passion

In recent years, more and more credibility and support is given to internship and service-learning programs at universities and colleges across the United States (see, for example, Hartmus, Cauthen, and Levine 2006; Hirschinger-Blank and Markowitz 2006; Lersch 1997; Parilla and Smith-Cunnien, 1997; Penn 2003; Swanson, King, and Wolbert 1997). Such programs provide students with a connection between the classroom curriculum and the "real world" of the criminal legal system. In particular, as evidenced by the authors' experiences with exposing CJ students to these practices, students are able to directly witness the problems and challenges of the system, especially as they are related to race/ethnicity, gender, and class inequities. In an effort to define and describe service-learning and its benefits, Everette B. Penn (2003) uses the acronym "E-A-R" to capture the concept. "E" stands for "education in the community that sets up"; "A" represents "action in the community, which promotes"; and "R" refers to "reflection on the concepts taught in a traditional class setting" (373). Such programs allow students the opportunities to experience working in the particular environments, or something close to the environments, in which they hope to work after graduating. Some students are fortunate enough to find paid employment during college doing the type of work they hope to be doing upon graduation. Many of our students found paying jobs that resulted from their college internships or service-learning. That is, a student may conduct an internship in a jail, a battered women's shelter, a juvenile delinquent program, and so on, and upon graduation be hired into that program.

Often, these internship, service-learning, or paid employment opportunities allow students to learn whether they will enjoy work in that area as much as they thought they would. Sometimes, they find that what they thought would be interesting and enjoyable is boring or frustrating, or for other reasons, they decide this is not the field for them. Criminologist James W. Marquart (2005) describes an internship he had at Western Illinois University as an undergraduate, where he worked in a juvenile delinquent institution housing both girls and boys. This four-month internship "led to my interest in studying prison organizations, except I was through with kids and wanted to observe adults" (217). Later, while Marquart was working on his master's degree in sociology at Kansas State University, the son-in-law of the assistant warden of the Missouri State Penitentiary was enrolled in a course in which he was the teaching assistant, and helped him secure the opportunity to work as a prison officer at "Jeff City." Marquart writes eloquently how this job expanded his beliefs about prison and how significantly his observations differed from the popular research at the time reported (e.g., Haney, Banks, and Zimbardo 1973). More specifically, after reading about the "Zimbardo experiment" he expected to find solely abusive guards who tormented prisoners and a frightening day-to-day prison life. Instead he witnessed cooperation between the prisoners and the officers in the running of the prison, and he found that prison life was not all "grim and guts" but sometimes "downright hilarious" (Marquart 2005: 218). He became passionate about studying the prison subculture and went on to get a Ph.D. from Texas A&M University. He notes that "for nearly two years, I worked as a prison officer and began a journey to the other side that still has relevance and influence in my life today" (221).

One innovative service-learning project allowed college students the opportunity to mentor juveniles whose cases had been waived to adult court and were awaiting trial in an adult jail (Swanson, King, and Wolbert 1997). Clearly, these are juveniles at the deepest end of the criminal legal system. A study was conducted on this mentoring project, based on the students' papers and a questionnaire they completed. The findings from the study confirmed that the three project goals were established: (1) students obtained "a deeper understanding of the problems of youthful offenders"; (2) students gained knowledge about jails as institutions and the impact of holding juveniles in adult jails; and (3) students were more able "to evaluate the problems and needs of juvenile offenders in light of various punishment alternatives" (ibid.: 263).

Similarly, Diane M. Hartmus and her colleagues designed a service-learning partnership for criminal justice students and the New York Office of Court Administration and at New York Court reform organizations. The college students worked as court monitors in local criminal courts, and this service-learning program helped them not only to acquire an understanding of the court processes but also increased "their sense of civic responsibility" (Hartmus, Cauthen, and Levine 2006: 22). Likewise, students enrolled in a juvenile delinquency course that employed service-learning found the students "came to view the youth in a positive light, reported learning how to work with youth, experienced a reduction in stereotypes, gained career insights, learned how to apply academic theory to real-life experiences and developed attitudes about how society addresses delinquency that were sympathetic to the youths' condition" (ibid.: 69).

Reasons Criminal Legal System Workers Choose Their Professions

Some research endeavors address why and how people select their occupations. Clearly, numerous reasons abound as to why individuals pursue jobs in policing, law, and corrections. And certainly, whether one desires to focus more on working with victims versus offenders, or in a more prestigious or elitist agency (e.g., as a judge or FBI agent) compared with an important but less financially or status-respected institution (e.g., as a prison or jail "guard"), these goals influence individuals' decisions. Notably, most of the earliest studies assessing individuals' motivations to work in criminal legal system professions, whether these were of policing, law, or prisons/jails, were conducted on males, and often on white males (see Raganella and White 2004). Ward reports that even though there has been a remarkable change in the racial/ethnic and gender makeup in the criminal legal system workforce over the past century, there are still notable disparities. Blacks and Latinas/os are not well represented in professional and administrative positions and are more concentrated in service occupations, such as lower-ranked police and corrections officers. Except for a comparatively high proportion of Asian American attorneys, Asian Americans are underrepresented in policing (all ranks) and administrative positions. Native Americans have representations in criminal legal system jobs that are comparable to whites (except for lawyers), but this similarity is likely the result of the inclusion of positions held by Native Americans on tribal land. There is a need for research to examine how diversity in the system's agencies affects the system's practices (Ward 2006). Thus, more recent studies include women and people of color in the samples, and also attempt to address (1) if there are gender and/or racial/ethnic differences in motivations for criminal legal system work career choices; and (2) if different recruitment techniques are necessary to recruit women of all races/ethnicities and men of color to criminal legal system jobs. This section is an overview of some of the findings from the studies assessing motivations for criminal legal system careers and how these do and do not vary based on race/ethnicity and gender.

Reasons Reported for Choosing Law Enforcement/Policing

Anthony J. Raganella and Michael D. White not only conducted an excellent recent study on new police recruits in the New York City Police Department and their motivations for careers in policing, but they also reviewed research published since the 1950s regarding individuals' motivations for pursuing law enforcement jobs. Their research review compared men's and women's reasons for desiring policing careers, and it also addressed whether racial/ethnic differences occurred in pursuing law enforcement jobs. Regarding gender, their review of studies on males' desires to be police officers in research published in the 1950s, 1960s, and 1970s concluded: "Although some early research indicated that individuals who entered policing were more likely to have authoritarian personalities, seeking power and control, most of the research from that time highlighted the desire for job security as a primary motivating factor" (Raganella and White 2004: 502). But this review also noted that male police officers in these eras often reported "helping people," performing a job that was "consequential," and the "adventurous qualities of police work" as reasons to pursue law enforcement careers (ibid.). Their review of research on women's desires to be police officers found that women pursued law enforcement careers for reasons very similar to men: the salary, job security, and helping others seemed to be the most commonly stated reasons.

Raganella and White's overview of the research on racial/ethnic differences and similarities on choosing policing careers indicated that both white and black officers stressed job security as an appealing feature, but African Americans tended to be more influenced by helping others and the economic benefits, while whites tended to be more influenced by family members and friends (this was based largely on Nicholas Alex's 1969 book, *Black in Blue: A Study of the Negro Policeman*). Regardless of whether race/ethnicity and gender are significant factors in distinguishing the choice of careers in policing, it is quite clear from the research that being a woman of any race or a man of color often results in some stress owing to racism and/or sexism on the job (e.g., Belknap 2007; Martin 1994; Martin and Jurik 1996).

Raganella and White's recent study collected data from 278 New York City Police Department academy recruits to assess these individuals' motivation for becoming police officers. They reported: "Findings indicated that motivations for becoming a police officer were similar regardless of race or gender, and the most influential factors were altruistic and practical, specifically the opportunity to help others, job benefits, and [job] security" (2004: 501). However, women more than men, and African Americans and Latinos/as more than whites ranked "helping people" as a more significant motivator in pursuing policing careers. When examining differences based on race/ethnicity and gender simultaneously, this study found:

The greatest differences were seen between White males and Blacks, both males and females. Black females put the highest value on the *opportunity to help people,* particularly when compared to White males. White males, alternatively, scored *good companionship with co-workers* significantly higher than Black females and Black males (Hispanic males matched White males in this case). Also, Black males rated *salary* higher than White males. Again, however, the overriding theme from the analyses involved the similarity of responses across race and gender, rather than the differences. (511)

Significantly, while not specifying law enforcement officers' desires to become police officers, one study examined how people's attitudes toward the police (ATP) were impacted by television, in particular such "reality" television "cop shows" as *COPS* and *America's Most Wanted.* Consistent with other research, they found that not only do African Americans have more negative views of the police (lower ATP) than whites in general, but viewing these "reality" crime television shows amplified the gap between blacks' and whites' ATP: Viewing "cop shows" impacted whites by increasing their (already higher) view of police (ATP), while decreasing African Americans' (already lower) ATP. The authors note that this is hardly surprising given the manner in which these shows typically portray whites as police officers and African Americans as criminals. When controlling for a multitude of variables in this large study, however, it was found that "cop shows" increased the ATP of men but not women, whites but not African Americans, and those without a college education (but not those with a college education) (Eschholz et al. 2002).

Another variation among officers by race was established in Bolton and Feagin's study of African American police officers working in southern U.S. cities, where they found that many of the officers "owe their job, at least in part, to support of black organizations and communities." In turn, this compels black officers to essentially give back to the black community, even though, as mentioned above, there is a struggle for black officers to gain trust among a community that has historically had negative interactions with law enforcement (Bolton and Feagin 2004: 50).

Reasons Reported for Choosing Work in Prisons, Jails, and with Offenders

Employment in the corrections portion of the criminal legal system is often viewed as one of the "occupations of last resort" (Britton 2003: 104). As this segment has not often been considered a top employment selection among individuals, it has also been a relatively understudied subject by criminologists. However, the limited research on why individuals choose occupations working with offenders indicates that there are significant differences based on such characteristics as the individual's gender, education, and whether the person wants to work with juvenile or adult offenders. The bulk of this research assesses workers' attitudes in terms of a rehabilitative or service orientation versus a punishment orientation. Regarding gender, women are more likely than men to report "wanting to help people" or a rehabilitative orientation as a reason to work with offenders (Belknap 2004; Griffin 2002; Jurik 1985; Jurik and Halemba 1984; Kissel and Katsampes 1980; Walters 1992; Zimmer 1986; Zupan 1986). Research fairly consistently finds education is positively related to a rehabilitative ideal among persons working with offenders: the more education, the greater the likelihood that a person working with offenders will hold a rehabilitative ideal (Burton et al. 1991; Cullen, Golden, and Cullen 1983). Finally, those working with juveniles tend to be more supportive of rehabilitative ideals (relative to punitive ideals) compared with those working with adult offenders (Caeti et al. 2003). A challenge faced by some working with offenders is *role conflict*, when they hold rehabilitative ideals but work in institutions with punitive ideals (ibid.).

In reviewing 1982 data from the National Longitudinal Survey of Youth, Britton (2003) determined that few youth (0.1 percent) conveyed any desire to work as a "prison guard," with 95 percent of youth aspiring to this job being male. Likewise, in her in-depth interviews with seventy-two female and male prison officers, Britton discovered that the majority of these women and men did not find their way into their prison jobs through strategic planning. Additionally, only a few had childhood dreams of even working in the criminal legal profession, specifically, policing. The most common previous work experience for the men in Britton's study was military service (44 percent), while clerical work was the most common prior experience for the women officers (37 percent). Britton concludes that "race and sex discrimination in the larger labor force mean that prison work is more attractive to women and African-American and Hispanic men. Lower levels of wage differentials by race and sex in the government employment sector have made these jobs even more appealing to workers from formerly excluded groups" (2003: 80).

Reasons Reported for Choosing Work in Law

Deceased U.S. diplomat, lawyer, and business executive Sol M. Linowitz (1994) wrote of exclusionary experiences of his and other marginalized attorneys in the 1930s and several years thereafter. Upon concluding his law school education, Linowitz recalled being dissuaded from applying to law firms that were not "Jewish" firms. Similarly, African Americans and women suffered from discrimination in the legal profession by being barred from entrance into law schools and professional lawyer associations until the 1960s and early 1970s, and were often blocked from practicing certain types of law, relegated to assignments that were seen as best suited for their gender/femininity, only assigned people of color and women as clients, and so on (e.g., Kornhauser and Revesz 1995; Linowitz 1994).

Born in 1931, L. Douglas Wilder, the first African American governor in U.S. history was sworn in as governor of Virginia in 1990. He majored in chemistry, planning to become a physician, but shortly after he graduated with his B.A. in 1951 he was drafted into the U.S. Army and served in the Korean War. Upon his return to the United States after receiving a bronze star for heroism in this war, he qualified for the G.I. Bill, but there were no law schools in Virginia at that time that accepted African American students, so he studied law and acquired his law degree in 1959 at a traditionally black college, Howard University. Although he and many of his friends began their undergraduate degree aspiring to be physicians, when walking home with a friend from a movie one day "he experienced an epiphany. 'You know, we don't want to be doggone doctors. As good as we talk, we ought to be lawyers. I'm going to be a lawyer" (Anonymous 1998: 49). After receiving his law degree he started his own firm and specialized in criminal defense. Wilder's experience is reaffirmed in reports of increases in African American law students in the United States in the mid-1990s, attributed to more support for and less discrimination against black students, but also to these students' belief that most change for African Americans "in the past decades has been achieved through the legal process" (Anonymous 1996: 55).

Moll (1990:15) argues that though women were particularly underrepresented in the legal profession prior to the 1970s, they "are now an important component of the law profession" by forcing the profession to consider gendered issues not previously regarded. Many of the earliest women lawyers (of all races and ethnicities) in the United States were committed to advocating for women's, American Indians', African Americans', and others' civil rights (Barteau 1997; Morello 1986). Arguably, dealing with these issues of equality (or inequality) in the legal workplace begins to force those practicing the law to think of these matters as they affect greater society. Nevertheless, people of color and women are still underrepresented in law school enrollments and the legal profession in comparison with their population within the United States (Kornhauser and Revesz 1995).

Attorney Susan J. Bell (1992: 7) names many reasons individuals wish to go to law school and become attorneys, including "to bring about social change, to assist others in need, for intellectual stimulation, for financial rewards, and for professional prestige." However, many argue that the monetary gain of an attorney's salary is the most important lure to becoming a lawyer (Moll 1990). Even still, undergraduates wishing to pursue a profession in *criminal* law are not overwhelmingly motivated by this financial lure, owing to the relatively low salaries for public sector attorneys. Indeed, many women pursue public sector law, working as prosecutors or public defenders, because the hours are more conducive to balancing careers with parenting than those that private firm jobs entail (see Belknap 2007).

Kornhauser and Revesz (1995) found that upon entering law school, women, African American, and Latina/o students were more likely to desire work in the not-for-profit sector of the legal profession, including public defense attorneys and prosecutors, than their white, Asian American, and male counterparts. (However, when controlling for other factors, such as age at time of graduation, academic performance, and financial debt after law school, the rates were statistically significant only for women and not students of color.)

The proportion of individuals wanting to pursue not-for-profit jobs decreases throughout the law school process.

The Authors' Passion to Practice

The previous sections of this chapter summarized existing research on why students of criminology and criminal justice choose these majors and what they want out of their majors. This chapter also reported on the research about individuals' reasons for becoming police officers, prison/jail workers, and lawyers, and the significance of race and gender in these decisions. In this last section, we two authors discuss our "passions for justice" and how our passions are nuanced by the important and harmful roles of racism, sexism, and classism.

Hillary Potter: Although I recall being quite fond of Nancy Drew mystery novels and crime-TV shows like *Charlie's Angels* in my youth, and this probably eventually led me to a career as a practitioner in the criminal legal system, the stage at which I am now was brought on by a gradually strengthened passion. My interest in crime and the criminal legal system has been the only field and area of study to hold my attention since the end of my junior year in college when I took a sociology course in deviance studies to fulfill an elective credit requirement. After changing my major for the fifth and final time to sociology and graduating a year later, I entered the criminal legal system workforce for what would be a ten-year stint in various community-based corrections programs and agencies. Certainly, the path that led me to my recent calling was developed through these experiences in the field, especially because my favorite media choices during my youth—those featuring amateur sleuth Nancy and *Charlie's* private investigator "angels"—were especially lacking in explicitly drawing attention to *in*justices. (However, a contemporary feminist criminologist analysis of these images might provide examples of the gendered, raced, and classed underpinnings of these representations of those working in the criminal legal field.) When beginning my postbaccalaureate career I was aware of the inefficiencies of the system, particularly for people of color, victims, and females, but it took several years for my disdain to develop into unremitting disillusionment. And, undoubtedly, my outlook and experiences as an African American woman further roused the perspective I would bring to fruition. Although it is especially important to have individuals working in criminal justice who are aware of the problems and who attempt to effect change for the better, I personally felt I would be more valuable in educating others through teaching at the college level, conducting research to highlight the inefficiencies and recommend changes, and participating in the criminal legal community in an independent capacity.

Since entering my doctoral program, I have continued to focus on criminology issues as related to people of color, victims, and women. Though my dissertation focused on the ways in which African American women experience intimate partner abuse as affected by culture and social structure, it was not my first choice of subjects. Nevertheless, the obstacles that prevented me from conducting research on my original topic led me to the project that resulted in a particularly rewarding endeavor. As those of us in criminology seek to convert our passions into practice, it is important to be receptive and accept that there are many paths to take. For example, many criminal justice/criminology undergraduates do not typically consider working in a prison until they attend a class tour and learn of this as an opportunity. My investigation into the way African American survivors of Hurricane Katrina labeled their survival behaviors in the aftermath of the storm was certainly not an intended project; I only engaged in the research after witnessing the myriad of disturbing images in the news media. However, this project and my other academic endeavors have remained loyal to my passion for the need to draw attention to the racialized, gendered, sexualized, and classed perceptions and realities of certain individuals and groups as related to crime.

Joanne Belknap: I can remember being confused as a small child at how different the expectations were for my sister and me compared with our three brothers, particularly regarding our freedom to roam, try new activities, vent our anger, and the nature of our responsibilities in our home and on our farm. These distinctions were enforced not only by our parents, but by other relatives, neighbors, religious leaders, teachers and principals, and so forth. The older I grew, the more my confusion turned to anger and frustration. Growing up in Denver, Colorado, and then in a farm community in Kentucky, I was also increasingly aware with age of the subtle and overt ways that racism and classism were behaviors that privileged me as a white girl whose parents had sufficient (legal) means to care for me. I struggled with feeling guilty about my race and class privilege (although we did not use these terms then, in the 1960s and 1970s), at the same time that I started recognizing I had unknowingly assumed racist and classist prejudices (e.g., poor people and people of color are more criminal than wealthier and white people; all doctors and lawyers are white). I also became aware of other types of oppression and discrimination, such as homophobia, anti-Semitism, and nationalism. (The first letter I wrote to a newspaper editor was about the hatefulness toward Iranian students at my university during the Iranian hostage crisis in 1979.) Ironically, despite my often vocal resistance to sexism, I was also noticing ways that I was sexist (against women and girls) in assumptions I never questioned (e.g., women should be the primary caretakers of children; men were due the "better" and higher-paying jobs). I also noticed, with some shame, that I had a more difficult time with and was less willing to vocalize my resistance to racism, classism, and other forms of oppression than of sexism.

I do not remember a time that I was not annoyed (at the least) or enraged (at the most) about the unfairness in the world. The time this hit me the most profoundly, and changed my passion to criminology, was when I visited a men's prison (an optional trip) in a course on urban public policy during my junior year in college (1980) at the University of Colorado. I was astounded by how many American Indian and African American men were in the prison of the largely white state of my birth. Old feelings of confusion, anger, and guilt emerged, and when I spoke to the professor of this course during his office hours, he suggested I pursue a master's degree in criminal justice. I worked on my master's at Michigan State University, originally with the goal to conduct prison reform, but like my colleague and coauthor, Hillary Potter, decided at some point that I could create the most change in the criminal legal system through teaching and research. Although I am sometimes disappointed by what I have accomplished, most of the time I feel as if the career I chose has been the best one for me, given my personality and abilities. However, I am continually awed and impressed with the people I routinely meet who have turned their lives around—from being a criminal to working with juveniles, or from being a victim to someone who advocates for victims. Yet also there are many people who work with victims and/or offenders who do not have these backgrounds themselves but have made the effort to learn how to best advocate for others.

Conclusion

Numerous reasons exist for criminologists and criminal legal system practitioners to become passionate about crime and the criminal legal system, and transforming this into practice. While many criminal justice/criminology students are influenced by the "*CSI* effect," that is, entertainment media representations of the system, just as many are propelled into the field as a result of more altruistic and personal motivations. These motivations are oftentimes shaped by an individual's gender, race/ethnicity, and class statuses and subsequent life chances and experiences.

The nature of the passions among criminal justice/criminology students tend to vary between the types of proposed employment (i.e., "dream job") among this group. Studies show that most criminal justice students wish to pursue a policing-related career, but those who find themselves working in the corrections field often experience rewarding careers. Interestingly, criminal justice/criminology students geared toward a law enforcement career tend to be less empathetic than other criminal justice/criminology students (such as those leaning toward corrections-based and counseling jobs) and students majoring in other subjects. Further, women are more empathetic than men, which may provide an explanation for why fewer women are entering policing positions and, thus, are more likely to be in counseling-related criminal legal system positions. Interestingly, the college experience for criminal justice/criminology students has been found to make them more empathetic throughout their college tenure.

Regardless of the reasons and motivations for entering into criminal justice as a major and a career, experiential learning is particularly important in testing one's passion. Although a number of criminal justice/criminology students may have previously encountered the inner-workings of the criminal legal system, for example, via relatives who work(ed) in the system or personal experiences as a defendant, many students' only exposure to the system has been through media representations (e.g., movies and TV crime dramas, news stories, TV crime documentaries). Internships, service-learning, and volunteer work, along with criminal justice/criminology instructors' use of practitioner, victim service worker, and offender guest lecturers, as well as corrections facility tours, provide students with firsthand exposure to their intended professions and aid them in reinforcing or redirecting their passions.

A good deal of extant research has determined that there are some differences in choosing careers in the criminal legal system by gender and race/ethnicity. Though factors such as job security, decent salaries, and excellent fringe benefits were cited as significant factors for entering into the various criminal legal system jobs, other factors, for instance, helping others and giving back to the community, were more significant among women and people of color.

In directing one's passion into practice, criminal justice/criminology students are encouraged to conduct a thorough self-assessment and to determine their rationale for committing to a career in criminal justice and criminology. How might these passions affect our performance on the job? Do our personal experiences as a victim of crime or as a convicted offender influence our career decisions, and in what way? How might our gender, race/ethnicity, and class alter the type of criminal justice career we pursue? Will these experiences negatively or positively influence our actions? These and many other questions and factors are a necessary consideration in making the most out of our passions and in effecting positive change in the criminal legal system.

Discussion Questions

1. What are some of the reasons, reported in studies of undergraduate students, that they chose criminology/criminal justice as a major? What do they want to do with their degrees in criminology/criminal justice?

2. What roles do a desire for punishment and personal empathy play in students' pull toward criminology/criminal justice majors/careers?
3. How can volunteer and paid work, internships, and service-learning help identify one's passion for criminology/criminal justice?
4. What are some of the ways in which individuals currently working in the field choose their professions? How are these related to gender and race?

References

Alex, N. 1969. *Black in blue: A study of the Negro policeman.* New York: Appleton-Century Croft.

Anonymous. 1996. The verdict is in: Blacks continue to flock to highly ranked law schools. *Journal of Blacks in Higher Education* 11:54–55.

Anonymous. 1998. Douglas Wilder withdraws from the presidency of his alma mater, Virginia Union University. *Journal of Blacks in Higher Education* 20:49.

Barteau, B. 1997. Thirty years of the journey of Indiana women judges: 1964–1994. *Indiana Law Review* 30:43–202.

Belknap, J. 2004. Women in conflict: An analysis of women correctional officers. In *The criminal justice system and women,* 3rd ed., ed. B. R. Price and N. J. Sokoloff, 543–561. Boston: McGraw-Hill.

———. 2007. The Invisible Woman: Gender, Crime, and Justice. 3rd ed. Belmont, Calif.: Wadsworth.

Bell, S. J. 1992. *Full disclosure: Do you really want to be a lawyer?* 2nd ed. Princeton, N.J.: Peterson's Guides.

Bolton, K., and J. R. Feagin. 2004. *Black in blue: African-American police officers and racism.* New York: Routledge.

Britton, D. M. 2003. *At work in the iron cage: The prison as gendered organization.* New York: New York University Press.

Burton, V. S., X. Ju, R. Dunaway, and N. Wolfe. 1991. The correctional orientation of Bermuda prison guards. *International Journal of Comparative and Applied Criminal Justice,* 15:71–80.

Caeti, T. J., C. Hemmens, F. T. Cullen, and V. S. Burton. 2003. Management of juvenile correctional facilities. *Prison Journal* 83(4):383–405.

Courtright, K. E., D. A. Mackey, and S. H. Packard. 2005. Empathy among college students and criminal justice majors. *Journal of Criminal Justice Education* 16(1):125–44.

Cullen, F. T., K. M. Golden, and J. B. Cullen. 1983. Is child saving dead? Attitudes toward rehabilitation in Illinois. *Journal of Criminal Justice* 11:1–13.

Eschholz, S., B. S. Blackwell, M. Gertz, and T. Chiricos. 2002. Race and attitudes toward the police: Assessing the effects of watching "reality" police programs. *Journal of Criminal Justice* 30(4):327–41.

Griffin, M. L. 2002. The influence of professional orientation on detention officers' attitudes toward the use of force. *Criminal Justice & Behavior* 29:250–77.

Haney, C., W. Banks, and P. Zimbardo. 1973. Interpersonal dynamics in a simulated prison. *International Journal of Criminology and Penology* 1:69–97. *Journal of Criminal Justice Education,* 15(2):219–37.

Hartmus, D. M., J.N.G. Cauthen, and J. P. Levine. 2006. Enriching student understanding of trial courts through service learning. *Journal of Criminal Justice Education* 17(1):22–43.

Hirschinger-Blank, N., and M. W. Markowitz. 2006. An evaluation of a pilot service-learning course for criminal justice undergraduate students. *Journal of Criminal Justice Education* 17(1):69–86.

Jurik, N. C. 1985. An officer and a lady: Organizational barriers to women working as correctional officers in men's prisons. *Social Problems* 32:375–388.

Jurik, N. C., and G. J. Halemba. 1984. Gender, working conditions and the job satisfaction of women in a non-traditional occupation: Female correctional officers in men's prisons. *Sociological Quarterly* 25:551–66.

Kelley, T. M. 2004. Reviewing criminal justice baccalaureate curricula: The importance of student input. *Journal of Criminal Justice Education* 15(2):219–34.

Kissel, P. J., and P. L. Katsampes. 1980. The impact of women corrections officers on the functioning of institutions housing male inmates. *Journal of Offender Counseling, Services and Rehabilitation* 4:213–31.

Kornhauser, L. A., and R. L. Revesz. 1995. Legal education and entry into the legal profession: The role of race, gender, and educational debt. *New York University Law Review* 70:829–964.

Krimmel, J. T., and C. Tartaro. 1999. Career choices and characteristics of criminal justice undergraduates. *Journal of Criminal Justice Education* 10(2):277–89.

Lersch, K. M. 1997. Integrating service learning in undergraduate criminal justice courses: Bringing academics to life. *Journal of Criminal Justice Education* 8(2):253–61.

Linowitz, S. M., with M. Mayer. 1994. *The betrayed profession: Lawyering at the end of the twentieth century.* New York: Macmillan.

Marquart, J. W. 2005. Understanding the power of social contexts on criminal justice institutions. *Journal of Criminal Justice Education* 16(2):217–25.

Martin, S. E. 1994. "Outsider within" the station house: The impact of race and gender on black women police. *Social Problems* 41:383–400.

Martin, S. E., and N. C. Jurik. 1996. *Doing justice, doing gender: Women in law and criminal justice occupations.* Thousand Oaks, Calif.: Sage.

Moll, R. W. 1990. *The lure of the law.* New York: Penguin Group.

Morello, K. B. 1986. *The invisible bar: The woman lawyer in America, 1638 to the present.* Boston: Beacon Press.

Parilla, P. F. and S. L. Smith-Cunnien. 1997. Criminal justice internships: Integrating the academic with the experiential. *Journal of Criminal Justice Education* 8(2):225–41.

Penn, Everette B. 2003. Service-learning: A tool to enhance criminal justice. *Journal of Criminal Justice Education* 14(2):371–83.

Raganella, A. J., and M. D. White. 2004. White race, gender, and motivation for becoming a police officer: Implications for building a representative police department. *Journal of Criminal Justice* 32: 501–13.

Swanson, C. K. King, and Nicole Wolbert. 1997. Mentoring juveniles in an adult jail: An example of service learning. *Journal of Criminal Justice Education* 8(2):263–71.

Tontodonato, Pamela. 2006. Goals, expectations, and satisfaction of criminal justice majors. *Journal of Criminal Justice Education* 17(1):162–80.

Walters, S. 1992. Attitudinal and demographic differences between male and female corrections officers. *Journal of Offender Rehabilitation* 18:173–89.

Ward, G. K. 2006. Race and the justice workforce: Toward a system perspective. In *The many colors of crime: Inequalities of race, ethnicity, and crime in America,* ed. R. D. Peterson, L. J. Krivo, and J. Hagan, 67–87. New York: New York University Press.

Zimmer, L. 1986. *Women guarding men.* Chicago: University of Chicago Press.

Zupan, L. Z. 1986. Gender-related differences in correctional officers' perceptions and attitudes. *Journal of Criminal Justice* 14:349–61.

Feminist Research Methods in Theory and Action

Learning from Death Row Exonerees

Historically, feminist methodology has emerged within a context of women scholars studying female subjects. This has been an essential and illuminating process in the development of social science research and has produced important advances for methodology. This chapter expands qualitative feminist methods to women scholars studying (predominantly) male subjects—in this case, death row exonerees. We have been explicit in our attempts to maintain our feminist integrity in the research process while studying a group of people whose lived experiences have not been central to most feminists concerns. Thus, we ask: how do we accomplish feminist methodology in the process of interviewing innocent individuals who have been exonerated of capital crimes? Given that our interview participants are predominantly men, how do we keep feminist concerns and techniques central to our method? In this chapter, we begin by briefly describing our current research and participants. We then outline our guiding principles of feminist methods and examine how we employ feminist methodology to study exonerees' lives. We conclude by discussing what we see as the lessons from this project for further expansion of feminist methods.

"Life after Death Row"

Since 1973, 122 men and one woman have been released from prison after having been exonerated of capital crimes. These individuals had been wrongfully convicted of crimes they did not commit, sentenced to death, and eventually exonerated based on substantial evidence of their actual innocence. To date, most of the academic literature addressing the wrongful conviction issue has focused on two primary concerns: documenting the extent of the wrongful conviction problem (Gross et al. 2004; Huff et al. 1996; Liebman and Fagan 2000; Radelet et al. 1992) and identifying the various legal and social factors that can lead to the conviction of an innocent person (Leo and Ofshe 1998; Olson 2002; Scheck et al. 2000; Westervelt and Humphrey 2001). Little scholarly research, however, has examined the emotional and practical consequences of a wrongful conviction for those unfortunate enough to experience it (see only Campbell and Denov 2004 and Grounds 2004). Thus, the questions guiding our larger research project are as follows: What is the impact of a wrongful capital conviction and incarceration on individuals who have been exonerated and released? What coping strategies do exonerees use post-release to negotiate reentry into family and community? What aids and impedes their reintegration? The purpose of this chapter is not to provide a detailed response to each of these questions, but instead to describe our strategies for exploring these questions. Still, we provide an overview of our research into the post-exoneration lives of these death row exonerees to lay the foundation for better understanding how we employ feminist techniques in this project.

From August 2003 to March 2006, we interviewed sixteen of these 123 people who have been exonerated of capital crimes. Our study does not include individuals who were erroneously convicted of non–capital crimes or those who eventually were released owing to legal error, though evidence of their guilt may be substantial. We focus solely on individuals sentenced to death who have been exonerated based on evidence of actual innocence. Our sixteen participants[1] were chosen from a list of death row exonerees maintained by the Death Penalty Information Center (DPIC).[2] The DPIC list includes all individuals exonerated of capital crimes since 1973, based on one of the following criteria: (1) the original conviction was overturned on appeal with acquittal at retrial, (2) the original conviction was overturned on appeal and charges were dropped by the prosecutor or dismissed by a judge, and/or (3) an absolute pardon was granted by a governor based on new evidence of innocence.

We chose individuals who varied along a number of factors: gender, race, state in which convicted, length of time in prison, length of time on death row, length of time since exoneration, and reason for exoneration (see table 1). We traveled to all the participants and interviewed them in their place of residence or somewhere nearby of their choosing. The interviews lasted from two hours to two days. Each interview was audio-taped and transcribed, producing transcripts ranging from 55 to 180 single-spaced pages. We also compiled field notes immediately following each interview in which observations and recollections of interactions with family and friends whom we had met were recorded. All but one exoneree gave us permission to use his or her real name in the research. Each person received compensation of $125, as well as a small and appropriate thank-you gift. In most interviews, we shared meals together

TABLE I
Biographical Details of Exonerees Interviewed

Name	Sex	Race	Age at Conviction	State Where Tried	Years in Prison	Years on Death Row	Year of Exoneration	DNA?	Actual Offender(s) Found?
Fain	M	W	35	ID	18.0	18.0	2001	yes	no
Melendez	M	L	34	FL	17.5	17.5	2002	no	yes
Tibbs	M	B	34	FL	2.0	2.0	1977	no	no
Gauger	M	W	41	IL	3.0	1.0	1996	no	yes
Krone	M	W	35	AZ	9.5	2.0	2002	yes	yes
Butler	F	B	19	MS	5.0	2.0	1995	no	no
Bloodsworth	M	W	23	MD	8.0	1.0	1993	yes	yes
Brown	M	B	25	FL	14.0	14.0	1987	no	no
Wilhoit	M	W	33	OK	6.0	5.0	1993	no	no
McMillian	M	B	47	AL	6.0	6.0	1993	no	no
James	M	B	23	OH	26.0	1.0	2003	no	no
Howard	M	B	23	OH	26.0	1.0	2003	no	no
Keaton	M	B	18	FL	2.0	1.0	1973	no	yes
Gell	M	W	23	NC	8.5	5.0	2004	no	no
Cobb	M	B	37	IL	9.0	4.0	1987	no	no
Taylor*	M	B	29	IL	13.0	10.0	2003	no	no

* This exoneree prefers to remain anonymous. We have chosen this pseudonym for him.

and chatted informally. Since these initial meetings, we have maintained regular contact with each participant to provide updates on our project and see how they are doing.

Table 1 displays a summary of biographical and case-related details of the exonerees who have participated in our study to date. Fifteen participants are men; one is a woman, the only female death row exoneree on the DPIC list. Six are white; nine are black, and one a Latino. The average length of time incarcerated is 10.8 years, though this masks incredible variation in time served by exonerees, which ranges from two to twenty-six years. Though all individuals were originally convicted of capital crimes and sentenced to death row, some received retrials at which they were reconvicted but sentenced to life in prison, and, as a result, moved from death row into the general population of the prison. Thus, in some cases, the average length of time served in prison is not equivalent to the average time spent on death row, which is a lesser period of 5.6 years with a range of one to eighteen years. The amount of time that had passed since exoneration ranges from 1.5 to 32 years. Three participants were exonerated as a result of DNA testing that was not available at the time of their wrongful convictions. In two of these cases, the DNA results revealed the identity of the actual offenders. The remainder were exonerated for a variety of other reasons: prosecutorial misconduct, police misconduct, false jailhouse snitch testimony at trial, coerced confession by the defendant, flawed forensic analysis at trial, mistaken eyewitness identification, ineffective assistance of counsel, and flawed expert testimony at trial. In three of those cases, the actual offender was identified. This results in five cases in which the actual offender was identified. Three of those offenders have since been prosecuted for those crimes. In one case, the actual offender was deceased by the time of our participant's exoneration.

Four of our participants had been accused of killing family members: Gary Gauger, his elderly parents; Sabrina Butler, her nine-month-old son; Greg Wilhoit, his wife; and Scott Taylor, his wife and young son (along with five others). As a result, they suffered the loss of their family members at the same time they were being accused, tried, convicted, and sentenced to death for those murders. Sabrina Butler's story exemplifies the horror of grieving for a loved one while facing a wrongful capital murder investigation and trial:

. . . when I was at the hospital when my son died [whom she was later convicted of killing], it was about fifteen, twenty different folks askin' me questions. . . . And I'm sittin' here holdin' him [Walter Dean, her nine-month-old baby]. And everybody's askin' me . . . I could have said I was a elephant! I don't know what I said. All kind of stuff. Everybody was askin' me, "What happened? Who did this?" And you know . . . and I'm sittin' there . . . [she begins to get emotional] . . . I don't know what I said, what I didn't say. I mean, you know . . . And, nobody would help me. *Nobody*.

Gary Gauger explains what it was like to come to grips with the violent death of his parents while being manipulated by the police into believing that he was the person responsible for their murders:

. . . within twelve hours, the police were telling me I'd done it. They had all the evidence. I'd failed the polygraph test. And I was in a very vulnerable, emotional state, looking to the police to help solve the murder of my parents. So that's why they had such an easy time with me. I was trusting them. I was very vulnerable. . . . I mean, they had me believing it enough that the next morning, after I'd been charged, I tried to inhale toilet paper [in order to commit suicide]. . . . The only way I could say I maybe had grieved a little bit was about a month and a half, two months after my arrest, I had a dream. And I was speaking with my mother. And then I realized, I said, "Oh, wait a minute, but you were killed." And then she faded away. I asked for a hug [he begins to cry and whisper]—Man, I didn't wanna do this [deep breath and silence]—um, I asked for a hug and then she faded away, and I started crying. And I woke up crying. . . . that was as close as I had come to mourning their murders, their deaths. . . . I feel like a plastic barrier holding back the ocean. You know, not much substance and a lot of weight.

Kirk Bloodsworth and Charles Fain were accused of killing young girls who also had been sexually molested, thus subjecting them to vile treatments by other inmates in prison and passionate public hatred. Delbert Tibbs, Walter McMillian, and Shabaka Brown are all black men accused of raping and/or killing white victims in the Deep South. Most exonerees did not come close to an actual execution date, though two are worth mentioning. Shabaka Brown came within fifteen hours of his execution before being granted a stay. He lost several teeth in the scuffle he had with prison guards when they came to measure him for his burial suit:

. . . the most telling thing during that time was when they took me out of that cell. And they had a civilian with them, with the Lieutenant. And the civilian had a tape measure in his hand. And they took the handcuffs off me and asked me to raise my hands, like that. And the tape measure went around my chest, and around my waist, and the inseams of my leg. And then it struck me. Son of a bitch's measuring me for a burial suit, you know. And I struck out. I mean, 'cause I was standin' there, and they was doing this so mechanically. I mean, it was almost like [bangs on the table] I was an inanimate object. And for some reason, something just . . . [Shabaka shouts in frustration]. And I was determined right then and there that if they were going to kill me, they were going to do it with some damn dignity. . . . This is how I lost these teeth.

Sabrina Butler believed that her execution date was imminent, though she had, in fact, received a stay. On March 8, 1990, the judge announced her execution date as July 2, 1990. This date was seared into her consciousness because it was two days before her dead son's birthday (the son she was wrongly convicted of killing). What the judge said subsequently was lost to her: the execution would be stayed pending appeals. She was a young black woman of nineteen in the Deep South—a high school drop-out and mother of two small children. She did not understand the legal process. She sat on death row, mourned her child, and worried about her other child languishing in foster care. As she awoke on July 2, she believed it would be her day to die:

> When that day came, I was the scaredest person in the world. That is a feelin' that I wouldn't wish on my worst enemy. I stood there at the little old door . . . the slot in it . . . and you [would] just stand there and look. And I thought, by me watchin' TV and stuff, that they was gonna come and get you, and you was gonna have this ball and chain on. And these people gonna be walkin' beside you. You goin' down this long hall, you know what I'm sayin'. Like they did in *The Green Mile*. . . . And I was scared to death. . . . You know, I was standin' there cryin'. I kept tellin' her [the woman in the cell next to Sabrina], "Yeah, they gonna kill me. They gonna kill me. Somebody call my mama, or somethin' and tell 'em that," you know, "I love 'em." . . . That whole day I just sat in my room. I couldn't sleep. I couldn't eat. [She's crying.] That is the most humiliating, scary thing that any person could ever go through. I was scared to death because I thought that they was gonna kill me for somethin' that I didn't do. And I couldn't tell nobody to help me.

No one came to get her. Her anxiety mounted. In the late afternoon when she asked a guard "aren't they supposed to come and kill me today?" she learned, only then, that she would not be put to death that day.

Stories like these ripple through the pages of the transcripts from our interviews. Our participants relate that their losses are profound and multiple, their recovery hampered by social and economic obstacles, their feelings of injustice inflamed, and their stigma at times overwhelming. Our challenge as researchers has been to gain access to our participants and to their stories and experiences—their feelings of loss and injustice, their beliefs about prison and the death penalty, their fears about and hopes for the future. Death row exonerees are often quite guarded in their interactions with those outside of their immediate family and/or legal team. These individuals have had their words twisted and used against them; they have been manipulated and misrepresented; they have been "used" and forgotten by politicians, criminal justice officials, and even other researchers. They do not trust with ease.

Greg Wilhoit depended on his defense lawyer, a hired attorney with a solid reputation in the community, to point out the numerous problems with the prosecution's accusation that he had killed his wife. The attorney instead asked Greg to provide a list of questions to ask the witnesses at trial, having developed none of his own, frequently joked with the judge and prosecutor in court, and once threw up in the judge's chambers after coming to court drunk. Gary Gauger depended on the judge at his trial to ensure that he received a fair proceeding. Instead, while Gary was testifying on his own behalf, the judge made misleading and crude gestures intended to indicate his disbelief of Gary's story. When the lawyers objected to the judge's behavior, the judge simply spun his chair to face the wall and remained as such for the remainder of Gary's testimony. Sabrina Butler explained that she now refused to do interviews for "free" as she had been "used bad" by others. Because we offered $125 for her time, she believed she could take us seriously.

We have had to establish ourselves as worthy of listening to their stories, as people worthy of their trust. We have adopted a feminist methodological approach because we find it best able to meet this challenge posed by our research process.

Feminist Methods in Theory and Practice

Since classics by Reinharz (1979) and Harding (1986) revolutionized how social science can and must incorporate gender and gender considerations into theory, analysis, and methodological development, feminist scholars have expanded sociology from a "value-free" social science into a socially relevant, activist-oriented, and grounded theoretical approach. According to Reinharz (1992: 6), feminist methods are "used by people who identify themselves as feminist or as part of the women's movement." We identify ourselves as feminist and are concerned that our approach to research maintains certain principles grounded in feminist theory and methodology. We also find that feminist methods provide the techniques that allow us to overcome most effectively the challenges unique to accessing death row exonerees. In this section, we will discuss four central principles of feminist method and how we realize these in our study of death row exonerees: (1) the belief that research is a collaborative process; (2) the centrality of trust and openness in this collaborative process; (3) the role of the "ethic of care" in research; and (4) the necessity of bringing issues of gender, race, and class to the forefront of research.

Each research project requires idiosyncratic adaptations of method, especially qualitative projects, in order to learn about and analyze the described phenomenon. Our project is no exception. We have chosen to examine rare and traumatic events, to combine our established expertise in wrongful convictions (Westervelt) and the death penalty (Cook) with our ideological convictions as feminists committed to ethical research that illuminates and enhances people's lived realities. Thus, we "mix and match" from the best practices and principles of qualitative research methods to meet the goals of our project—to record, analyze, and learn about the impact of a wrongful capital conviction directly from the exonerated death row inmates.

Fundamentally, social research is best conducted within a collaborative setting between the scholars and the participants in the research (Ely 1991). Accordingly, we, as researchers, do not own or control the means and the outcomes of the research. Feminist research can create "a sense of connectedness and equality between researcher and researched" (Patton 2002: 129). Our role in the collaborative process is to help participants—in this case, exonerees—to tell their own stories, which in turn have consequence for modern society and criminological and sociological theory (Patton 2002). As facilitators, we are guided by the principle that we neither criticize nor categorize the participants or their experiences. Bringing their voices to the public issues of capital punishment and wrongful convictions requires us to let their voices be heard as authentically as possible, in their own words (Cook 1998) without "filtering" by our own interpretations or categorizations into psychological "disorders" or social [mal]adaptations. Because we hope to explore and understand the flesh-and-blood realism of their experiences, we cannot reduce their stories to statistical patterns or disengaged numerical measures of various aspects of their stories. Thus, our feminist methods are inductive rather than reductive.

Furthermore, as individuals who have been talked about, classified, categorized, and legally processed as if they were murderers, these participants have rarely been granted an opportunity to speak for themselves. Their lawyers talked for them (with varying degrees of effectiveness); the prosecutors spoke against their right to live; witnesses spoke against them; journalists spoke with authority about their cases; jurors convicted them, and judges condemned them to death. All the while, the participants in this study felt powerless to respond effectively in their own words and rarely believed they were truly heard. As noted above, the judge overseeing Gary Gauger's trial spun his chair to face the wall rather than listen fully to Gary's testimony. Our project provides an opportunity for the exonerees' authentic voices to be heard, thus affirming the value and meaning of their lived experiences.

We have made a number of choices in our research process to increase the level of collaboration between us and our participants. We always allow them to choose the location of the interview in order to ensure they are as comfortable as possible. We typically do not prefer to interview in a participant's home but instead recommend quiet places with no phones and/or children, such as hotel or library conference rooms. However, we have completed interviews with several exonerees in their homes because they clearly were most comfortable in that setting. We also provide all participants with a copy of the final transcript and allow them to make any changes. Again, the point is to ensure the accuracy and authenticity of their stories, which is enhanced by giving them as much input into the final "product" as possible. We have rejected numerous attempts by other researchers and funding agencies who ask us to subject participants to a psychological evaluation and/or survey before the interview. We believe it essential to rely on exonerees for their own assessments of their well-being, both past and present; they must be allowed to author their own stories rather than being placed into prefabricated categories of emotional and/or psychological conditions. Exonerees view their post-release reintegration and coping as a process, and they frequently compare their current states of mind with their memories of times past. So, though they may "objectively" suffer from depression or post-traumatic stress disorder, if they were to be given a battery of tests, they would see themselves as more psychologically, socially, and emotionally sound (or damaged) today than they were several months or years previous. Thus, we think it essential to allow them the opportunity to speak for themselves and claim their own stories, free from the labels placed on them by others (Goldman and Whalen 1990; Goodley 1996; Hones 1998).[3]

Unfortunately, the power of labeling can never fully be escaped, and these people's stories are powerful testimonies to the enduring consequences of ascribed stigmas, socio-legal classifications that render a human being "worthy" of capital punishment, as well as the capacity of hope, faith, and fortitude. Part of our feminist epistemological framework draws from Patricia Hill Collins (1991), who teaches that dualistic approaches employing mutually exclusive categories are less helpful than "both/and" frameworks that recognize complexities of identity and ownership of authentic selves. So, while on the one hand, our participants have been frightfully traumatized, stigmatized, and bereaved, at the same time, they have survived on hope, dreams, and desires for justice. As Delbert Tibbs, one of our participants, comments, "you have to make medicine out of poison."

We have chosen a semistructured interview method known as the "life history technique" for recording the life stories of our participants because this method is premised on the assumption that an interview is a collaborative event (Atkinson 1998; Goodley 1996; Hones 1998). Interviewing participants has an important legacy in feminist methodology. Hilary Graham (cited in Reinharz 1992: 18) refers to interviewing as "the principle means by which feminists have sought to achieve the active involvement of their respondents in the construction of data about their lives." The life history technique emphasizes this "active involvement" of all research participants (scholar and subject) and allows the participant to dictate the direction of the interview as much as the researcher. For example, we found that more than one participant created opportunities to discuss at length the adequacy (or inadequacy) of the current political administration's handling of current events, including those not directly related to criminal justice or death penalty issues. No matter which direction we took with the interview, several exonerees came back over and over to politics. Ray Krone spent quite a bit of time discussing how he adapted to prison life itself, and life on death row in particular, even though our primary focus was on his life once he was released from prison. When participants took these directions in our discussion, we followed their lead, believing that we can learn as much by discussing what they deem important as we can from following our own interview schedule.

The interview process also liberates participants from the confines of a "survey" or set of predetermined answers (on a scale of 1 to 10, for example) to questions prepared in advance by the scholar. It provides the participant time to reflect on what is most salient to him or her about the experiences being discussed. It also allows for unexpected "tangents" to emerge into full-blown themes that might be unanticipated by the researcher, as is typical when using this type of grounded theory approach (Glaser and Strauss 1967). An interesting "tangent" occurred when we interviewed Tim Howard in Ohio. While we were talking, his attorney called, and Tim mentioned that we were there interviewing him. This attorney had represented Tim successfully on appeal, culminating in his exoneration and release after twenty-six years in prison. Tim invited him to join us for the afternoon. This afforded us another perspective on Tim's story that we had not anticipated or planned.

As Tierney (1998) notes, a collaborative interview process is particularly important for marginalized peoples and those who have experienced powerlessness and exploitation, as is certainly true for our participants, because it increases the level of trust between the researchers and the participants and reduces the possibility that the interview itself will become just another form of exploitation as viewed by the participants. More than one exoneree has told us that researchers came to interview them who were never heard from again, leaving the exonerees feeling used and exploited. This brings us to the second principle of feminist methodology essential to our research—the establishment of trust.

The process of conducting interviews of death row exonerees has been an exercise of trust, respect, and relationship building. These are guiding principles of qualitative and feminist methods (Patton 2002). Because the people we are interviewing have been so terribly exploited (wrongly accused, convicted, and sentenced to death), the degree to which they are able to trust us, or anyone, varies. We do not assume from the start that they should or would want to talk to us. We begin the process of building trust with our decisions about how to first contact our participants. We try to gain access to exonerees through networks of scholars, attorneys, and activists who work with and are trusted by the exonerees. Some of these individuals we know and some we do not. For those we do not know, we provide references to allow them to check on our credibility and ethics as researchers before they put us into contact with the exonerees with whom they work. We rarely "cold call" exonerees but prefer instead to have these other trusted individuals contact them on our behalf, or at the least we initiate contact through an introductory letter. This approach seems to have worked well for us, such as when attempting to set up an interview with Shabaka Brown:

To be honest with you, the only reason I'm sittin' at this table is because of Mike Radelet [a close friend of Shabaka's who is a colleague of ours]. I mean, that's the truth. . . . I trust [his] judgment. We talk a lot. We talk when I'm at work or at home. We e-mail each other. I trust his judgment. He said ya'll was cool people.

Though the contact information for many exonerees can be accessed through paid online "background check" services, we have chosen not to pay for such information but instead to continually rely on these more trusted network members for access. By doing so, we hope to relay to exonerees that we are interested in hearing about their experiences but that any contact with us is up to them; they have control over their own stories and to whom they tell them.

We also attempt to build trust by following up with exonerees on any requests made of us. Two specific examples come to mind. First, while traveling in North Carolina, the son of one of our participants needed some immediate help in an emergency situation. The participant called Saundra to ask for advice on how best to negotiate the situation for his son in North Carolina. Saundra made some inquiries of colleagues and provided as much information as she could to help them better address their problem. Sabrina Butler also made a request of us to help her get a copy of the transcript of her second trial, at which she had been acquitted. During this retrial, her former husband testified that he had been the last person to see her baby alive, not Sabrina. This testimony had stunned her because though she knew that she did not kill her child, she did not, to that point, know what had happened to her child. She wanted the transcript in order to reread that portion of his testimony. However, because she was acquitted at this trial and thus the transcript was not needed for a possible appeal, the court did not automatically make one. She asked us to help her get a copy. We pursued every angle possible to locate the trial transcript for Sabrina, including finding the name of the court stenographer on duty during her trial (more than ten years ago) and attempting to make contact with this person at her new home in Texas. Although we were unable to find the transcript, we did provide Sabrina with copies of all of the legal documents that we had in our files, and she seemed to appreciate our extended efforts on her behalf.

Trust also is enhanced, we believe, by a forthright acknowledgment and exploration of the identity of all participants; therefore, if anyone is interested in our lives or asks us personal questions, we reply as fully as possible. We willingly reveal relevant details of our personal lives and histories to participants. We cannot hope to gain openness and honesty from people if we are closed and guarded about ourselves. In principle, this is considered by some to be sound feminist practice (Oakley 1981). For us, it is essential in helping us bridge the gap between our experience and theirs. This is even more important given that we are two middle-class white women interviewing working-class and poor men (mostly), many of whom are African American or Hispanic. Thus, we engage in self-disclosure when asked or appropriate, as long as it does not silence or infringe on the participants' telling their own stories.

We believe that another element of the establishment of trust is that the listener believes the speaker. Crowden (cited in Reinharz 1992: 3) suggests that understanding someone comes from "seeing [him or her] with a loving eye," and we would add, hearing with a loving ear, even if participants are not particularly lovable (Presser 2005; Scully 1988). We do not argue that "believing the speaker" means relying on the speaker as the sole source of information. To the contrary, we collect extensive documentation on each exoneree before our interview, including all publicly available legal documents, newspaper articles, scholarly books or articles, and even film clips. We use these materials to become intimately familiar with the details of each case and as a reference to check exonerees' own memories of such details. Instead, we argue that "believing the speaker" means to give credence to the story being told by the participant, to give it weight and indicate acceptance of his or her feelings, beliefs, and claims.

In this project, the participants have fruitlessly proclaimed their innocence for decades, having not been heard or believed by powerful entities (prosecutors, judges, juries) and the public, a deafness to their voices that nearly resulted in their deaths. For example, when Kirk Bloodsworth was released from prison after DNA evidence revealed he was not the man who raped and murdered nine-year-old Dawn Hamilton (Junkin 2004), he returned to his hometown and his family home on the eastern shore of Maryland. Though Kirk had proclaimed his innocence since the beginning and believed that the DNA results finally vindicated him and gave credence to what he had been arguing all along, many in his community, as well as the prosecutors in the case, did not agree. Many townspeople believed he got out on a "technicality" and continued to treat him as if he were guilty. The prosecutor in the case only enhanced the community's hostilities by continuing to state her belief in Kirk's guilt. The barber who had cut Kirk's hair since childhood refused to do so any longer; parents would clutch their children when he passed them in the local grocery store; neighbors yelled "child killer in the neighborhood!" when he went door-to-door looking for odd jobs because no one would employ him for long; former coworkers wrote "Child Killer" on his truck in dirt; he received death threats and hate mail. Ten years after his exoneration and release, the prosecutor in the case finally submitted the DNA from the case to the national DNA databank and discovered the true identity of the actual rapist and murderer of Dawn Hamilton. When she met with Kirk to tell him this news, she apologized to him, providing him with the recognition and belief that he had so longed for: "And then just like water off a duck's back, my pain disappeared. My anger, it was all gone." He goes on to explain what he wanted most upon his exoneration: "I wanted to be loved again. I wanted people to respect me. And I didn't want people to think I was a child killer anymore. Out of everything, you know, that was the biggest thing. . . . I wanted love and acceptance." He wanted to be heard and believed.

Thus, to believe the participants in this research is essential for their truths to be illuminated, understood, and perhaps compensated and affirmed. We are not "studying" them, so much as we are learning from them about the nature of personal fortitude, faith, forgiveness, anger, rage, obstacles, frustrations, racism, sexism, debilitation, hope, and despair. Such belief is an essential foundation of trust.

A third guiding principle of our methodology, borrowed and adapted from Gilligan (1982), is an "ethic of care" for ourselves and for our participants, recognizing and honoring the relational dynamics involved in research collaboration. This ethic of care we apply to our care for each other and our families and begins with our mutual trust. We have full lives; we are both busy women with families, jobs, and a multitude of responsibilities. This research is more time-consuming than some and has required extensive travel, taking us away from family and other responsibilities at home and work. We have each taken turns being overwhelmed with various aspects of our personal needs such that our capacity to focus on the research has vacillated. Fortunately, when one of us is stressed out, the other pulls more of the load. We care for and about each other, and our quality of life. This "ethic of care" emerged very early in our working relationship in that one of our first conversations about this project revolved around our concerns about how this might affect our families. Saundra's son was only two years old when we began this research, and as such we agreed that his needs were to be our first priority. We resolved, for example, to schedule interview trips far enough apart to not take Saundra away from home for too long or too often. It is our pact with each other.

Our ethic of care also applies to the participants in the project. Because we typically interview them only once, and we live long distances away from them, we maintain contact in a variety of ways. We send holiday gifts to each person; we call and write to them regularly to inquire as to their general well-being; we share their joys and provide advice or support when asked. We try to keep them in contact with each other by filling them in on each other's lives whenever they ask about someone. Recently, on an interview trip to Chicago, we took one exoneree, Delbert Tibbs, on a day trip to visit another exoneree and close friend, Gary Gauger, as they had not been able to see each other for some time. We realize, also, that there is a limit to what we can provide; we are not lawyers, and our resources are limited. But our affection and concern for each is real. This guiding principle helps us to deal with the stressful aspects of the work because we do not see these conversations as one-time obligations, but rather as ongoing relationships that enhance our lives and our understanding of broader social issues of justice.

The final guiding principle of our research drawn from feminist concern is the necessity of bringing issues of gender, race, and class to the forefront of the interview process and analysis (Collins 1991; Donnelly et al. 2005). As noted earlier, we are two white, middle-class, well-educated women interviewing mostly males who are predominantly working or lower class and who have varying levels of education. More than half of our participants are African American or Hispanic. Rather than approach our participants with a "color-blind" demeanor (Donnelly et al. 2005), we openly problematize the complexities of class and race/ethnic structures in our interviews. For many of the participants, negative racial stereotypes had significant impact on the circumstances leading up to their wrongful convictions. Delbert Tibbs, for example, was convicted on the basis of false cross-racial eyewitness identification. Walter McMillian, a black man, was convicted of killing a white woman in Alabama in a trial where the (white) judge was named for Confederate General Robert E. Lee. Sabrina Butler was a young mother of two small children, black, poor, and on welfare in Mississippi, and was portrayed in the media as an unfit mother and "welfare queen" in the early 1990s. We cannot be "blind" to these racialized and class-based patterns of structural oppression if we are serious in our efforts to understand and fully analyze exonerees' experiences.

Implications for Feminist Theory and Methods

Our experience in learning from death row exonerees over the past several years teaches us that the gender of the research "subjects" should not be the determinant of whether feminist methods should be used in a research project. The guiding principles of feminist methodology can apply equally as well to an examination of the lives of men as it can to those of women (Messerschmidt 2000, 2004). The use of feminist methods should be determined by the nature of the data a researcher is seeking, not the gender of the participants. Feminist methods are particularly well-suited if the researcher seeks an understanding of participants as whole people with often conflicting beliefs and feelings who exist within a larger web of obligations, relationships, and structures of power.

This is particularly true if one seeks to understand participants who have been marginalized, disenfranchised, or exploited. By defining the research as collaborative and the "subjects" as active participants, the feminist method allows participants agency and an opportunity to own their stories and be heard and accepted in a way often denied to them otherwise. By recognizing from the outset the class, racial, and gendered structures of oppression that may be at work in their lives, this method gives voice to the larger structural processes that shape their experiences and that often go unseen and unheard by others.

Thus, this method provides a framework for building trust with those participants who may be unsure about the research process and creates opportunities for understanding individuals and groups who may very well be inaccessible when approached in any other way.

Finally, we add that a feminist approach is unique in that it treats both participants and researchers as whole persons. Our participants are more than "just" death row exonerees. They are fathers, mothers, sons, daughters. They have jobs and dreams for the future that often do not revolve around their status as "exoneree." We try to interact with the whole person as much as possible, even though our contact was initiated because of their "exoneree" status. When we write or talk on the phone, we as often ask about their children as we do about the most recent activities related to their cases. Greg Wilhoit called us when he became a grandfather for the first time. We sent Sabrina Butler some information about an eye disease when she told us of some ongoing headaches she was experiencing. We listen to a CD that Perry Cobb made for us of his singing, his occupation before his wrongful conviction. We attended the book launch party for Kirk Bloodsworth's biography, *Bloodsworth* (Junkin 2004), and met many of his family members and his lawyer.

This same principle applies to us as researchers as well. We live within larger webs of obligations, relationships, and structures of power that impact on how we approach research and how we approach a research participant or even a particular interview. Detachment from one's topic or research participant may sound effective in theory, but it often prevents connection and true understanding in practice. As researchers, we bring experiences and emotions to the table when conducting an interview. To the extent that sharing those pieces of one's self with the participant can aid in achieving a better understanding of the participant's own story, the feminist method recognizes its value. Therefore, we find that feminist methods are adaptable, flexible, and promote unifying themes of analytical and ethical importance that can allow a more equitable exchange among research participants and a more complete picture of the lived experiences, in this case, of death row exonerees.

Discussion Questions

1. How does this study of death row exonerees differ from past research in the area of the wrongful conviction of the innocent?
2. What are the four guiding principles of feminist methods that are incorporated into the analysis of death row exonerees?

3. How have the researchers created a collaborative research process?
4. How do the researchers establish trust between themselves and the participants, and why is that important?
5. How are feminist methods flexible and adaptable, particularly in studying death row exonerees?

Acknowledgments

We express our sincere gratitude to the following people: Michael Radelet, Rob Warden, Chris Powell, Susan Sharp, Sarah Tofte, Mike Maume, Babette Boyd, Peter Neufeld, and Barry Scheck, as well as all of the amazing people who have participated in this project from whom we have learned so much. Both authors contributed equally to this paper.

Funding for this project has been provided by the External Proposal Development Incentive Program, Office of the Associate Provost for Research, University of North Carolina Greensboro, and the American Sociological Association's Fund for the Advancement of the Discipline Award supported by the American Sociological Association and the National Science Foundation.

Notes

1. We prefer the term research "participants" (rather than "subjects") because it provides an inclusive and egalitarian framework around all of us participating in this project—scholars and subjects.

2. For more information, refer to the Death Penalty Information Center's Web site: http://www.deathpenaltyinfo.org.

3. We do not argue that such psychological measures are useless or without value but simply that they are not a substitute for and are no more reliable or "true" than the stories that participants tell of their experiences in their own words.

References

Atkinson, Robert. 1998. *The Life Story Interview*. Thousand Oaks, Calif.: Sage.
Campbell, Kathryn, and Myriam Denov. 2004. "The Burden of Innocence: Coping with a Wrongful Imprisonment." *Canadian Journal of Criminology and Criminal Justice* 46:139–63.
Collins, Patricia Hill. 1991. *Black Feminist Thought: Knowledge, Consciousness, and the Politics of Empowerment*. New York: Routledge.
Cook, Kimberly J. 1998. *Divided Passions: Public Opinions on Abortion and the Death Penalty*. Boston: Northeastern University Press.

Donnelly, Denise, Kimberly J. Cook, Debra Van Ausdale, and Lara Foley. 2005. "White Privilege, Color Blindness and Services to Battered Women." *Violence against Women* 11:6–37.

Ely, Margot, with Margaret Anzul, Teri Friedman, Diane Garner, and Ann McCormack Steinmetz. 1991. *Doing Qualitative Research: Circles within Circles.* New York: Falmer Press.

Gilligan, Carol. 1982. *In a Different Voice: Psychological Theory and Women's Development.* Cambridge, Mass.: Harvard University Press.

Glaser, Barney G., and Anselm L. Strauss. 1967. *The Discovery of Grounded Theory.* New York: Aldine de Gruyter.

Goldman, Marion S., and Jack Whalen. 1990. "From the New Left to the New Enlightenment: The Methodological Implications of Public Attention to Private Lives." *Qualitative Sociology* 13:85–107.

Goodley, Danny. 1996. "Tales of Hidden Lives: A Critical Examination of Life History Research with People Who Have Learning Difficulties." *Disability and Society* 11:333–48.

Gross, Samuel R., Kristen Jacoby, Daniel J. Matheson, Nicholas Montgomery, and Sujata Patel. 2004. "Exonerations in the United States, 1989 through 2003." Unpublished manuscript. Available at: http://www.law.umich.edu/newsandinfo/exonerations-in-us.pdf.

Grounds, Adrian. 2004. "Psychological Consequences of Wrongful Conviction and Imprisonment." *Canadian Journal of Criminology and Criminal Justice* 46:165–82.

Harding, Sandra. 1986. *The Science Question in Feminism.* Ithaca, N.Y.: Cornell University Press.

Hones, Donald F. 1998. "Known in Part: The Transformational Power of Narrative Inquiry." *Qualitative Inquiry* 4:225–48.

Huff, C. Ronald, Arye Rattner, and Edward Sagarin. 1996. *Convicted but Innocent: Wrongful Conviction and Public Policy.* Thousand Oaks, Calif.: Sage.

Junkin, Tim. 2004. *Bloodsworth: The True Story of the First Death Row Inmate Exonerated by DNA.* Chapel Hill, N.C.: Algonquin Press.

Leo, Richard A., and Richard J. Ofshe. 1998. "The Consequences of False Confessions: Deprivations of Liberty and Miscarriages of Justice in the Age of Psychological Interrogation." *Journal of Criminology and Criminal Law* 88:429–96.

Liebman, James, and Jeffrey Fagan. 2000. "A Broken System." Parts 1 and 2. Available at http://justice.policy.net/cjedfund/dpstudy.

Messerschmidt, James W. 2000. *Nine Lives: Adolescent Masculinities, the Body, and Violence.* Boulder, Colo.: Westview Press.

———. 2004. *Flesh and Blood: Adolescent Gender Diversity and Violence.* Lanham, Md.: Rowman and Littlefield.

Oakley, Ann. 1981. "Interviewing Women: A Contradiction in Terms." In *Doing Feminist Research.* ed. H. Roberts, 30–61. London: Routledge and Kegan Paul.

Olson, Robert K. 2002. "Miscarriage of Justice: A Cop's View." *Judicature* 86:74–77.

Patton, Michael Quinn. 2002. *Qualitative Research and Evaluation Methods.* 3rd ed. Thousand Oaks, Calif.: Sage Publications.

Presser, Lois. 2005. " Negotiating Power and Narrative in Research: Implications for Feminist Methodology." *Signs: Journal of Women in Culture and Society* 30 (4):2067–90.

Radelet, Michael L., Hugo Adam Bedau, and Constance E. Putnam. 1992. *In Spite of Innocence*. Boston: Northeastern University Press.

Reinharz, Shulamit. 1979. *On Becoming a Social Scientist: From Survey Research to Participant Observation*. San Francisco: Josey Bass.

———. 1992. *Feminist Methods in Social Research*. New York: Oxford University Press.

Scheck, Barry, Peter Neufeld, and Jim Dwyer. 2000. *Actual Innocence*. New York: Doubleday.

Scully, Diana. 1988. "Convicted Rapists' Perceptions of Self and Victim: Role Taking and Emotions." *Gender and Society* 1:61–84.

Tierney, William. 1998. "Life History's History: Subjects Foretold." *Qualitative Inquiry* 4:49–70.

Westervelt, Saundra D., and John A. Humphrey, eds. 2001. *Wrongly Convicted: Perspectives on Failed Justice*. New Brunswick, N.J.: Rutgers University Press.

Chapter 3   Shana L. Maier and Brian A. Monahan

Dispatches from the Field

Negotiating Difference and Diversity in
Criminological Research

Imagine for a moment that you are a white, middle-class male who grew up in an affluent neighborhood and are currently a student at a university studying sociology and criminal justice. For an assignment, your professor asks you to interview a leader of a female gang to explore how her life experiences—such as poverty, drug use, violence, educational attainment—influence her behaviors. You begin to panic and want to run in the opposite direction. After class, you meet with your friends, exasperated at the thought of undertaking such a seemingly impossible task: "Can you believe that my professor gave me this assignment? Why can't I just study something I know about, like drinking or gambling among college students? How in the world am I supposed to interview a female gang leader? We have nothing in common!" This kind of reaction would certainly be understandable: studying crime and deviance can be intimidating, particularly as it often involves dealing with people, places, and situations that are entirely unfamiliar to students.

The truth is, although most students profess to be intrigued by the criminological research of others, many seem to have difficulty envisioning themselves as researchers investigating similar subject matter. In talking with our colleagues and our students to explore this further, we have come to realize that much of this apprehension among intrepid researchers stems from an often overlooked issue in crime and deviance research: the fact that those who conduct criminological research are often quite different from their respondents in terms of observable physical characteristics (e.g., race, gender, ethnicity, age), social status, social biography, or socioeconomic placement.

Crime and deviance researchers have, in recent years, increasingly alluded to the fact that the relative positions of researchers and their subjects can shape who and what is studied, the kinds of questions researchers ask, and how data gets collected and analyzed (Arendell 1997; Horowitz 1986; Lofland and Lofland 1995; McCorkel and Myers 2003; Wesely 2006). The present chapter seeks to build on this existing body of research by exploring issues of difference and diversity as they affect the research process and by illustrating some of the general strategies and specific techniques that researchers use in dealing with these issues in their own research.

Methods

To explore the role that difference and diversity play in criminological research, we conducted interviews with twenty-nine leading or emerging scholars who study matters of crime and deviance. Although many of these researchers alternately use quantitative and qualitative methodologies in their research, we limit our inquiry here to qualitative research. Qualitative methodology—which typically involves some combination of interviews, observation, or ethnographic placement in the social world being studied—is employed when the goal of the research is to grasp the meanings and nuances of an area of study; it is designed to capture social life as participants experience it (Bachman and Schutt 2003). Proponents embrace the qualitative research approach because it shifts the focus to the experiences and views of study participants and enables researchers to contextualize observation and interview data within the natural environment of the subjects' social worlds (Fleisher 1998b). In this chapter, we focus on qualitative research because it is our belief that issues of difference and diversity are most pronounced in the qualitative research setting.

In developing our sample, we began with purposive sampling; an initial selection of researchers was culled from a review of leading academic journals and papers presented at recent American Society of Criminology meetings. This was then followed by a snowball sampling technique, whereby we asked our colleagues and initial respondents to recommend additional participants. The twenty-nine interviews were conducted between August 2005 and March 2006, with twenty-six of the interviews conducted by telephone and three carried out in person. More than half ($N = 15$) of the respondents possessed greater than ten years of research experience (the total range of research experience ranged from three to thirty-five years). Nearly all ($N = 24$) of the respondents held doctorate degrees in sociology, anthropology, criminal justice, or criminology; three were doctoral students pursuing a degree in one of these fields, one (a staff member at a non–university research center) held a master's degree, and one (a staff member at a university research center) held a bachelor's degree and had no plans to matriculate further.

The researchers studied a wide range of crime- and deviance-related topics including prostitutes, strippers, and other sex workers; members of the "club culture"; drug dealers; drug users; white-collar offenders; gang members; juvenile offenders; female offenders; incarcerated offenders; active offenders; and victims of deviant or criminal activity (e.g., rape victims, battered women, abuse victims).[1] Researchers cited a number of factors that influenced their general areas of inquiry or specific topics that they researched: a few noted that long-standing personal interests that provided the impetus for their research; for some, professional curiosity drove their research; for others, it was notable personal, professional, or volunteer experiences that shaped their research interests; a few maintained that their decisions about who and what to study were determined largely by funding opportunities (this factor was most commonly cited by those in our sample who were currently, or had been previously, affiliated with a research center); still others claimed that they select research topics based on what they feel will help fill perceived "gaps" in the scholarly literature (i.e., topics or populations that, in their estimation, have not previously been thoroughly or appropriately studied).

During the interviews, we asked the researchers to discuss differences between themselves and their subjects and inquired about the strategies and techniques they used to deal with these differences during the qualitative research process (e.g., gaining access, entering the field, gathering data). Drawing on their responses, we identify several general strategies and specific tactics commonly used by researchers to negotiate the field research process.[2] Our primary goal in this chapter is not to provide a "how to" manual (although we do offer tips and techniques whenever possible); rather, we aim to spur the reader to give more thought to the role of difference and diversity in the research process, to take into account some of the ways that one might be different from those he or she encounters in the research setting, and to consider possible ways to constructively deal with those differences.

Our findings reveal that there is not an established collection of techniques and strategies for dealing with difference and diversity that will work for all researchers. Rather, the appropriate strategies for dealing with differences between researcher and subject are determined by the nature of the research, the characteristics of the sample, and the experience and research approach of the researcher. Further, negotiating difference and diversity must be viewed a process—one that requires constant attention, openness, and flexibility from the researcher. In the sections that follow, we outline some of the ways that researchers negotiate issues of difference and diversity in two key phases of the research process: (1) gaining access to a sample of interest and (2) operating in the field setting.

Negotiating Difference and Diversity to Gain Access

Gaining access to people involved in criminal or deviant activity—or victims of such activity—is often a difficult task. Some research participants welcome the opportunity to share their stories and knowledge with researchers, whereas others are exceedingly reluctant to participate in such research. Crime, by its very nature, involves breaking the law, and deviant acts are so because they bump up against moral boundaries, so it is understandable that offenders may be reluctant to be "studied." When the researcher is noticeably different from potential sample members (e.g., race, gender, socioeconomic status, occupation), as is often the case in criminological research, gaining access to the desired population can become even more difficult. Researchers suggested two key strategies that one could use to help overcome issues of difference and diversity in order to gain access to a desired sample: (1) *do your homework* to become familiar with those you intend to study; and (2) *break the ice* with potential respondents so that you can become a familiar presence in their social worlds before actual data collection is under-way.

Do Your Homework

Developing a familiarity with the subject matter is obviously an important aspect of any research, but we raise the issue here because our respondents maintained that research success rests on successfully negotiating the potential hurdles of difference and diversity in order to gain access to research participants. Researchers must become as familiar as possible with the issues, people, and locations that they plan to study. In many instances, familiarity will be gained by extensively researching the targeted population by surveying the academic literature or reviewing public records, media content, and other archival source material.

Familiarity may also stem from prior interaction with a targeted population, perhaps in a professional capacity (e.g., a lawyer who later studies criminals, a volunteer in a battered women's shelter who later studies battered women) or from the shared social biography or parallel life experiences between the researcher and her or his subjects. For example, one drug culture scholar noted how his experiences during his young adult life increased his comfort level with different types of people: "As a result of sex and drugs and rock-n-roll issues in my life, I spent most of my teen years and twenties supporting myself in working-class jobs. I learned to be comfortable with a wide variety of people and my misspent youth is sort of this perverse investment that has paid off in my career." A gang researcher thought her personal familiarity with the gang's neighborhood through prior research and volunteer work helped her with her later work: "I had an ability to converse with them about the reality of the place they lived. I knew who the gangs were, I knew about the park and the school and the difficulty in getting the kids to school. I could talk with them about all that beforehand. . . . And my familiarity with their living arrangements and their experiences definitely helped."

Developing a familiarity with one's subject matter and potential respondents is essential to successful research; it can enhance the overall research design, improve field instruments, allow researchers to anticipate possible concerns respondents might have about participating, and help researchers develop and demonstrate confidence while in the field setting.

Break the Ice

Research is all about trust and rapport (Denzin and Lincoln 1994; Fleisher 1998b). This is especially true in criminological research, given the kinds of issues and behaviors often studied. A researcher cannot just show up in the field and expect to immediately be able to gather detailed ethnographic data. Our researchers suggest that, whenever possible, researchers should make themselves known in the community and among potential sample members well in advance of data collection. This can help to assuage respondents' fears about whether you mean them harm and enable them to become more comfortable with your presence as a researcher in their world. When doing research on criminals, deviants, or victims, trust is crucial. Researchers often ask questions about sensitive issues or behaviors (e.g., drug or alcohol use, sexual activity, deviant behavior, heinous crimes, unknown offenses, traumatic events, and so on) that might make respondents uncomfortable. A certain level of trust and comfort must exist in order for researchers to be able to broach such matters with the hope of getting honest responses. A sex work researcher with whom we spoke underscored the value of getting to know members of the potential sample: "Initially, the contact is a little awkward and they may be more cautious of you but . . . the more that they see you, it doesn't seem like you are just there as a researcher. You sort of know these people, and that builds trust." Similarly, a domestic violence researcher in our sample suggested that her subjects were very familiar with her because she already worked at the shelter where they resided. She explained:

In the shelter I think I had a level of trust and rapport already built with women because I was already working there. I was already in the setting. I didn't go into the setting hoping to gain access. I went in there with honest intentions of volunteering and then realized there was a potential for a project. I could build the trust with the women on honest grounds because I was actually there trying to help and work with them and then the research just happened to come along opposed to just appearing that I was there to get my data and get out.

Many researchers, however, have neither preexisting ties to the target population nor shared social biographies with potential sample members and must figure out other ways to establish contact with potential respondents. Sometimes it is possible to just show up and hang around a potential research setting to establish connections. Such an approach might work when studying college students in social situations or exotic dancers in strip clubs, but it is probably not advisable for those who wish to study riskier populations such as gangs or active offenders. When connections through other means (e.g., parallel life experiences or preexisting ties to the population of interest) are not available, many researchers rely on "informants" (sometimes referred to as "sponsors" or "field recruiters" or "connections") to assist them in their efforts to connect with potential respondents. There is, in fact, a long tradition of the use of informants in ethnographic crime and deviance research (Adler 1993; Fleisher 1998a, Klockars 1974; Liebow 1967; Shover 1996; Walker and Lidz 1977; Whyte 1943; Wright and Decker 1994, 1997). Informants are often individuals who are part of the population the researcher wants to study, or have a close connection with members of that population (e.g., a member of a gang, a probation officer with access to offenders, a prison official, a social worker, a drug dealer, a community leader, and so on). Ideally, the informant is someone who is known and trusted by possible research participants so that he or she is best able to "vouch" for the researcher's trustworthiness and intentions. An added advantage of enlisting informants is that they can educate the researcher on suitable behavior in the field, appropriate questions to ask, and proper terms or jargon (Lee 1995). In sum, researchers should try to rely on preexisting relationships to gain access to research populations whenever possible (see also Lofland and Lofland 1995).

Interestingly, for several of the researchers in our sample, initial contacts with informants materialized through classroom interaction with students. For example, an ethnographer who has extensively researched active violent offenders discussed how the assistance provided by a former student proved invaluable in shaping the research design and gaining access to the eventual sample: "We have an ex-offender who is a former student with whom we've worked closely and we worked through him. I mean, this was pretty serendipitous—this was a guy who after a lecture one day came up and said, 'You were lecturing about what active criminals are like and with all due respect I want to tell you that you're full of shit. I'm an ex-offender and what you described is not what I know to be the case.' So we started from there and that worked out well." We heard of similar instances of serendipitous classroom connections used to forge access to respondents, such as a researcher who had a student/ex-convict offer to put her in touch with his niece, or the ethnographer who was able to use a student's relative—a heroin user—to help gain access to the field to conduct drug research.

In sum, researchers use a variety of methods to make initial connections with those they wish to study. Most stressed the importance of not trying to get into the field "cold." First, they become as familiar as possible with the people and locations they plan to research. This familiarity could be gained through reviewing academic literature, media reports, or other archived information. Some may already be familiar with their population owing to prior work or volunteer experience. Second, when preexisting connections do not exist, some suggested use of informants, often part of the population of interest, to "break the ice" or vouch for their credibility.

Negotiating Differences in a Field Research Setting

Issues of difference and diversity must remain a central concern, even after a researcher has gained access to an appropriate sample and successfully entered the field environment. Even if subjects permit a researcher to enter their social worlds and "hang out" with or interview them, such an arrangement often remains very tenuous. Researchers must tread carefully when in the field; even a seemingly minor misstep on the part of the researcher can jeopardize further access to the sample and threaten the long-term viability of the project. Researchers must pay careful attention at all times to how they are presenting themselves when in the company of actual or potential research subjects. In this section, we outline the four strategies and tactics most commonly suggested by the researchers in our sample for negotiating difference and diversity in the field research setting. These include: (1) be "real," (2) be honest with respondents, (3) provide constant reassurances about protection of subjects, (4) remain open-minded.

Keep It Real

Imagine for a moment that your professor has just asked you to conduct an ethnographic study of one of the following: prostitutes, pimps, robbers or burglars, incarcerated violent juvenile offenders, female gang members, drug dealers, white-collar criminals, rape victims, or battered women. Which one would you study? What are some questions that come to mind as you think about how you would study members of this population? For most students, some of the first questions that arise when presented with such a scenario are How am I supposed to act? Should I dress a certain way? How should I talk to them? These issues are related to what Erving Goffman (1959) has termed "presentation of self," which has to do with how social actors present themselves to those with whom they interact. The issue of presentation of self is inextricably rooted in issues of difference and diversity—if researchers were studying people who were very similar to themselves, then there would be no need to ask questions about how to act, dress, or talk.

Depending on who and what is being studied and the types of questions to be asked, being different presents a substantial challenge in gaining access to the population of interest or in establishing and maintaining a connection among that population. Thus, in virtually all research some amount of impression management is required. Our researchers repeatedly emphasized the importance of presentation of self in the field research setting; specifically, they stressed the importance of not pretending to be someone you are not. Most felt that research subjects could easily detect when they were trying to "fake" a membership role or trying too hard to "fit in," and that this could threaten the viability of a study. One experienced hate-crime scholar commented: "I find a lot of value in not pretending. I never tried to pretend I had any insight into their world. I have seen other people try to be something that they are not in the field, and I think that is dangerous and exhausting. You can always be exposed." Another scholar who explores female offending agreed on the importance of being "real": "Don't try to be something you're not. Don't go in there thinking you are all that. Just go in as a normal person who wants to talk to somebody about stuff in their lives. Be human. Be real. Don't try to put on something that is not natural for you. To do anything else—maybe they won't trust you still—but to do anything else they would probably see through it."

An experienced ethnographer who has studied active offenders shared a similar sentiment: "In our research, we've always decided that, you know, like Popeye says, 'I am what I am.' For us, we thought that if we tried to pretend that we were more street savvy or that we were 'of the street' that [our respondents] would sniff us out and think that we were fakes and that we were trying to be something that we really aren't." Along the same lines, a club-culture field researcher commented: "I always tell students that you can't hide the fact that you are educated. You can connect and keep it real and talk slang, but after awhile, because you do age, even talking slang you seem silly. People always try to gauge how genuine you are."

All of the twenty-nine researchers made it clear that they were strongly opposed to making wholesale alterations to one's personality or presentation of self and stressed the importance of being "real." However, several advocated taking steps to appear professional and to avoid seeming completely out of place in the research setting or in respondents' company.

Many of the researchers admitted to spending considerable time deciding what to wear prior to conducting interviews or spending time in the field, with most attributing these efforts to a desire to avoid accentuating any socioeconomic or status differences (e.g., clothes, shoes, or jewelry) that would identify them as belonging to a different social class. One prostitution researcher stated: "I would always wear very dressed down jeans . . . never anything that would seem showy in any way in terms of economics." A sex-work scholar also tried to minimize her class position: "I try to wear clothes that are very plain and nothing with labels. Nothing that identifies me in a particular class." A researcher who interviewed women living in public housing reported: "I dressed in a way that did not create a hierarchy. I strip myself of the appearance of being someone in power," while another researcher, who interviewed incarcerated female offenders, spoke of the instance when she learned of the potential ramifications of not attending to seemingly minor details like style of dress:

The first time we went to the detention facility I dressed with a sweater set with pearl buttons and pearl earrings and dress slacks. And my professor, my research colleague, showed up in jeans and a semicasual shirt and sneakers. And she had interviewed people in a prison setting quite a few times. So I realized I was overdressed. And I thought you know what—nice way of rubbing it in their face [by dressing nicely]. They are sitting there in these obnoxious orange jump suits that say "property of" on the back and you are coming in wearing pearls.

Another prominent presentation-of-self theme among our sample is how one ought to speak when in the field. Although the researchers were quick to admit that it is important to be familiar with the terms and slang that respondents might use, nearly all were vociferously opposed to the idea of researchers trying to adopt the languages or communication styles of one's subjects in order to fit in. Instead, they suggest that the key is to know and understand how subjects speak without using their language to try to establish acceptance. One researcher who studied single mothers living in gang neighborhoods told us: "I learned jargon in the process of doing the interviews. But I didn't then adopt that jargon to use with subsequent interviews. I didn't adopt it as though it were my own jargon." An experienced researcher who has interviewed both corporate crime offenders as well as incarcerated street offenders stressed the dangers of attempting to mimic subjects' jargon or communication style: "I don't think it's a good idea to try to adopt the style of speaking or the style of communicating that your subjects are using with you because it's not authentic. I think it's important to be authentically who you are."

Of course, it works the other way as well; if you tend to speak in a manner similar to your respondents, it is not required that you blunt those similarities to appear more "researcher-like." Being "real" and authentic—whether in terms of general comportment, dress, or manner of speaking—is essential to the qualitative research process. The style of dress, language, and behaviors that a researcher adopts for the field setting is a product of the nature of the research, the characteristics of the sample, and the researcher's personal and professional experiences. One thing is certain: trying to adopt an unfamiliar language or style of dress or otherwise cultivating an entirely new researcher persona is not an advisable means of bridging differences. Only the researcher can really determine if he or she can be successful in using certain terms or dressing or acting in a certain way, or if doing so will make him or her look like a "fake."

Straight Talk

Qualitative research, as we noted earlier, is all about trust. Getting people to participate in a study and to answer questions honestly ultimately requires that they trust the researcher. Our researchers contend that being as honest and forthright with respondents as possible is vital to establishing trust. Indeed, the two most experienced researchers in our sample each emphasized the importance of being candid with one's subjects: "Gaining trust is really about being upfront. Tell them who you are and what you want," said one, while the other noted, "the first step is to let them know what it is you are doing and why it's interesting and how their participation in that project is important."

Potential research subjects are unlikely to allow a researcher into their world if they do not know or understand that researcher's intentions. Even after subjects understand a researcher's purposes, they may remain fearful of being exploited, revealed to the police, or comprised in their dealings with social service agencies (with a resulting loss in assistance or benefits). An ethnographer who focuses on active offenders confirmed that "we tried to make our role as clearly defined for them as possible from the start. We let them know what we were doing, why we were doing it, and what we were interested in them for." Unless potential research participants are sure of the researcher's intent, they are not going to trust him or her enough to speak with or "hang out" with him or her. Researchers must establish trust by being honest with subjects *before* they engage them and *throughout* the research process. Constant candor is key.

Reassure Respondents

Another way to foster a trusting relationship—which is, again, a crucial part of overcoming challenges that might stem from differences between researchers and their subjects—is for the researcher to constantly reassure respondents that the information and accounts they provide will not be traced back to them or used against them in any way. Some populations—particularly those that might be studied in crime and deviance research—tend to be initially untrusting of researchers because they often lump them into that group of authority figures (e.g., law enforcement officers, government officials) that they have been culturally conditioned to distrust. Therefore, researchers should regularly provide reassurances about anonymity and confidentiality from the outset and continue to do so throughout the duration of the field research.

Such assurances are, of course, built into the research process; any university-affiliated research dealing with human subjects must be approved by the university's Institutional Review Board [IRB], which requires researchers to outline what measures they will take to protect their subjects from any possible harms related to the research. Making sure that respondents are aware of these built-in protections can go a long way toward establishing trust and alleviating any concerns they may have about their participation. We were told by a researcher who has conducted in-depth interviews with battered women: "I make it clear that I don't work for the courts, I don't work for the agency, I don't work for anybody that can take away their benefits. . . . That seems to help." Another researcher, who conducts pre- and post-release interviews with incarcerated juvenile offenders as part of a study on recidivism, uses a similar approach: "I always try to reiterate that whatever they tell me will not be used against them in a negative way, that their probation officer or the people at the institution are not going to find out, and that the information is only going to be used in a general way."

It is incumbent on researchers to make sure that subjects understand they will not "rat them out" and to assure respondents that they will take all necessary steps to guarantee that participation will not cause them harm. A gang researcher discussed how she actively avoids soliciting certain information from her respondents and makes it clear to them what topics should not be broached in their responses:

We spend a lot of time in the interview making sure that the respondents know in answering some of the questions that they could be getting very close to information that we don't want to know about it because it could put us in a difficult position. For example, we might want to know in general about their criminal behavior but if they start describing a particular case with all the details of it we stop the interview and tell them not to tell us that information because we can then find ourselves in a situation—especially if they are talking about a future event. We warn them, "Don't tell us any more about that." We want the general bits, but we don't want the specifics. I think those techniques gradually build confidence in the respondent that we are serious about protecting them.

Some researchers go to great lengths to ensure the strictest levels of confidentiality; a researcher who studies active offenders explained that one tactic used to maximize confidentiality is to avoid any and all identifying information about respondents in order to facilitate trust and open, honest discourse: "I absolutely convince them that I don't want their names or where they live or any personal information about them. It really gets them to open up because all I want is the data. The data on what they do, how they do it, and why they do it. You are getting very detailed information, but it is removed from identifiers, so they feel comfortable talking to you." A researcher who studies prostitution takes her efforts to ensure the anonymity of her subjects even further, revealing that she conducts interviews by phone whenever possible. She reported that her participants were more at ease speaking with her over the phone because there would be no way she could identify them if she ever passed them on the street or came into any physical contact with them.

Be Neither Judge nor Jury

One of the exciting aspects of qualitative research is that you get to hear some compelling stories that you may not have considered or expected to find. But sometimes these stories—particularly those conveyed by respondents in certain types of crime and deviance research—can be immensely disturbing and emotionally upsetting to the researcher (Goldman 2001; Pryor 1996; Wesely 2006). Nonetheless, researchers must remain composed and professional even when confronted with grotesque details or disturbing accounts. Above all, they cannot seem judgmental or position themselves as morally superior to their respondents. Good qualitative research requires getting subjects to open up, and the surest way to fail at this mission is to act shocked by what your subjects are sharing with you, or worse, to sit in judgment of them. Researchers repeatedly reminded us that disconcerting facts and disturbing accounts are a staple of crime and deviance research. It is imperative that researchers react appropriately—listen carefully and demonstrate interest, but never look shocked or appalled—in order to reduce respondents' apprehension and allow them to further open up about the details of their lives and activities.

An ethnographer who has spent considerable time with active offenders highlighted the importance of avoiding appearing judgmental of their answers: "We tried not to be judgmental about what these offenders had done. We went in knowing that if these were the people we were interested in, they would've been involved in a lot of stuff, some of which would be pretty bizarre and stuff we would have moral objections to. But we did not let on that we were appalled at some of what we were told." One drug researcher explained that being nonjudgmental breaks down possible barriers that may arise from differences: "I think that my willingness to hear what they have to say without being judgmental about some of their behaviors that they might be talking about or doing in front of me [is the key to breaking down barriers and gaining trust]. That is especially true with drug users. I can get those who have a lifetime of using drugs to respond immediately to that [being nonjudgmental] because they are so used to being constantly judged."

While conducting research on strippers, another deviant population, one researcher commented: "I think the key is appearing and responding in ways that are not judgmental. Even if someone would tell me something completely shocking or tell me they had sex with twenty men in three days or they did all these drugs or whatever, . . . I never respond in a way that would seem judgmental or horrified by something they were telling me." Refraining from appearing shocked or appalled is also essential when interviewing victims of violence. A domestic violence scholar attempts to ensure that her respondents continue to share painful details by reacting in a certain way: "You have to walk this odd line between expressing empathy but not expressing shock, especially if what they are telling you is very painful for them. Somehow making them feel more normal about it opens them up to tell you more and more painful details. You have to act like you have heard this, like you have heard fifty women tell you they got hit in the head with a hammer."

In sum, although researchers may be very different from their subjects and may hear about or witness deviant activity or traumatizing victimization, it is crucial that they not appear judgmental about participants' behavior or lifestyle. Although researchers may not go as far as normalizing participants' experiences or encouraging their activities, it is best for them to not act as if whatever they are hearing or witnessing bothers them in any way. One has to remember that things that might seem outlandish or appalling to the researcher (e.g., excessive alcohol or drug use, risky sexual behaviors, violence) might, in fact, be quite normal within the day-to-day world of the people being studied. To appear judgmental is to highlight some of the very differences between researcher and subject that you have worked to overcome, and this could derail the research process or substantially limit the candor and honesty of respondents' accounts.

Summary

Let us return again to the scenario with which we opened this chapter: imagine you are a college student who has been assigned to interview someone who is quite different from you along a number of social dimensions—race, gender, social status, socioeconomic placement—and possesses very different life experiences from your own. After your having read this chapter, we hope that you would no longer consider a panic-induced sprint in the opposite direction or an exasperated plea for a more palatable research topic to friends or faculty as viable options. Instead, we are optimistic that, by drawing on the broad lessons and specific strategies and techniques discussed in this chapter, you would be willing and able to embrace the potential rich and rewarding experience of trying to gain an in-depth understanding of individuals and social worlds that are entirely different from those that you typically encounter.

Diversity is a fundamentally important, yet overlooked, aspect of criminological research. In many cases, the members of criminal or deviant populations being studied are often quite different—in terms of race, gender, ethnicity, social class, educational attainment, and so on—from those who seek to research them. In this chapter we have explored the role of difference and diversity in criminological research and identified some of the ways that researchers confront and overcome issues and obstacles that can arise when researching individuals who are involved in criminal or deviant activities, or who are victims of such activities.

For this research, we conducted interviews with twenty-nine leading or emerging scholars that conduct qualitative research in the areas of crime and deviance. During the interviews, we asked these researchers to discuss what they saw as the most salient differences between themselves and their subjects and how they deal with these differences in their research. Their responses indicate that, above all else, dealing with difference and diversity in one's research is a process—it requires constant attention, acute awareness, and flexibility from the researcher. Further, there is not a single strategy or particular collection of techniques for dealing with these issues that will work for all researchers.

The appropriate strategies for dealing with differences between researcher and subject are determined by the nature of the research, the characteristics of the sample, and the experience and research approach of the researcher. However, we were able to identify a number of common strategies and techniques among our sample that can be used to overcome potentially significant differences between researcher and subject in order to gain access to the targeted sample: become familiar with those you intend to study and take steps to become a familiar presence in potential subjects' social worlds prior to data collection. In addition, several researchers indicated the use of informants to "break the ice" for them—a practice commonly used in ethnographic crime and deviance research (Adler 1993; Fleisher 1998a, Klockars 1974; Liebow 1967; Shover 1996; Walker and Lidz 1977; Whyte 1943; Wright and Decker 1994, 1997). In terms of dealing with difference while collecting data in a field research setting, the researchers in our sample repeatedly suggested that *being yourself*, *being honest* with respondents, *constantly reassuring respondents* as to the protections against risks associated with participation in the research, and *remaining open-minded* were essential techniques for overcoming any barriers that might arise owing to issues of difference and diversity.

Our goal in conducting this research was to highlight an overlooked issue in crime and deviance research—differences between researchers and subjects—and to spur readers to consider these issues in light of the tremendous influence they can have on researchers and their research. We hope this chapter will serve as a resource that will prove helpful to students, teachers, and scholars alike. Students can draw on the issues discussed in this chapter to demystify the research process and realize that the observable characteristics (e.g., race, ethnicity, gender, age), social status, social biography, or socioeconomic placement of researcher and subject—no matter how different— should not preclude you from doing the kind of research that you seek to do.

If these issues of difference and diversity are thoughtfully considered and thoroughly attended to, researchers may find themselves able to have much fuller, more engaging discussions with their subjects, which can open up new lines of inquiry, provide access to unexpected research settings and populations, and yield unforeseen insights into who and what is being studied.

Discussion Questions

1. Refer back to the hypothetical scenario posed in the opening paragraph of this chapter. Given what you have read, how would you go about conducting an interview with a leader of a female gang?
2. Explain two techniques researchers use to gain access to research subjects or research settings.
3. Why is it pertinent that research subjects become familiar with the researcher?
4. Why is it important to "be real" while conducting research?
5. Why should researchers constantly provide reassurances about anonymity and confidentiality to their subjects? List at least two ways researchers can provide this reassurance.
6. Explain why researchers refrain from adopting the language of their participants as their own.

Notes

1. The demographic profile of our sample is as follows: thirteen participants were men and sixteen were women. Participants ranged in age from twenty-four to fifty-nine years at the time of the interview, and the mean age of participants was forty-two. Most of the sample members (N = 26) were white, two were Latino/Hispanic, and one was multiracial.

2. Some of the researchers with whom we spoke did not see themselves as being all that different from their subjects and, thus, did not see much need to negotiate what they did not believe to be an issue. However, the majority of our respondents recognized difference as a salient issue in the research process.

References

Adler, Patricia A. 1993. *Wheeling and Dealing.* New York: Columbia University Press.
Arendell, Terry. 1997. "Reflections on the Researcher-Researched Relationship: A Woman Interviewing Men. *Qualitative Sociology* 20:341–68.

Bachman, Ronet and Russell Schutt. 2003. *The Practice of Research in Criminology and Criminal Justice.* Thousand Oaks, Calif.: Pine Forge Press.

Denzin, Norman and Yvonna Lincoln. 1994. "Introduction: Entering the Field of Qualitative Research." In N. Denzin and Y. Lincoln, eds., *Handbook of Qualitative Research*, 1–18. Thousand Oaks, Calif.: Sage.

Fleisher, Mark S. 1998a. *Dead End Kids: Gang Girls and the Boys They Know.* Madison: University of Wisconsin Press.

———. 1998b. "Ethnographers, Pimps, and the Company Store." In Jeff Ferrell and Mark S. Hamm, eds., *Ethnography on the Edge: Crime, Deviance and Field Work*, 44–64. Boston: Northeastern University Press.

Goffman, Erving. 1959. *The Presentation of Self in Everyday Life.* New York: Doubleday.

Goldman, Marion S. 2001. "The Ethnographer as Holy Clown: Fieldwork, Disregard, and Danger." In David G. Bromley and Lewis F. Carter, eds., *Toward Reflexive Ethnography: Participating, Observing, Narrating*, 53–75. London: JAI.

Horowitz, Ruth. 1986. "Remaining an Outsider: Membership as a Threat to Research Rapport." *Urban Life* 14:409–30.

Klockars, Carl B. 1974. *The Professional Fence.* New York: Free Press.

Lee, Raymond M. 1995. *Dangerous Fieldwork.* Thousand Oaks, Calif.: Sage.

Liebow, Elliot. 1967. *Tally's Corner: A Study of Negro Streetcorner Men.* Boston: Little, Brown.

Lofland, John and Lynn Lofland. 1995. *Analyzing the Social Settings: A Guide to Qualitative Observation and Analysis.* Belmont, Calif.: Wadsworth.

McCorkel, Jill A., and Kristen Myers. 2003. "What Difference Does Difference Make? Position and Privilege in the Field." *Qualitative Sociology* 26:199–231.

Pryor, Douglas W. 1996. *Unspeakable Acts: Why Men Sexually Abuse Children.* New York: New York University Press.

Shover, Neil. 1996. *Great Pretenders: Pursuits and Careers of Persistent Thieves.* Boulder, Colo.: Westview Press.

Walker, Andrew L., and Charles W. Lidz. 1977. "Methodological Notes on the Employment of Indigenous Observers." In Robert S. Weppner, ed., *Street Ethnography: Selected Studies of Crime and Drug Use in Natural Settings*, 103–23. Beverly Hills, Calif.: Sage.

Wesely, Jennifer K. 2006. "Negotiating Myself: The Impact of Studying Female Exotic Dancers on a Feminist Researcher." *Qualitative Inquiry* 12 (1): 146–62.

Whyte, William Foote. 1943. *Street Corner Society: The Social Structure of an Italian Slum.* Chicago: University of Chicago Press.

Wright, Richard T., and Scott H. Decker. 1994. *Burglars on the Job: Streetlife and Residential Break-Ins.* Boston, Mass.: Northeastern University Press.

———. 1997. *Armed Robbers in Action: Stickups and Street Culture.* Boston: Northeastern University Press.

II

Inquirers

Professionals, Activists, and Researchers

"Comforting the Troubled and Troubling the Comfortable"

Reflections on Lawyering for the Poor

DA and EP: We are setting out to write about the effect of race, gender, and class on the practice of poverty law. That is to say, how our racial, gender, and socioeconomic identities and differences (from each other and our clients) affect the way we practice law on behalf of people who are poor.[1]

Biographical Background

DA: I am a white, forty-year-old Jewish male, raised in a middle-class, two-parent home. I attended public schools from elementary school through college, then a large private law school. Although I would not describe my childhood as one of excessive wealth, I certainly did not experience deprivation, or anything close to it. I have been married for fourteen years and am challenged frequently by two children, ages ten and seven. My wife and I both work full-time but are fortunate to have jobs that enable us to work flexible schedules. (Michelle has her own private clinical psychology practice.) For nine years, from the birth of our oldest child to the time when our youngest started public school, we each worked four days a week, taking one day off to care for our children. We live in a small college town fifteen miles outside of Philadelphia.

In many obvious but significant respects my background and personal circumstances are remarkably different from my clients'. To the extent that these differences affect my ability to build rapport with clients, gain their trust, be empathic, and understand the context of what brought them to my office, I think these differences are material.

For example, imagine a scenario[2] in which a single mother relying on public assistance obtains a good job with attractive hours that permits an extended family member to care for her two children under six. However, just days before the job is to commence, the employer informs the mother that there is mandatory job orientation which was scheduled on a different shift than the one on which she was hired to work. Unable to find child care on such short notice, the mother faces a Solomon's choice, and either way a tremendous cost will be exacted. The state removed the children from their mother and placed them in foster care because the children were left alone in their apartment for three hours at a time, twice in one day.

Imagine hearing this story from a client and consider what reaction might be provoked depending on your background and experiences. Certainly a lawyer who is a single parent will process this story differently from one with a parenting partner and a plethora of financial and family resources. A single mother may empathize with the difficult choices often confronting working parents. A single mother who has been poor at some point in her life may understand the powerful lure of a job that promises to enable a family to escape welfare. In my case, even as a parent with an embarrassment of riches when it comes to supports and resources, for some reason that is beyond my consciousness (but may be attributable to some deep-seated pathology) I am able to empathize with the plight of the client in this scenario. Rather than harshly judge the mother's unfortunate choice, I would seek context, since in lawyering, context matters. Seeking out details of the client's life to shed light on the resources and options available to her, and contrasting those with the resources and options the state could offer as an alternative to foster care is the way to defend a case like this. Unlike some cases, this one had a happy ending. Ultimately, we were successful in persuading a state social worker and her supervisor (whose personal background we will never know about) to reconsider their decision, and within a week the children were returned to their mother, with state-subsidized daycare referrals for the future.

I will also never forget one of my early encounters with a new client when I was just a twenty-four-year-old lawyer, fresh out of law school. I remember bounding down the stairs of my office to the waiting room, greeting my client with great enthusiasm, but having my bubble burst by the warm but pointed plea from the client: "Lord, I know I am poor, but can't I get a real lawyer?" Why did I not look like a real lawyer? I wore the lawyer's uniform of the day—a business suit (which I rarely wear these days). Nonetheless, my appearance in some respect did not comport with my client's expectations. Did she expect someone who looked like her? Did she hope for an attorney who looked like one on television? Or did she just not believe that someone who looked so young could be trusted to handle her important case competently? Until I turned thirty, I wore a jacket and tie to work every day, in part for my client's confidence, in part for my own. If I did not feel like a real lawyer, at least I could try to look like one. Now, as I have turned forty, I go to great lengths to avoid wearing jackets and ties; perhaps my loss of hair has had one redeeming effect—at least I now look more like a lawyer.

. . .

EP: I am a white, thirty-two-year-old female raised in an upper-middle-class family with what I felt growing up was more than its share of mental health and substance abuse problems. In retrospect, I am not certain my family was any more "dysfunctional" than many others; perhaps it is just that my parents were particularly inept at compensating for their deficiencies. They were young when they married, privileged in ways they probably did not fully appreciate, and too wrapped up in their own growing pains to think much about appearances. That being said, they were loving parents who attended to our daily needs, and I never wanted for anything material. What I did want for, the lack of which has repercussions potentially equally lasting although less easy to identify, is a sense of safety in the world.

I have been married for almost four years, have a twenty-one-month-old daughter, and am expecting my second child. A year ago, my husband, child, and I moved from Wilmington, Delaware, to Berkeley, California, pursuing a dream of a life I had wanted since I attended college at Stanford and fell in love with the open, sunny, hopeful air of the San Francisco Bay Area. My husband is a restaurant man—a chef by training, now a manager of a busy, high-end restaurant—and has odd hours, as one might expect. Together, we manage to limit our child's day-care week to no more than thirty hours, and we share equally in the child-care and household management tasks that threaten daily to swamp us. Unlike many of my women friends (women with similar educational and career profiles), I spend no time lamenting my husband's inadequacies around the house; instead, I am constantly burdened by a sense of my own inadequacies—an awareness that I am too quick to reach overload, too slow to stay on the chores for which I am responsible, too exhausted by my toddler's unceasing demands.

Like Dan, my background and personal circumstances are strikingly different from those of my clients, at least in those ways that are evident to public scrutiny. Unlike Dan perhaps, I have always felt much closer to my clients in a more personal respect—I easily identify with their insecurity, their expectation that they will not be heard, their fear of failure, and their mistrust of intimacy. These are the ghosts of my past. Unlike my clients, however, I was able to break with my past through sustained effort at counseling (paid for by my family, supported by family and friends) in the years that I was attending elite college-preparatory, college, and postgraduate institutions. This is not to say that I believe that our clients' problems are a result of individual pathology, treatable with a good dose of high-quality mental health treatment. Instead, I recognize that I did not face the intractable, endemic social problems that arise from and prey on poverty—homelessness, unemployment, discrimination, mental and physical illness, and substance abuse, to name a few. Too often, I believe, the American ideal of self-reliance masks these social factors, scapegoating individual frailty. It is so much more palatable to the public to present social problems as susceptible to medical "cures," doled out on an individual basis, than to face the more fundamental redistributive issues inherent in any real or lasting economic and social change.

Although today I no longer share many of my clients' emotional frailties either, I do not easily forget their scars; it is these scars I have developed on my own battlefield that I believe make me more empathic with my clients' failings. At the end of the day, it is the connections I am able to forge with my clients that sustain me in the face of their crushing circumstances. Even where connections fail, it is the aspiration—the gesture toward some future in which they too will know, if only fleetingly, if always imperfectly, that they are as capable of self-advocacy as anyone—that drew me to this work and will keep me in it.

· · ·

DA: Eliza's reflections on her ability to identify with our clients inspired me to think again about the importance of gender, race, and background as it relates to my ability to connect to my clients. I suppose when all is said and done, we are all brothers and sisters, no matter where we come from. We are human beings before being lawyers and clients. And our law degrees must not come at the expense of our humanity. For some, compassion, empathy, and rapport come naturally; for others, it must be learned. Eliza and I got where we are traveling different paths, but we now share the same core ideology about our clients' plight—that they have been beaten down by a system that does not distribute justice equitably, and that it is our job to empower and ensure that they get their fair share.

Professional Background

DA: Since 1990, when I graduated from law school, I have worked at a medium-size legal services program in Delaware. "Legal services" refers to the loosely associated cadre of law offices nationwide that provide civil (that is noncriminal) legal services to people who are poor.[3] In the 1960s, the national legal services program was born as part of President Lyndon Baine Johnson's War on Poverty.[4] Since its inception, there has been a highly charged political spirit to the work: eradicating poverty was the end; litigation, the means. The cases brought by legal services lawyers, just to name a few, challenged inequitable funding of public schools,[5] welfare rules that trampled on constitutional rights,[6] and irrational restrictions on noncitizens' right to work.[7]

I first learned of the legal services program when I was in college in the mid-1980s, when President Ronald Regan was trying to dismantle the program.[8] I became involved in a progressive community action program through my university's sociology department, which opened up my eyes to economic, racial, and gender injustice rampant in America. I saw how lawyers through grassroots organizing, class action litigation, and other forms of radical advocacy could effectuate meaningful systemic change for the disenfranchised. I went to law school knowing that I wanted to become a social activist lawyer and chose to go to school in Washington, D.C., which was ground zero for public interest law.

Looking for permanent legal services positions is sort of like being drafted into a professional sports league, minus the lucrative bonuses. There is very little control over where one may be chosen to work. Even the large programs do not have many openings, and there are scores of applicants for every advertised position. As a result, I, like other law students committed to the idea of working in legal services, had to engage in a broad job search and be prepared to move wherever necessary.[9] By some bizarre stroke of good fortune, I was in the enviable position of choosing between legal services programs—one in Virginia, along the North Carolina border, and one in Wilmington, Delaware, twenty miles outside of Philadelphia.

For the past sixteen years I have worked in the same legal services office, but in two different components of Community Legal Aid Society, Inc. (CLASI) in Delaware. For the first eight years at CLASI, I worked in both the poverty and disability programs as a staff attorney, representing individual clients with low incomes or disabilities. I worked mostly in family court, representing parents whose children were placed in foster care; in housing court, trying to stave off evictions from public or subsidized housing; and in administrative hearings, helping families obtain public benefits to which they were legally entitled. For the past eight years, I have served as the legal advocacy director of the Disabilities Law Program at CLASI—training, mentoring, and supervising attorneys, and coordinating the impact work our program conducts on behalf of people with disabilities. During the past year, I have also become a deputy director of CLASI, handling administrative duties in addition to advocacy.

I am essentially a civil rights lawyer for people with disabilities and people who are poor.[10] Depending on what day you are asking, I am either tilting at windmills, or making some modest progress on behalf of clients. Although I cannot imagine another job providing me with a better opportunity to right wrongs and accomplish justice for the disenfranchised, the limitation of the law's ability to serve as a vehicle for radical change has become more prominent in my mind.[11]

In one of my more nihilistic moods I bemoaned to a friend of mine who had practiced poverty law that in more than fifteen years I had yet to lift a single client out of poverty. Certainly I had helped people—by getting them important public benefits they were entitled to, by getting them out of institutions, or by preserving their parental rights. But even when I had obtained sizable monetary judgments for clients, they still remained poor people. My friend noted wisely, "that may be so, but poverty lawyers alleviate pain, and that is a noble calling." He was right. Whether poverty lawyers make a difference depends on how the analysis is framed. Troubling the comfortable is fun, but comforting the troubled is what matters most.

· · ·

EP: Yesterday in the playground, watching my daughter play, I overheard a conversation between a father and his two young children that represented a model of parenting worlds apart from the families I work with as a legal aid lawyer in dependency court. It was a forty-something father responding to concerns expressed by his children about the fact that two older kids were riding down the hill to the playground on skateboards without wearing helmets. It says enough about the Berkeley parenting scene that the children independently noted this, but it was the father's response, and the exchange that followed, that stood out to me. "They're okay," he told his kids. "But shouldn't they be wearing helmets?" "Well yes, it would be safer to wear helmets." "Maybe they can't afford helmets," the kids offered. "It's possible," the father responded, "but I don't think so. I think probably they just haven't thought hard about it; it may be that they will need to have a fall to really think hard, and I hope they don't get hurt."

What is there to fault about this exchange? I could think of nothing. The father was not judgmental, was open to discussing it, and ultimately left open several possible scenarios, challenging his children to reject what I had expected to be the moral: "you must wear a helmet when you ride a skateboard." As I thought about this, I realized that my instinct had been to judge the father—to dismiss him as yet one more overprepared, overvigilant, overeducated Berkeley parent trying to be "perfect." I wanted to say that he was no better a parent than my clients, who had no preparation, formal or informal, for the colossal feat of parenting, and that they did as a fine a job under concerns he could never imagine. But is this true? And then I realized (or, I hope, remembered) what I truly to believe to be the answer: it doesn't matter. I have chosen a career of defending the parental rights of indigent parents not because I believe they are the "best" parents a child could hope for, but because I believe they are good enough.

After graduating from college with a bachelor's degree in English "with an emphasis in creative writing," I was fortunate to land an internship with a legal services organization in Wilmington, Delaware—Community Legal Aid Society, Inc. (CLASI). This is where I first met Dan. During my interview, I described to Dan my interest in working in the field of child welfare. I probably labeled my interest "child advocacy" back then; my only relevant experience had been a brief stint during college as a volunteer with a program that conducted child assault prevention workshops with kindergarten students. I confessed that I had considered an internship with the New York City District Attorney's office that prosecuted child abuse cases and had also applied to become a CASA—a court appointed special advocate—for children making their way through the foster-care system. Dan suggested that working at CLASI would provide an alternative view into the child welfare system; I would be assisting him on cases in which he represented parents with disabilities whose children had been removed from their care by the state resulting from charges of neglect.

During my internship with CLASI, I fell in love. The objects of my affections were the clients I was fortunate to meet—women of all racial and ethnic backgrounds, all of them poor, many of them struggling with mental health problems, substance abuse and addiction, abusive relationships, and any number of other social ills. The women were, for the most part, survivors, strong, intelligent, funny women struggling to be heard in a world where the cards were stacked against their voices mattering. I related to them in a way I am often shy about admitting because of our otherwise obvious dissimilarities. Perhaps most strikingly to myself, I felt drawn to the work of helping them without a sense of a larger mission and without any particular regard for how they had come into these circumstances. It was not until much later that I learned that the representation of indigent parents in child welfare proceedings implicates constitutional rights and principles dating back to our founding as a nation. This was the legal support for my instinctual belief that these parents were "good enough." Based instead on an affinity for the clients, I went to law school.

I chose NYU because of its reputation as a top-tier law school with a unique commitment to public interest law and because Dan had told me about a professor there, Martin Guggenheim, who had successfully championed parents' rights in child welfare proceedings before the United States Supreme Court and had created at NYU a unique clinic that offered students the opportunity to represent indigent parents in child welfare proceedings in New York's family courts. I knew child welfare practice was what I wanted to do, but I never considered myself has having an explicitly "social activist" agenda. In a way, I think I was insecure about my status as a privileged white female from the upper middle classes of American society; in a way I think I was simply naive about what the term meant. Today, I continue to avoid explicitly "activist" descriptions of what I do, preferring to describe my work in the affective, emotional terms so often attributed to women.

During my summers at law school I worked in two very different capacities—first, at a small juvenile rights law firm that engaged in very little direct representation and focused instead on advancing the rights of juveniles through legislative advocacy, public policy and education efforts, and impact litigation, and next at the nation's oldest and largest independent legal services provider assisting in the representation of a relatively large number of parents in child welfare cases in family court. As graduation approached, I went back to Dan and proposed the idea that we create a fellowship application that would allow me to return to work at CLASI, devoted solely to child welfare cases. Together, we created a proposal that envisioned a mix of direct client representation, community outreach and education, and public policy advocacy. I was awarded a Skadden Fellowship, a two-year public interest fellowship funded by the law firm Skadden Arps. When my fellowship ended, CLASI agreed to keep me on as a staff attorney, eventually assuming a position partially supported by the family court through which I represented a high volume of indigent parents in child welfare cases on a court-appointed basis.

How Issues of Race, Class and Gender Are Introduced to Law Students and New Lawyers

EP: It was a hot, humid, ordinary day in Philadelphia's family court. The immense stone walls and cavernous waiting room did nothing to diffuse the heat. The crush of bodies in the waiting room boiled. A black sea of faces. Children squirming in their seats, running circles around the lines of chairs, being scolded in varying degrees of harshness. Two calls a day—9 a.m. and 1 p.m.—that was all the family court administration offered. You come and you wait until your case is called. If the morning calendar is not finished by lunchtime, it spills into the afternoon, further delaying those who report at 1 p.m., hopeful to be out of there by closing time. Sometimes you wait all day and your case is never called. It is summer, so school is out. That means the children who have not been removed come with you. Or maybe it is your neighbor's kids, or your sister's—whomever you have agreed to watch that day. Children are not allowed in the courtroom, so you need to find someone to sit with them while you go into court. Cases last, on average, no more than twenty minutes, so once you get in, you can be sure they will not have long to wait.

This was the scene I was introduced to in my second summer of law school, as I trailed the attorneys who would come to court each day to beg whatever scraps of justice they could extract for their clients that day: more services, mainly, or more time—time to complete service plans, time to see their children, time to be heard by the court. Today's client was an older black woman.

By older I mean she was in her thirties. She had already had more than one child removed from her care and placed for adoption, her parental rights involuntarily terminated by this same court. She was a drug addict, and the child we were there about today had been removed from her care at birth because of her positive toxicology screen for cocaine when she was admitted to the hospital in labor. The child was born without cocaine in her system, but she had been placed in foster care directly from the hospital, and the state had indicated its intent to push for a fast-track to adoption; under a new federal law, with the court's consent it could forgo otherwise mandatory reunification efforts in favor of an immediate termination of parental rights action.

As an intern, I tagged along with the staff attorneys on "intake" days—those days when you show up at first call and interview potential clients, make quick decisions about which cases to take, turn away many more. There was something about this mother that appealed to me. I was only an intern, so I had to go to my supervising attorney to make my case. "She's serious this time," I told him. He rolled his eyes. Even the most intrepid parent advocate can be rendered cynical after years of disappointment when it comes to representing clients with drug addiction; you invest so much of yourself on their behalf, they seem to be doing so well that you are even convincing the state's attorney and the court, and then they relapse, and you are back where you started. Or I should say, the child is back where she started. My supervising attorney was not convinced. "We're not going to pick this one up, Eliza," he told me. "But she's already gotten herself into a long-term drug treatment program where, if you succeed and progress through the levels of treatment, your child can join you, and they provide all kinds of long-term support and assistance," I pleaded. "Oh all right, I'll talk to her," he conceded, and off he went to interview the client in the moments before the case was called.

Later that day, as I sat in the back of the courtroom and watched the client and her attorney sitting at the table before the judge, who sat high above them behind a solid wooden desk in a courtroom of aged wood paneling, peeling at the corners, that belied the respect the court system held for these cases, I felt a naive sense of hope. In law school, through my clinical experience and a select number of seminars, I had learned about why we consider the parental right fundamental, why it is constitutionally protected. I had learned that as a young republic, we believed in individual autonomy and sought a civic structure that enhanced and fostered such autonomy. Families, it was believed, were the best petri dishes for a heterogeneous community. Where the state seeks to interfere in the family and to inculcate values through childrearing, we should tread with the utmost caution. But then why, I could not help but wonder (with the help of law professors who guided my thoughts in this direction) was the waiting room outside this courtroom almost entirely filled with black families?

"All rise." Court is in session. The state presents its case: crack addict mother, repeat offender, crack baby, lost cause. My supervising attorney makes his vain attempt: new commitment, demonstrated initiative, unique program potential, sacred relationship . . . "Whatever," the judge interrupts, sitting back expansively in his chair and spreading his arms to each side, portraying a black-winged vulture ready to strike. "You speak to me about this person as a mother?" he asks the attorney, turning now to face the client herself. "You're not a mother, you're a carrier." I feel my own eyes swell with tears. I cannot erase the angry ball in my stomach, a mixture of horror (at justice so demeaned), guilt (at my part in bringing her before this judge), and pain (that any woman should be so stripped bare of her humanity and her maternity by a man in power). What did I know then of what it means to be a mother? Nothing, really, and yet I knew what it meant to be a woman, a human being capable of reproduction, a subject of all the world's judgment and expectation when it comes to our rights and (for much of the world more powerfully) our responsibility as "carriers" of the next generation.

It is a lonely place on the side of the courtroom where the parent sits in a dependency hearing. On the other side sit the state's attorney and the case-worker (one, maybe more). Just next to or in front of the state's table, but care-ful not to cross the dividing line of the courtroom, is the table for the child's representative—either a nonlawyer advocate and her counsel or a court-appointed lawyer for the child. On average, you can expect that the other adults in the room (save, perhaps, the judge) will be overwhelmingly female. Usually your client is female, although sometimes you will represent a father if the mother is not available to care for the children. I had thought, at times, that the other adults in the courtroom discounted my commitment to parent representation as naïveté resulting from not being a parent. This hunch was proved true the summer I appeared by my clients' side with my pregnant stomach an inescapable portent of "motherly sentiment" to come. "Does it feel any different," one female district attorney asked me one day, "to repre-sent your clients now that you're going to be a mother yourself? If it doesn't now, just you wait."

Twenty-one months after the birth of my first child, seven months pregnant with my second, I can say it does not feel any different. I am still pained when I see a child mistreated; perhaps my pain is more acute because of my new identification with the child, but that kind of pain is not so relevant to the work I do. I believe all parents, regardless of their crime, are entitled to a competent defense when their parental rights are threatened, but that has never been where my heart is in this work. Instead, I gravitate to the center, to the 85 per-cent of child welfare cases that do not involve physical or sexual abuse. These cases are made up instead of the more intransigent, pervasive problems en-demic to poor America: homelessness, mental illness, lack of education and social support, inadequate access to medical care. To me, the task of defending parental rights does not force a confrontation with a parent's individual pathology, because in the vast majority of cases the reason a child is removed from her parent's care has little to nothing to do with individual pathology and everything to do with societal injustice and inequality. Does this make me the "social activist" lawyer I avoid calling myself? Maybe it does, but for me, as a woman, as a parent, it is the most gratifying job I can imagine.

. . .

DA: Law school for me began almost twenty years ago, and so the distance in time has allowed me to reflect without worry of post-traumatic stress disorder flashbacks. I do not remember my experience fondly. Perhaps it was because my expectations were so high. Naively, I thought that I would learn how to solve problems for real people. Instead, the first-year law school curriculum goes to great lengths to ensure that students are learning in a universe unconstrained by reality—a universe in which the "people" studied do not have faces, genders, races, or classes. In fact it seemed as if removing humanity from the curriculum was the pedagogical end, and repetition was the means. Time after time, sympathies led to one result in a case, yet "the law" militated toward another. The not-so-subtle message to law students was that lawyers and judges think with their brains not their hearts.[12] Of course the absurdity of such an approach is the conceit that "the law" neutrally applied dictates reliable results. In the real world, clear cases get resolved before they get to a judge. It is the hard cases, ones where laws conflict, or interpretations are ambiguous, that get decided by courts. And in the cases that affect poor people, like the child welfare cases Eliza discussed, the law does not seem to matter at all. Cases where the legal standard is whether the parents are providing "adequate care"[13] or acting in the "best interest of the child"[14] do not have meaningful legal standards at all. The applicable laws are so pliable that judges can move mountains of evidence to get to the result they wish.

This of course begs the rhetorical question—if the laws are so malleable, then are not these cases more easily susceptible to racial, gender, and class biases? The child welfare system that Eliza and I have immersed ourselves in from the beginning of our careers is rife with biases. Biases against people with awful choices: poor people who cannot afford or locate appropriate day care and leave their children unattended out of desperation; women who are prisoners to domestic violence; people of color whose cultural mores regarding parenting may deviate from those of the majority culture.[15]

If poverty law does not attract young attorneys who are race conscious in the first place, the practice of poverty law certainly makes them more race conscious. When our waiting rooms are filled with people of color, telling stories of abject poverty, bureaucratic nightmares, and health-care travesties, it certainly makes us consider the role of racism in creating or perpetuating poverty.[16] When we see deplorable public housing projects and shamefully under-funded public schools almost completely devoid of white people, one cannot help but confront the issues of race. That poverty disproportionately affects people of color and women ensures that poverty lawyers will be confronted by issues of class, race, and gender bias inherent in our legal system and in society at large. The trick is how we deal with it when it hits us in the face. Recognizing it is the first—and perhaps the easiest—step. Eradicating, or at least mitigating, its effects, is the real challenge.

Does Diversity Matter?

DA: The fundamental attribution error (FAE) is a well-known psychological phenomenon in which human beings tend to underestimate the importance of context and overestimate the importance of ingrained personality when trying to understand other people's behavior.[17] This bias is insidious but very important in the practice of law. Lawyers, especially poverty lawyers, are always sizing up clients and their cases. With limited resources to ration, and many more clients seeking services than we could possibly serve, inevitably we subjectively evaluate which cases are meritorious, and which are not. Judges, whether in personal injury cases or child welfare cases, are always sizing up parties and witnesses. Who is telling the truth? Whose story is more compelling? Is this parent worth trusting? Can I safely return this child to her care?

Often being of a different race, gender, and class from my clients, I have had to counteract the FAE when I try to understand my clients' predicaments. I am not always successful. I am sure I have misjudged a client whose story I just could not relate to. I try to be conscious of my own biases and prejudices, and make sure that I go out of my way to understand the context of our clients' lives. But, would it not be ideal if we had poverty lawyers who were once poor themselves? Who better to empathize with the client who is applying for public benefits than a lawyer whose family was once on welfare? Who better to comfort the mother who has lost her child to foster care than a lawyer who once was in foster care? Who better to identify with a victim of domestic violence than a lawyer who once was a victim herself? Surely, diversity does not ensure a bias-free law firm. Everyone has biases. But, I think we would improve our ability to minimize the effects of the FAE and other biases that skew our case selection process if we were able to recruit and retain lawyers who share some demographic characteristics with our clients.

I spent some time in the beginning of my career advocating for victims of domestic violence. One could argue a man representing a female victim of domestic violence is at best unnecessary, at worst, foolish. I cannot refute that point. I may be able to identify with my client, but will my client identify with me? No matter how sensitive, patient, and comforting, I am still a man, and that cannot feel right to some women. On the other hand, there may be some benefit to having a man validate a battered woman's position; it may empower her to have a different kind of relationship with a man if she has been accustomed to being bullied, abused, or disbelieved by men. At least it may present an alternative way of being in a relationship with men. This same principle may extend equally well to other differences. For example, a low-income client, accustomed to being treated poorly by her societal "betters"—those with higher incomes and more public visibility—may eventually come to feel empowered by having an advocate who shares the profile of those at whose mercy she has so long suffered. Is there possibly some closing of the societal gap when she is heard for the first time as their equal, if only because her voice is channeled through a lawyer?

Eliza's comments in the previous section about how becoming a parent did not change her view of her work on behalf of parents is worth mentioning here. I do not disagree; it may not have changed her view of the work. But maybe it did change her work, or at least how effective she became. Experiencing the pressures of parenthood, appreciating the plethora of supports she and I enjoy, understanding the pain of separation from our children, may help us be better lawyers for our clients caught up in the child welfare system. Certainly, it would matter to our clients to hear from us: "I have been there, I understand what you are going through."

.   .   .

EP: The flip side of how we choose good legal services lawyer-candidates is how we, as legal services lawyers, choose good clients. Many, but far from all, legal services programs exercise discretion over which clients to represent. These choices are often made on the basis of one or more interviews with the potential client and as thorough a review of her paperwork as you are able to do within the time constraints imposed by any pending litigation. You will probably also attempt to speak with several possible witnesses. In a child welfare case, for example, these will include the parents' and children's therapist(s), the children's schoolteacher, any involved medical professionals, and those family members or friends whom the potential client has identified as particularly knowledgeable about the case.

Once you have gathered as clear a picture of the legal situation as you are able to do—or once you feel adequately comfortable that the client has told you more or less the truth—you make a decision whether this case has "merit." As Dan suggested, these decisions are rarely free of subjective valuation. How could they be? Thus, the issue of diversity in hiring has profound relevance. Even assuming that programs try their best to achieve diversity, does a lawyer who looks like the client, or comes from the same place (ethnic, cultural, socio-economic, or racial) ensure better representation? At a minimum, that lawyer will no doubt have to struggle less with the fundamental attribution error to which Dan referred. After all, she would more readily see the client's situation through the client's eyes, have a more "true" (as opposed to imagined) understanding of the client's choices and motivations, and even perhaps have once been in the same situation herself. Does this mean she will be better able to empathize with the client?

I have never had the benefit of lawyering from this position. Instead, I have always had to acknowledge a distance—ethnic, cultural, socioeconomic, or racial—from my clients. At times, it is they who have given voice to this difference. I am less disturbed when clients make the (common) assumption that because they are getting their lawyer for free, their lawyer will somehow do an inferior job. This seems like a rational assumption, and I consider it my duty to demonstrate otherwise through my actions. I am more disturbed when a client perceives me as a lawyer for "the state" (our adversary in child welfare cases), referring to the child welfare agency and me with a plural "you." To the client, this must seem obvious. After all, she is poor and black and single, newly separated from her children by the state, and I, along with the other attorneys in the courtroom and the social workers, am white, middle-class, and often, because of the fact I am in court with the same attorneys and social workers and attorneys day after day, drawn into small talk about our families in the waiting room between hearings.

As much as I acknowledge these apparent differences and see real merit to a more diverse legal community serving the needs of our diverse clients, I also believe there is a value or criterion that is not readily captured by labels such as race, class, or gender. It is, to me, the dirty little secret of case selection. We are better lawyers for the clients with whom we connect. It is, of course, important that all lawyers who work for legal services share a commitment to the principle of equal justice for all. In civil matters, this translates into a shared belief that state action that deprives individuals of basic human rights—economic support, housing, family integrity—must be sharply scrutinized and held to the letter of the law. Perhaps this shared commitment alone is enough. But I have found, in my child welfare experience, that it is the clients with whom I feel empathy born of relationship for whom I will go the extra mile—driving them to visitations with their children or other appointments, or to look for a job or housing; helping to move them into new housing; calling around to find a counselor better suited to their particular needs. Do I tell myself that if I had infinite time and support staff that I would do the same for all my clients? Yes. But even if this is true, the reality is that a legal services lawyer never has adequate time and support staff, let alone infinite. Thus, subjective choices become all the more critical a part of the job. Assuming diversity facilitates empathy, this makes diversity matter all the more, for both lawyer and client.

Conclusion: The Impact of Race, Gender, and Class on Affective Lawyering

DA and EP: We are avid believers in "affective lawyering."[18] Affective lawyering is an alternative construct to "instrumental lawyering." Instrumental lawyers emphasize efficiency—rationing limited resources as prudently as possible by narrowing the scope of representation, focusing on "winning," and tightly controlling the lawyer-client relationship. Affective lawyers, on the other hand, emphasize client empowerment—broadly construing the scope of representation, focusing on the lawyer-client relationship, spending time building rapport. That is not to say that affective lawyers do not care about winning. Instead, we believe that winning is much harder to achieve without being affective.

Affective lawyering takes time, patience, and courage. It is rendered more difficult when your race, socioeconomic status, or gender is different from your client's. Displaying empathy to a victim of domestic violence comes naturally to Dan, but whether it is always well received coming from a man is another question. Building trust and rapport with an African American client who has been disenfranchised by a bureaucracy for reasons she believes are in part racist, in part culturally biased, can be tricky. Fully appreciating the burden poverty imposes on our clients is especially difficult when we have never experienced it ourselves.

The legal profession remains dominated, at least at the top of law firms and the courts, by white males. In legal services programs, lawyers who are women and/or people of color are not only more common, but also more prominent.[19] As discussed in the previous section, we believe that our clients are the better for it. Although diversity does not ensure quality representation, it certainly goes a long way toward facilitating it. Affective lawyering can be considered a "gendered" approach to lawyering because of the more emotion-focused language it employs and the explicit value it places on "process" and "relationship" as opposed to outcomes. For these reasons, some may say it is not surprising it has not taken greater hold in the top law firms and in the courts.[20]

To illustrate how diversity can shape legal services programs and the cases they will handle, consider how these programs develop case priorities, that is, how programs across the country choose which cases to handle with their limited resources.[21] A program that takes an instrumental approach might devote significant resources to defending eviction actions—cases in which successful results are easily quantified (by how many evictions are prevented); the duration is relatively limited (the case can often be closed soon after the eviction is prevented); and the number of people helped can be quite high (which pleases funders). In contrast, programs that take an affective approach might devote their limited resources to domestic violence work—cases in which results are not necessarily amenable to measurement (can you count as a win a case in which you obtain a protection from abuse order, but the victim soon after returns to the batterer?); the legal issues can proliferate (custody, property division, and housing are all issues likely to arise); and the demands on the lawyer are such that case turnover is not high (the number of clients served may be modest and thus harder to justify to funding sources).

It is not always clear that the affective model can or should be adopted in its purest form where time does not permit the kind of "rapport building" that is an essential prerequisite of working within the affective construct. On the other hand, there are many situations in which the possibility of "winning," at least in the foreseeable future, is far from evident. In these cases, we believe it is necessary to engage the client in the process of seeking a positive outcome over the long haul and to be prepared to confront the client to remain in the relationship when she wants to give up in the face of seemingly overwhelming obstacles.

If legal services programs were less diverse, clients with cases demanding an affective approach would be terribly underserved. Legal services programs, like the larger legal community, would be dominated by white males, and as a result their case priorities would be skewed toward an instrumental, results-focused orientation. Although more people might be helped, many vulnerable segments of the poverty community—women, children, people with disabilities—would be left in even more precarious circumstances, as they would not have the possibility of free legal assistance available to them.

And at least for us, the practice of poverty law would not be nearly as rewarding. We do not measure our effectiveness with wins and losses. We are relentlessly challenged by intractable problems and frequently cheered by small victories. We do the best we can, given our limitations in brainpower, creativity, and experience. We play to our strengths.

Discussion Questions

1. Consider whether the affective/instrumental dichotomy is a false one. That is to say, can cases really be divided up neatly into two mutually exclusive categories? In what ways is the dichotomy false, and in what ways is it true?

2. Are you able to discern any differences in the philosophies of the authors that could be rooted in their gender?

3. The authors self-identify as white and members of the middle or upper middle class. Yet, the authors emphasize the importance of diversity among poverty lawyers. Are there different conceptions of diversity besides race, gender, and class? What are they, and how could they be relevant to the practice of lawyering for the poor?

4. Do you think that affective lawyering could be employed in other areas of the law besides the practice of poverty law? What about in criminal law? Personal injury law?

5. Do the authors challenge or complement your preconceived notion of lawyers? What was your conception of lawyers before reading this chapter? Has it changed?

6. Have you considered law as a career goal? How has this chapter affected your thinking about the practice of law, if it has at all?

Notes

We were first introduced to the phrase we have used to title this article by Steve Banks, a lawyer for the Legal Aid Society of New York, in an interview with Elizabeth Koblert in the magazine. *New Yorker*, December 27, 1999.

1. The authors are listed in alphabetical order, as this was a truly collaborative effort in which we share equally the credit and blame.

2. This is not a hypothetical situation, but instead is a synopsis of a case I handled early in my career.

3. For more detail about the history of legal services and its compelling history, there are numerous sources to consult. See, e.g., Robert Hornstein, Daniel Atkins, and Treena Kaye, "The Politics of Equal Justice," *American University Journal of Gender, Social Policy and the Law* 11 (2003): 1089.

4. William P. Quigley, "The Demise of Law Reform and the Triumph of Legal Aid: Congress and the Legal Services Corporation from the 1960's to the 1990's," *St. Louis University Public Law Review* 17 (1998): 241, 245.

5. *San Antonio School District v. Rodriguez*, 411 U.S. 1 (1973) (rejecting a challenge to the linking of property taxes and school funding).

6. *Shapiro v. Thompson*, 394 U.S. 618 (1969) (welfare benefits must be provided to new residents of a state if they are provided to long-time residents).

7. *Sugarman v. Dougall*, 413 U.S. 634 (1973) (noncitizens must be eligible to hold permanent state service positions).

8. When Reagan was governor of California, California Rural Legal Assistance (a legal services program) sued the state to increase the state's minimum wage and to provide food benefits for the hungry.

9. Law schools boast that they do not teach lawyering, but rather teach students how to think like lawyers. However, I rightly suspected that clients would retain me to actually do lawyerlike things, perhaps file complaints and litigate cases, rather than just to reflect and ponder. I hoped that if just one program would be foolish enough to hire me, I could figure out those tricky details once I got there.

10. These are not mutually exclusive categories. Most of our clients with disabilities are poor, and many of our clients in poverty have disabilities.

11. For example, courts and legislatures have dismantled federal entitlement programs such as Aid to Families with Dependent Children (see the *Personal Responsibility and Work Opportunity Reconciliation Act of 1996*, 42 U.S.C. 601, et seq.); limited the ability of civil rights plaintiffs to receive attorney fee awards (see *Buckhannon Board & Care Home, Inc. v. West Virginia Dept. of Health and Human Resources*, 532 U.S. 598 [2001]); and comprehensively tied the hands of legal services programs in prisoner rights, abortion rights, and drug-related housing cases, just to name a few (see *Omnibus Consolidated Rescissions and Appropriations Act of 1996*, Public Law No. 104–134, §504, *U.S. Statutes at Large* 110 [1996]: 1321, 1353, 1356 ["OCRAA," or "the 1996 Act"], reenacted in the *Omnibus Consolidated Rescissions and Appropriations Act of 1997*, Public Law 104–208, §502, *U.S. Statutes at Large* 110 [1997]: 3009).

12. One legal academician has pointed out quite to the contrary that

proper use of and effort to invoke passion is not a sophistic or rhetorical appeal to irrationality or sentiment, but a means of achieving justice by helping the Court to hear and understand the real human dimensions of a legal controversy. The opposite of truth is not passion, it is falsehood. Refusal to acknowledge and respond to the "concrete human realities" that are the lifeblood of many legal disputes, by following an abstract, conceptual, logical approach to judging, does not reflect a greater commitment to truth, but at most an intellectual preference for a dispassionate, rationalistic method of deciding cases.

Steven Wizner, "Passion in Legal Argument and Judicial Decisionmaking: A Comment on *Goldberg v. Kelly*," *Cardozo Law Review* 10 (1988): 179.

13. In child welfare cases in which the child is first being removed from the parent, the legal standard is typically whether the parent can provide adequate care. See e.g., 10 *Del. C.* 901 (8). In Delaware, adequate care is unhelpfully defined as "a type and degree of personalized attention that will tend to advance a child's physical, mental, moral, emotional, and general well-being." 10 *Del. C.* 901 (1).

14. In termination of parental rights cases, which is the final phase of a child welfare proceeding, the state typically must meet statutory grounds amounting to parental unfitness or abandonment and must also show that termination is in the child's best interest. See, e.g., 13 *Del. C.* 1103. Best interest is defined in Delaware, and everywhere else, very nebulously. See 13 *Del. C.* 722.

15. Just looking at the data on the disproportionate representation of children of color in the child welfare system reveals the importance of race in poverty law. In 2005, 35 percent of children in foster care were black. U.S. Department of Health and Human Services, Administration for Children and Families, Administration on Children, Youth and Families, Children's Bureau, AFCARS Report, 2005; http://

www.acf.hhs.gov/programs/cb. The latest census statistics indicate that blacks constitute only 13 percent of the population. Either we believe that parents of color are inherently deficient parents, or there must be some other reason. One explanation is that reporters of abuse or neglect may be biased. For instance, one study conducted by child advocates found that doctors suspected and reported physical abuse more often in minority children than in white children. Wendy G. Lane, David M. Rubin, Ragin Monteith, Cindy W. Christian, "Racial Differences in the Evaluation of Pediatric Fractures for Child Abuse," *Journal of the American Medical Association* 288 (2002): 1603–9.

16. Two researchers at Harvard Medical School, Linda Clayton and W. Michael Byrd, in their book, *An American Health Dilemma: A Medical History of African Americans and the Problem of Race; Beginnings to 1900* (N.Y.: Routledge, 2000) conclude that racism in the health-care system has played a major role in the relatively poor health outcomes of blacks in America.

17. E. E. Jones and V. A. Harris, "The Attribution of Attitudes," *Journal of Experimental Social Psychology* 3 (1967): 1–24.

18. We were introduced to the concept in Peter Margulies, "Representation of Domestic Violence Survivors as a New Paradigm of Poverty Law: In Search of Access, Connection, and Voice," 63 *George Washington Law Rev*iew 63 (1995):1071.

19. In the legal services program we worked in together (which has about twenty lawyers) two-thirds of the attorneys are women, and the managing attorneys of all its three offices are women. In other dimensions of diversity we also do fairly well, though not as well as with gender, at least when compared with the private sector. We have two attorneys with disabilities (one of whom is blind) and two attorneys of color.

20. While the opportunity to practice affective lawyering may not arise very often in corporate law cases, some of the larger private law firms do have pro bono programs. In such programs, firm lawyers are partnered with public interest organizations to co-counsel public interest cases free of charge to the client and the organization.

21. Legal services programs have many more clients seeking representation than resources enable them to provide.

When the Stakes Are Life and Death

The Promise and Peril of Public Sociology/

Criminology for Capital Cases

> *On April 30, 2001 I went before the Delaware Parole Board, as was anticipated. . . . I spoke. I addressed the reason why my life had been filled with such violence and [why I] committed the acts which I had over the years. It was so quiet you could hear a pin dropping to the floor, and all eyes were on me.*

This was the second-to-the-last bit of correspondence I received from Abdullah Tanzil Hameen. At the time of writing, Hameen had been on Delaware's death row for more than nine years. I had known and worked with him on his legal case for the last four of those years. Hameen's was not the first capital case I worked on, nor was it, strictly speaking, one of the more egregious ones I have come across. In some of the other cases, defendants were convicted on the basis of confessions that bore all of the telltale signs of police coercion. In others, defendants were found guilty based on the testimony of a single witness who had both a lengthy criminal record and plenty of reasons to cooperate with prosecutors. What Hameen's case held in common with these cases, and in fact most capital prosecutions, was that his poverty put him at the tender mercies of a judicial system that affords little in the way of adequate legal representation for those who cannot bankroll their own defense. His case was similar in another way as well. He was convicted on the basis of testimony from his codefendant who, in exchange for fingering Hameen as a murderer, was able to avoid a death sentence. What distinguishes Hameen's case, particularly with respect to other cases that I have been involved with, is Hameen's admission of guilt. Although he vigorously challenged the state's theory of the crime, Hameen openly and candidly acknowledged his responsibility for the shooting death of Troy Hodges.

In many ways, my involvement in his case begins with that admission of guilt. I was in graduate school working toward a Ph.D. in sociology with an emphasis in criminology when I became interested in racial inequities in capital sentencing. I became aware of the issue after the American Society of Criminology, the primary professional organization for U.S. criminologists, issued a formal position statement against capital punishment.[1] Initially, my work was that of a public activist. I endeavored to raise public awareness about wrongful conviction cases and the disproportionate number of African American men sentenced to death. I wrote letters and essays, gave public talks, organized fundraisers, and participated in rallies with anti–death penalty organizations. Shortly after being interviewed by a Philadelphia daily newspaper regarding one such rally, the nature of my work changed. Letters from prisoners and their families began to pour into my university mailbox. Many of the letters were inquiries from prisoners facing lengthy sentences for drug-related crimes. A few were from African American men on Pennsylvania's death row who, in the brief space of a single page of notebook paper, endeavored to convince me of their innocence. Although I was unsure of what I could contribute to their cases, I reviewed all of the death penalty cases and agreed to help out with three.[2] I selected each based on my belief, after reviewing case files and court transcripts, that the defendants were innocent of the capital crimes they had been charged with. I felt compelled to tell these men, often at great length, that I had no formal legal training and that, from my vantage, a master's degree in sociology was of little use for navigating the complexities of habeas law or the byzantine procedural dictates of the penal system.[3] I quickly learned that my lack of legal expertise was of little significance to them. They needed all the help they could get, they needed it quickly, and, as one of the men wrote to me, "a master's degree is better than nothing."

My work varied from one case to the next, although it usually involved a good bit of legal research. I identified relevant appellate decisions and wrote reports on how the points on which those cases were decided stacked up next to the defendant's own. Occasionally, I did a bit of investigative work, tracking down current addresses for witnesses and venturing out to photograph the geography of the crime scene and the escape routes the defendant was purported to have taken. Although I enjoyed this work immensely, I became increasingly conflicted over the amount of time I was devoting to it relative to my graduate studies. My work on these cases was strictly activist in orientation. I did not approach these men with the intent to research them or the situation in which they found themselves. The death penalty was not even the subject of my dissertation. Indeed, I managed a rather tidy division between my activism and research. Or I did until my colleagues began to challenge me about the nature of my death penalty work. Was this "real" sociology/criminology? If it was, what was the research angle? If it was not, why bother? Family, friends, and students asked questions of a more political nature. Would I do this work if I knew the defendant was guilty of murder? What was the point of defending prisoners whose murder convictions had been upheld by numerous appellate courts?

It was in this context that I became acquainted with Hameen's case. I met his wife, Shakeerah Hameen, through an anti–death penalty organization based in Delaware called B.L.A.C. (Because Love Allows Compassion). The organization was for the family members of death row inmates, and I routinely invited members to share their stories with students in my undergraduate criminal justice classes. Shakeerah showed up in my class one night and, at the end of her session, she invited me out for coffee to discuss her husband's case in greater detail. I told her my doubts about getting involved with someone who was guilty of murder. She offered a detailed account of Hameen's case and argued that the racial injustice of capital punishment extended beyond wrongful convictions. Shakeerah was a passionate and persuasive spokesperson on her husband's behalf. I agreed to review his case file.

At first glance, this is the case of a drug dealer (Abdullah Hameen) who shot and killed another dealer (Troy Hodges).[4] Prosecutors were initially unsure if the shooting occurred during the course of a robbery or whether it was the outcome of a drug deal gone bad. Although there was no evidence that the shooting was premeditated, Hameen was charged and convicted of first-degree murder, a capital offense in Delaware. During the penalty phase of his trial, Hameen maintained that the shooting was both "accidental" and in self-defense. Both the judge and the jury found his explanation contradictory and nonsensical. The jury voted unanimously in favor of execution. The judge affirmed their decision and set the initial execution date for December 7, 1992.

Hameen was certainly guilty of murder, he acknowledged as much during the trial. But was he guilty of the kind of murder that the death penalty is meant to punish? Appellate courts, including the U.S. Supreme Court, have routinely held that executions are to be reserved for the worst of the worst. Did Hameen's case qualify? It was this question that prompted me to agree to drive down to Smyrna, Delaware, for a face-to-face visit. I was interested in Hameen's explanation of the crime and, in particular, how his narrative fit with the evidence presented at trial as well as the ways that it contrasted with the theories put forward by both the prosecution and defense. How did he account for his testimony that the murder was both accidental and in self-defense? Why did he pursue such a risky strategy when his life was on the line?

The questions that interested me were the very same ones Hameen was anxious to address and, in fact, were questions he knew he had to incorporate into his plea to the Delaware Pardons Board to persuade them to spare his life. His case had been working its way through the appellate court system, and his execution date had been postponed several times. When we met in 1997, he was running out of legal options. What Hameen wanted from me was a narrative strategy that would render his world, a world of poverty, racism, violence, and street-level hustles, meaningful and comprehensible to the predominantly white, upper-middle-class professionals that sat on the Pardons Board. In other words, he was looking for a translator, someone who could assist him in recounting the events that lead up to the shooting in a way that board members would find, if not reasonable, then at least plausible. This was a task that was particularly well suited to a sociologist. After all, much of our research is spent explicating how context shapes and gives meaning to behavior. I accepted his offer on the spot. For me, the task represented both an opportunity to put sociology to work in the "real" world and a test of my personal convictions regarding guilt. For Hameen, the task represented nothing less than a last-ditch effort to defend his life.

In the remainder of this essay, I elaborate on our effort to create a narrative that told Hameen's story in a way that resonated with the worldly expectations of members of the Pardons Board. I begin first by summarizing the case against Hameen and then detailing the logic offered by the judge and jury to support a sentence of death. It is this logic that we endeavored to combat in writing Hameen's statement to the board. Next, I describe the role public sociology played in this case. By "public sociology," I am referring to the use of sociological theory and research to inform public debates regarding political, legal, and moral issues (Baiocchi 2005; Burawoy 2004; see also Mills 2000). Here, sociological theories, methods, and concepts are put to use in civil society for the purposes of enriching debates, informing policy, and generating new forms of knowledge. With respect to Hameen's case, sociological research on narratives, as well as on the intersubjective character of the race and class divide, were crucial to formulating a strategy to save his life. In the last section of this essay, I examine both the implications and consequences of our narrative strategy for Hameen's case and for capital cases more generally.

The Case against Abdullah Hameen

The state's case against Hameen begins on the night of August 5, 1991. That night, Hameen accompanied a local drug dealer by the name of Tyrone Hyland to the Tri-State Mall in Claymont, Delaware. They were there to meet a third man, Troy Hodges, who was a part-time college student with a drug business going on the side. By all accounts, Hodges was a relative novice in the drug trade. Hyland and Hameen were not. Both men were older than Hodges, both were from a much rougher neighborhood just across the border in Pennsylvania, and both were dealers with histories of using violence to defend their turf. In Hameen's case, modest success in the drug game came at a price—there were multiple "contracts" out on his life. During the summer of 1991, he carried a gun with him wherever he went.

The state's attorney surmised that Hyland and Hodges were the principal parties to the drug transaction and that Hameen was there to back Hyland up in the event of trouble. The meeting took place in Hyland's car. Hyland was the driver, Hodges sat in the front passenger seat, and Hameen sat directly behind him. An argument ensued between Hyland and Hodges over money. Hodges had agreed to bring $10,000 in cash in exchange for an unspecified amount of cocaine; however, he showed up with only $5,000.[5] According to a statement Hameen gave to police a few weeks after the murder, Hyland covertly passed a cocked gun to Hameen during the course of the argument. As the discussion between Hodges and Hyland grew increasingly heated, Hyland began slowly driving through the parking lot and indicated that Hodges should get out of the car. When Hodges exited (it was unclear if he was shoved or jumped out of the car), Hameen shot him at close range in the torso. Hodges ran a few paces before collapsing on a sidewalk. He died a few days later from massive hemorrhaging caused by the gunshot wound.

Although laws in each state differ, prosecutors generally charge a person who kills another person during the course of a heated argument ("in the heat of passion") with murder in the second degree. Second-degree murder carries a lengthy prison term, but it is rarely, if ever, treated as a capital crime. In the current era, the death penalty is primarily reserved for murder in the first degree, which is typically defined as killing with "malice aforethought" (i.e., premeditation). There are a few exceptions to the premeditation rule. In Delaware, as in most states, a murder that occurs in the course of a felony—even if the murder was not premeditated—is considered a first-degree murder and thus, a death-eligible offense. Prosecutors applied this rule, known as the felony-murder rule, to Hameen's case. Although Hameen did not know the victim, bore him no ill will, and clearly had not planned to kill him, he was charged with first-degree murder. Prosecutors argued that Hyland, Hodges, and Hameen were not simply three men who got into an argument that resulted in the death of Hodges. Rather, the murder occurred during the course of a felony. Thus, it was not necessary for prosecutors to explore Hameen's state of mind. Nor did they need to establish premeditation. To win a capital conviction, they needed only to prove that Hameen had been involved in a felony during which a murder occurred.

Initially, prosecutors could not settle on an underlying felony charge. They juggled three possible scenarios before the jury. The first was that Hyland and Hameen were engaged in drug trafficking. Because neither money nor drugs were confiscated from the crime scene, this was difficult to prove. In the second scenario, prosecutors argued that the drug transaction was a setup that Hyland and Hameen had arranged for the purposes of robbing Hodges. To establish this, they used the presence of a weapon and the absence of drugs to establish that this was a classic "rip off" scheme. The third felony scenario presented by prosecutors was that this was a conspiracy to commit a robbery or to engage in drug trafficking or both. For that, they relied on statements from Hyland. In closing arguments and at the judge's admonition, prosecutors chose the second scenario, robbery, and argued that Hameen was guilty of felony-murder based on his participation in a robbery that resulted in the shooting death of Hodges.

Although it was a controversial prosecutorial strategy and one that became the basis of a series of subsequent appeals, it proved effective. Hameen's attorneys, two public defenders with a huge caseload, few resources, and no experience with death penalty cases, elected not to present a defense. The trial court judge denied them funds to hire an expert witness to challenge the state's claims that the gun, which was never recovered, belonged to Hameen. They were also denied funds to hire a forensic expert to refute the prosecution's argument that the gun had been fired at close range. The limited resources they did have were quickly expended trying to defend against the three hypothetical felonies. Indeed, prosecutors worked these felonies like a shell game. They argued one felony, and when their own witness said something that contradicted the argument, they pulled that felony and substituted another one in its place. This happened throughout the entire trial. In the end, defense attorneys called no witnesses, hired no experts, and refused Hameen's request to testify that the shooting had been in self-defense. In the case of the latter, they worried that a self-defense claim could contradict Hameen's earlier statement to police that the shooting was accidental. And so, when it came time to present their defense, Hameen's attorneys simply stood before the jury and told them the state had not proved the case beyond a reasonable doubt.

It was not a particularly convincing argument. In early November 1992, the jury found Hameen guilty of first-degree, felony-murder.

The Sentence of Death

Death penalty cases are tried in two phases. In the first, the jury decides whether the defendant is innocent or guilty of the capital crime that he or she has been charged with. In the event of a guilty verdict, the trial moves into a second phase. Here, jurors determine whether the defendant should be given a sentence of life in prison or death. The proceedings mimic adversarial aspects of the guilt/innocence phase of the trial. The prosecution goes first and presents evidence of statutory aggravating circumstances. Aggravating circumstances are formally established by the state legislature and include characteristics of the offense and the offender that render the murder particularly egregious. Typical aggravating circumstances include the murder of a police officer, multiple victims, murder for monetary gain, and a defendant with a history of criminal violence.

Following presentation of the state's case, the defense calls its own witnesses, who provide testimony as to mitigating circumstances. Defense attorneys have considerable latitude in defining mitigating circumstances. State legislatures, for example, typically allow jurors to consider various aspects of the defendant's life, including his or her age, employment history, family upbringing, education, familial obligations, and remorsefulness. Before a sentence of death can be imposed, jurors must carefully weigh aggravating circumstances against mitigating ones. If there are more mitigating circumstances then aggravating ones, jurors cannot sentence the defendant to death. If, however, jurors can show that aggravating factors outweigh mitigating ones, they can elect that the defendant be executed. In some states, including Delaware, the jury's decision is considered an advisory one to the judge. The judge performs his or her own weighing test, considers the jury's findings, and makes the final decision as to the penalty.

In Hameen's case, both the judge and the jury recommended a sentence of death. In the judge's written opinion, he listed three statutory aggravating circumstances that the state had proven "beyond a reasonable doubt." First, both the judge and the jury found that Hameen committed the murder of Hodges during the course of a robbery. Second, they found that the murder had been committed for the purpose of monetary gain. Although defense attorneys argued that these were one in the same, the trial court judge held that because the state legislature had established each as a unique aggravating circumstance, they could be counted separately against Hameen.[6] The third count, and indeed the most damning one, was that Hameen had previously been convicted of murder. That murder had taken place during a bar fight in Pennsylvania eleven years prior. It was not difficult for state prosecutors to argue that Hameen was a man with a propensity for violence and one who displayed callous indifference to human life.

It is not enough, of course, for the judge and jury to find that the state had proved the case and that the defendant met the criteria for aggravating circumstances. They must also establish that these outweigh any mitigating circumstances raised by the defense. Hameen's defense lawyers raised a total of twelve mitigating claims. These included: (1) that Hameen was a victim of and witness to domestic violence as a child; (2) that he grew up in a substance abusing and dysfunctional family; (3) that he has a son whom he loves and who loves him; (4) that he has a family who loves and cares for him; (5) that he had a job prior to incarceration; (6) that he lacked appropriate role models in his community; (7) that he has remorse for the murder victim; (8) that he has positive personality traits and is intellectual; (9) that the murder was not premeditated; (10) that the death occurred during a meeting to commit felony drug trafficking; (11) that Hyland, the principal party to the drug deal, had been granted a plea deal; and (12) that Hameen has worked throughout his adult life to better himself.

Before rendering the sentence, the trial judge itemized each of these claims and noted why they did not mitigate a sentence of death. For example, the judge noted that Hameen's father was an alcoholic and his family dysfunctional; however, he argued that by the time Hameen was eight years old, he had been placed in the custody of his maternal great-grandmother and that she appeared to be "loving and nurturing." With respect to his son, the judge found that Hameen's trouble with the law and frequent incarcerations ". . . do not indicate that [his] love [for his son] was a high priority." Further, the judge discounted Hameen's claim to feel remorse for the victim. The judge argued that Hameen's explanation that the shooting was accidental contradicted his response to a question from prosecutors regarding whether such an event could happen again. Hameen acknowledged that it could. In the judge's written opinion ordering the execution he summed up the official position of the trial court as to Hameen's account of his life and crimes: "The Court considers and rejects [Hameen's] background and upbringing as a mitigating factor that outweighs the heinous nature of this crime and the propensity of [Hameen] for violence. [Hameen's] siblings have not made a career of shooting people. They were subjected to the same familial and societal deprivations. Society did not create [Abdullah Hameen's] lack of concern for human life . . ."

Challenging the logic of the court's decision, particularly the argument that social conditions were essentially irrelevant to the crime, became the basis of my work on this case. Although I was deeply troubled by Hameen's previous murder conviction and his demonstrated capacity for violence, I also felt an abiding sense of injustice with respect to the way the sentencing phase of the trial had been conducted and decided. The failure to consider Hameen's poverty and, in particular, the violent streets on which he had come of age, struck me as a fatal error in the logic of sentencing. Hameen's environment certainly could not mitigate his guilt. He had committed murder and acknowledged as much. However, his environment was absolutely a relevant factor to consider in mitigating a sentence of death, and it was crucial to understanding why he accounted for the crime as both accidental and defensive. The court has a responsibility to not only understand the nature of criminal violence and but also the defendant's capacity for redemption. From my perspective as a sociologist, the trial court had been glib in its dismissal of socioeconomic factors, and this undermined the justness and legitimacy of the sentence.

Public Sociology in Capital Cases

Although public sociology has recently come into vogue with the publication of Michael Burawoy's (2004) widely circulated article, "Public Sociologies: Contradictions, Dilemmas, and Possibilities," its potential remains largely unrealized in the U.S. criminal justice system.[7] The death penalty, given its persistent legacy of race and class discrimination, is ripe for sociological incursion. Although it is a penalty that is, in theory, reserved for the "worst of the worst," this is rarely the case in practice. As numerous studies of capital sentencing have shown, the best predictor of whether a convicted murder will be sentenced to life in prison or executed is poverty. Other characteristics, including those relevant aspects of the offense, such as age of victims, number of victims, and the character of the murder itself, are weakly linked, if at all, to the likelihood that a convicted murderer will receive the death sentence (Baldus et al. 1986; Gross and Mauro 1989). Further, racial politics are strongly implicated in both the likelihood that a jurisdiction will adopt the death penalty as a sentencing option and as an determinant of sentence in individual cases (Jacobs, Carmichael and Kent 2005; Paternoster 1991).

In the wake of recent controversies over wrongful convictions and racial disparities, now is a particularly urgent time for sociologists and criminologists to use research and theory to weigh in on the political and moral desirability of capital punishment. The role of sociologists should not be confined to participation in broader public debates, however. It is also vital that sociological research be put to use at the level of individual case processing. Here, Hameen's case offers but one example of how a public sociology might critically and productively inform the court's sentencing decisions.

Using the written opinion of the trial court judge as a guide, it appears that the court's decision to sentence Hameen to death rather than to life in prison boils down to two sets of interrelated issues. First, the judge and jury found Hameen's accounts of the shooting contradictory and nonsensical. They read this as a sign that Hameen was neither remorseful, nor sufficiently honest and forthcoming about his responsibility for the murder. The second set of issues involves, of course, Hameen's criminal lifestyle and, particularly, his previous murder conviction. Here, they used Hameen's siblings as a point of comparison to gauge the effects of poverty and childhood abuse on the decisions Hameen made in his adult life. Because his siblings did not exhibit the same criminal and violent behavior in adulthood, the court concluded that poverty and other environmental factors were irrelevant to understanding both the nature of the crime and the character of the defendant.

By the time I became involved in Hameen's case, it was too late to reargue aggravating and mitigating circumstances before judge and jury. It was not too late, however, to put forward a set of arguments challenging the trial court's logic to the Board of Pardons.[8] In Delaware, the Board of Pardons makes a recommendation to the governor for removing or reducing a criminal sanction. The governor cannot modify a criminal sanction without the recommendation of this board. Petitioners to the Board of Pardons can address this body directly and at length, as can representatives from the Attorney General's office and members of the victim's family. Hameen and I assumed, I believe correctly, that the members of the pardons board would rely on a logic similar to that of the trial court to evaluate the worthiness of Hameen's plea for mercy. Our goal was to present a narrative to the board that situated the facts of the case within the larger context of Hameen's life and to do so in a way that restored Hameen's humanity. Because the space of this essay does not allow for an extended elaboration of the narrative we crafted, I focus here on the ways we accounted for the apparent contradictions in Hameen's statements by linking them to the unique sociocultural context he inhabited.

During an interrogation that occurred in the weeks following Hodges's death, Hameen gave a tape-recorded statement to police officers acknowledging his guilt but contending that the gun discharged "accidentally." Later, during the penalty phase of his trial, he claimed the shooting was in self-defense. But how could this be? Both prosecutors and defense attorneys treated these statements as contradictory and mutually exclusive. Indeed, both sides interpreted the self-defense claim as an indicator of intentionality—that in the moments leading up to the murder, Hameen made a conscious decision to wound or kill Hodges. The presence of intentionality, according to a legalistic interpretation, undermines Hameen's initial claim that the shooting was done accidentally. Intentionality is not present in the event of an accident. Rather, the shooting simply happens.

Hameen's defense attorneys, while woefully inexperienced in death penalty cases, understood that his tape-recorded statement to police narrowed down the range of possible explanations he could subsequently offer to a jury. In spite of his limited education, Hameen was an extremely intelligent man. He understood the point his attorneys were making, but he disagreed with their strategy and repeatedly requested that he be allowed to testify the shooting was in self-defense. His attorneys refused. When he was found guilty, they relented and allowed him to testify during the penalty phase. In that hearing, he apologized profusely to the victim's family and to the court for the murder. He maintained that it was an accident and that it "just happened," but he also acknowledged, in response to a question from prosecutors, that it might happen again. When asked how something that was accidental could happen again, he explained that it was because the shooting was in self-defense. In the judge's written opinion, he characterized this as contradictory testimony and asserted that Hameen did not feel remorse for the killing, only ". . . remorse that he is in the situation in which he finds himself."

After reviewing the trial transcripts and having numerous conversations with Hameen and members of his family, I came to believe that the shooting of Hodges really was both accidental and defensive in nature. To make this case to the Pardons Board, I helped Hameen craft a narrative that was based on a key principle of sociology—that individuals strategize their actions but do not do so in conditions of their choosing. In other words, socioeconomic context shapes both the obstacles and choices that individual actors are confronted with on a day-to-day basis. Racism, poverty, and a violent upbringing did not *cause* Hameen to engage in violence in the sense that they stripped him of his own agency. Rather, these social structures narrowed the range of choices available to him as he struggled to survive in his environment. By linking Hameen's actions to a larger social context, we neither sought to excuse his conduct or minimize his responsibility. Instead, we endeavored to show how his violence was socially situated, and a meaningful, albeit tragic, response to unique set of social conditions.

Hameen's statement to the board began with a lengthy acknowledgment of his responsibility for the shooting death of Troy Hodges and an elaboration of his remorsefulness. He then explained that he could not offer an account of that night without referencing the circumstances in which he found himself that summer as well as aspects of his personal biography. In his own words, he stated:

At the outset I feel compelled to emphasize that I am not seeking to . . . make excuses for my behavior, nor do I feel or believe that my actions are the direct result of being a victim of poverty, racism, or the tremendous challenges each of these pose for poor families attempting to raise their children in crime-ridden neighborhoods. . . . As was pointed out in my sentencing hearing, "Many individuals survive similar if not worse conditions without resorting to criminal activity." On the other hand, for me to ignore or minimize the circumstances that caused me great pain as a child and the violent, impoverished environment in which I found myself as a young man, would be dishonest, as these experiences were paramount in my feelings about myself and others, and central to the decisions that I made. In recounting these experiences, then, I am not seeking to minimize my responsibility for what I've done, I accept full responsibility, rather, I am seeking to explain the choices that I made and the reasons why some of my perceptions and reactions were misdirected and flawed.

He acknowledged that the gun was his, though he denied taking it to the meeting with Hodges for the purposes of robbery or providing "muscle" at a drug transaction. He explained that he carried the gun with him at all times that summer. In fact, he was armed for much of his adult life. This was as much a product of the neighborhood where he lived—one that was notorious for an outrageously high murder rate and a stunning lack of policing resources—as it was a necessary element of the illicit drug market in which he worked to supplement his meager income mowing lawns for the city of Chester.

That summer began ominously. He was the victim of an attempted robbery in June and shortly after found himself pulled into an increasingly violent dispute involving several members of his family. The dispute was linked to Chester's drug economy and the turf battles that ensued in the wake of large-scale police raids. Hameen did not deny being a tough talker in those disputes and issuing threats to his enemies. His threats made his situation all the more precarious. He shortly discovered that other local dealers had put a contract out on his life. He took this seriously and changed key aspects of his behavior, including curtailing his social life and travels, limiting his interactions to close friends and family members, and keeping his gun by his side at all times. He was on edge anticipating threats and fatigued from sleeping with "one eye open."

On the night of August 5, he agreed to accompany Hyland to the mall so that Hyland could meet a "friend." He insists he was unaware that it was a drug transaction until Hyland and Hodges emerged from the mall arguing. He acknowledged having his gun on him and said that he was incorrect when he told police that Hyland had handed it to him during the argument. As the argument grew heated, Hyland ordered Hodges out of the car. Hameen, by this time, had his gun out and across his lap. As Hodges exited, he turned toward the car and reached for something behind his back and underneath his T-shirt. Hameen, thinking Hodges was reaching for a gun, fired. He shot once in the direction of Hodges's hand. He denied ever knowing that Hodges was hit.

Although this was not brought out at trial, Hameen was correct in noting that Hodges had something clipped to the back of his trousers. It was a pager rather than a gun, and presumably Hodges was reaching for it to contact a driver who sat waiting with the remainder of the cash in a nearby section of the parking lot. Hameen explained to the board that the shooting was accidental in that he mistook the pager for a weapon and that he intended to maim but not kill Hodges. But, as he also recounted, the shooting was very much in self-defense. He spent the summer trying to anticipate danger, and in that moment he believed Hodges was poised to shoot him. He fired when he saw something dark clipped to Hodge's pants. In the context of his world, he believed that hesitation made the difference between life and death. He did not know, he admitted, how much of the events of that summer influenced his interpretation of Hodges's behavior and whether there would have been a different outcome had there not been a contract out for his life.

In the remainder of his narrative, he recounted his upbringing and, in particular, his rocky relationship with a father who was physically abusive and often absent. He pointed out that his father encouraged him to be a "fighter"— one who stood up to his enemies and never backed down from a challenge. He touched on the first murder, the outcome of a fistfight that occurred between him and another man with whom he had been arguing with at local bar. He was just seventeen and had, in fact, accompanied his father to the bar. When someone hollered that the other man had a gun, Hameen turned and shot him. He was armed with a gun his father had helped him acquire. He plead guilty to manslaughter and served three and a half years in an adult prison.

The remainder of his narrative filled in the details of his poverty, his neighborhood context, and his family upbringing. It was the story of a man who grew up very fast and who grew accustomed to "doing what [he] had to do" to survive. He acknowledged making a number of bad choices, noting in particular his involvement in illicit drug markets, but he also emphasized how poverty, illiteracy, violence, and obligations to family narrowed his range of options. He observed that while in prison, away from the temptations and threats of the street, he had a clean disciplinary record and, in fact, had voluntarily enrolled in a number of educational and self-improvement classes. He was, by his own account and the accounts of others, a model prisoner.

Members of the board were moved by his testimony, and we were told by Hameen's attorney that a majority cast a straw vote in favor of commuting his sentence to life in prison without the possibility of parole. It was not to be. State's attorneys were given the last word. They asked for an extension to track down members of Hodges's family who might be willing to testify that Hameen's original sentence should be carried out. After several weeks, they were able to locate Hodges's sister. Although she was not present for the presentation of Hameen's case, she testified that he was "garbage" and that he was incapable of change. She requested that he be executed. The board obliged. In their public pronouncement they noted, "While board members concluded that Hameen truly was sorry for his crimes and that his attempts at rehabilitation were genuine, they said they did not find sufficient justification to overturn a jury's unanimous recommendation."

Abdullah Tanzil Hameen was executed on May 25, 2001.

Conclusion

When I initially agreed to write this article, I thought that it would serve as a cautionary tale about public sociology. In most graduate programs, sociologists and criminologists are trained to thrive as academics, not as policy wonks or public advocates. We learn how to select issues of theoretical and conceptual interest, how to set up our studies in ways that address gaps and omissions in previous research, how to analyze and present our data convincingly, and how to market our work to other sociologists and criminologists. Although we are occasionally asked to address the policy implications of our findings, we all too often do so as an afterthought. Rarely are we encouraged or motivated to put our work to critical public use. In the wake of Hameen's execution and my own excruciating suspicion that sociology had failed him, I encountered the hoopla surrounding public sociology with skepticism. Who are we, after all, to believe that we are qualified to tinker in legal and political battles when the stakes are as high as life and death?

In the course of researching this article, I came to answer this question differently than I would have at the outset. Sociologists have every reason to put themselves on the front lines of legal and political battles, *especially* when the stakes are life and death. Three aspects of Hameen's case bring me to this conclusion. First, the trial court's dismissal of the role that social conditions, particularly poverty and racial inequality, played in the crime reflects a naive and inaccurate understanding of the relationship between social structures and human behavior. Behavior is never divorced from the social contexts in which it is enacted. Violence is a social process, an event that emerges in the course of social interaction. It is not a character trait that an individual intrinsically possesses. The fact that Hameen's siblings, raised in a similar context, did not engage in violent behavior does not signify the irrelevance of environment to the crime; rather, it suggests that the interplay with human agency is both nuanced and complex. Sociologists and criminologists have an urgent responsibility to educate courts on this basic principle.[9]

Second, Hameen's case speaks to the significance of narrative for influencing sentencing decisions. Good trial lawyers have always been cognizant that compelling and persuasive narratives are necessary for convincing jurors how to best interpret and evaluate the facts of any given case. Sociologists and criminologists can play an important role in shaping those narrative strategies, particularly when a defendant's lifestyle and circumstances are unfamiliar or foreign to courtroom practitioners. Hameen's account of the murder as both accidental and in self-defense was read by the judge and even his own lawyers as evasive and contradictory. However, when considered within the context of his life, these accounts become infinitely more plausible and reasonable.

The third reason is one Hameen wrote in a letter to me that I reread while writing this article. He was responding to a letter I wrote, one in the aftermath of the board's decision to postpone the hearings while attorneys for the state endeavored to locate Hodges's family members. I was concerned about what this might signal in terms of the board's final decision. He wrote, "Whatever the outcome, I told my story and stayed true to it. It's part of the history of this case. It will outlive us both." I realized as I reread this that Hameen's death is neither a story about the triumph of public sociology or its failure. It is, rather, a story about the possibilities of public sociology/criminology. Although we were unable to stop the state from carrying out an execution that I believe was unjust, we did succeed in making Hameen's voice a part of the historical record and memorializing his life. As public sociologists working on capital cases, we must look to both the present and the future. As Hameen noted before he died, his goal in work-ing with me was to "speak truth to power" so that he might not only save his life but the lives of other condemned men and women. Public sociol-ogy/criminology creates the possibility that Hameen and others like him can influence politics and law in the future by using their stories to narrate the injustices of the present.

Discussion Questions

1. What is public sociology and criminology?
2. How was public sociology / criminology used in this case?
3. How might it be used in other death penalty cases?
4. Was the author correct in arguing that this was not a story of the failure of public sociology and criminology? Why or why not?
5. The author suggests violence is socially produced. How did Hameen's nar-rative demonstrate this?

Notes

1. For more information on the American Society of Criminology and its position on capital punishment, see http://www.ASC41.com.

2. I did not take on the drug cases because a U.S. appellate court had recently ruled that lengthy sentences, even for minor sorts of cocaine-related offenses, is constitu-tional. Short of establishing the defendant's innocence (something none of these men claimed), there was little that could be done to reduce the length of their prison terms.

3. Habeas law refers to the writ of habeas corpus, which allows a person held in cus-tody to challenge the legality of his or her confinement.

4. *Cornelius Ferguson, a/k/a Abdullah Tanzil Hameen v. State of Delaware*, 642 A.2d 772 (Delaware, 1994). All subsequent information and quotations from the court records are from this source.

5. Alvin Wiggins had accompanied Hodges to the mall but did not accompany him to the meeting. He testified that Hodges had $10,000 with him, but left half of it in his car.

6. The trial court's decision was upheld on appeal.

7. Notable exceptions include the work of Michael Radelet and Richard Leo, both of whom do research on policy-relevant issues and routinely testify in death penalty and wrongful conviction cases.

8. In Delaware, the board is comprised of the lieutenant governor, chancellor, secre-tary of state, state treasurer, and auditor of accounts.

9. In many respects, this is analogous to the use of social scientists as expert wit-nesses in the cases of battered women who murder their abusers. In these cases, re-searchers frequently present social scientific data demonstrating why battered women

remain trapped in abusive relationships and why their violence qualifies as a form of self-defense (Bowker 1996).

References

Baiocchi, Gianpaolo. 2005. "Interrogating Connections: From Public Criticisms to Critical Publics in Burawoy's Public Sociology." *Critical Sociology* 31 (3):339–51.

Baldus, David, et al. 1986. "Arbitrariness and Discrimination in the Administration of the Death Penalty: A Challenge to State Supreme Courts." *Stetson Law Review* 15:133–262.

Bowker, Lee. 1996. "Sociologists, Gangs, and Battered Women: Representing the Discipline in the Courts." In *Witnessing for Sociology: Sociologists in Court*, edited by Pamela Jenkins and Steve Kroll-Smith, 149–63.

Burawoy, Michael. 2004. "Public Sociologies: Contradictions, Dilemmas, and Possibilities." *Social Forces* 82 (4):1603–18.

Gross, Samuel, and Robert Mauro. 1989. *Death and Discrimination: Racial Disparities in Capital Sentencing*. Boston: Northeastern University Press.

Jacobs, David, Jason Carmichael, and Stephanie Kent. 2005. "Vigilantism, Current Racial Threat, and Death Sentences." *American Sociological Review* 70:656–77.

Mills, C. Wright. 2000. *The Sociological Imagination*. New York: Oxford University Press.

Paternoster, Ray. 1991. *Capital Punishment in America*. New York: Lexington Books.

Chapter 6   Susan Caringella and Drew Humphries

Getting from Here to There
A Guide for Aspiring Academics

This chapter is aimed at college students who may aspire to become academics, in other words, college professors, who teach, conduct research, and participate in the life of the college or university. If you are anything like the way we were as undergraduates, the idea of becoming a professor is a romantic aspiration, too vague to be useful in getting you from where you are into graduate school and from there to a job and tenure. In this article, we give you a road map, along with helpful advice for the journey. And because the journey is long and difficult, it is important for you to understand the rewards. Faculty members are paid for doing what they love doing: educating students, conducting research, and engaging in the intellectual development of our discipline.

The occupational details are attractive. Salary and benefits are competitive. For an eight- to nine-month teaching job, you will make more than the median household income. Colleges are closed for holidays; faculty members are not required to teach in the summer. Faculty members exercise considerable control over their schedules, which helps in balancing work and family or personal obligations. They decide what to research and where to conduct the research. However appealing financial security, flexibility, and autonomy may be, a passion for justice or the search for knowledge comes closest to describing what drives us to be academics.

Academic careers can be broken down into a series of stages that raise different questions about one's personal life, political commitments, and ethical values. In the first two sections of this essay, "Undergraduate to Graduate School," and "Making the Most of Graduate School," we emphasize the steps of getting from one place to another, giving comparatively less attention to issues raised in these steps. However, in the last two sections, "Your First Job" and "Getting Tenure," we have organized the discussion around personal, academic, political, and ethical issues, paying less attention to describing the methods.

From Undergraduate to Graduate School

One of the things Humphries liked about her undergraduate education was the chance to talk about ideas. Such conversations typically took place at exam times, when students had finally learned enough to argue about the nature of deviance, the causes of the civil war, or what metaphysics actually referred to. Recognizing the pleasure that these conversations brought her was the first clue that academia was in her future. As professors, however, we are aware that an intrinsic interest in criminology, a passion for justice, or a commitment to social activism is a more common first step. Either way, the problem is the same: how does one go from a passion for justice to an academic career? The short answer is that you apply to graduate school. The long answer follows.

Some basic facts about graduate schools can be helpful. The task of selecting a school can be overwhelming, and it is a good idea to do some research. Some graduate schools offer master of arts degrees; some offer Ph.D. degrees. Master's-level programs are typically aimed at professionals; they serve to credential newcomers and upgrade credentials for those already in the criminal justice field. Job candidates with M.A. degrees may teach full-time at two-year colleges or part-time at four year colleges or universities—unless a nontenured position, for example, director of internship program, opens up, although there are fewer of these. At four-year colleges and universities, a Ph.D. is an entry-level requirement for a full-time appointment, even though when demand is high, some universities may hire candidates before they finish the dissertation.

Because the quality of the graduate program you enter has an impact on your job prospects, you should aim high. Spend some time identifying the very top schools, which would be your "reach schools," the strong schools, where your chances of admission are good, and your "safety schools," where you know you would be accepted. Application fees are high ($50-$100), which tends to limit the number of applications candidates can afford to submit. In addition to quality, graduate schools vary in content areas or specializations. Some are known for their emphasis on quantitative research; others for opening new fields (e.g., forensics), or for specific approaches (e.g., critical or feminist criminology). Gathering information about different specializations has been made easy; college and universities have extensive Web sites that list course offerings, faculty members, and faculty publications. The photos, titles of faculty publications, and course titles that you find there will give you some idea about the program's commitment to diversity.

With some sense of the choices, you can approach the admissions process. It may seem intimidating, but it breaks down into simple steps. The more you know about these steps, the more you are able to shape the process. The typical admission packet that graduate programs require includes GRE scores, letters of recommendation, a personal statement from the candidate, and transcripts. Undergraduate papers may also be submitted as indictors of a student's intellectual development. The GRE now includes a writing component in addition to returning verbal and analytic scores, which indicate to a committee whether the level of your communication and reasoning skills are in line with the demands of graduate-level work, especially the graduate statistics and method sequences. The better you can write and reason, as indicated by GRE, the better your chances of admission. Preparation courses are worth the time and money for everyone. If you tend to freeze on standardized tests despite preparation, it is worth including an exceptional piece of research or other writing that shows that you are a strong writer and a clear thinker.

Letters of recommendation for graduate school come from academics. Performance reviews from job supervisors are unhelpful as indicators of academic potential, not because responsibility or integrity are irrelevant to admission decisions, but because your ability to write, to think, and to reason are important to decisions the admissions committee makes. Undergraduates err in thinking that the request for a letter of recommendation is a terrible inconvenience. On the contrary, writing recommendations is part of the professor's job, and you should go in expecting a resounding, "Of course, I would be happy to write on your behalf." There are, however, legitimate reasons for an instructor to turn down a student. A professor may not know or remember you. After all, our records are rudimentary. Knowing that you got all B+ and A grades in a class is not enough to generate an effective or helpful letter of recommendation. Or, a professor may remember you, but if you did less than B+ work in the class, he or she might decline your request rather than write a letter that would hurt your chances of admission.

Once a professor agrees to write on your behalf, you should make an appointment to sit down with him or her to go over your case for graduate school. Be prepared to bring four things to this meeting: GRE scores, a résumé, a personal statement, and your transcripts if they are not readily available online. These documents paint a picture of who you are as an aspiring intellectual. Do the documents tell a coherent story? Does the story account for weak spots, perhaps a shaky B average? Does it back up high grades with evidence of research activity, scholarly interests, or special recognition? You should be thinking about the overall portrait that you want to present to your letter writers and ultimately to the admissions committee.

The résumé is important because it provides the convincing biographical details that most professors are unaware of and that paint a well-rounded picture of you for an admissions committee. Some types of employment can be relevant for graduate school. For instance, full- or part-time jobs in the criminal justice system give you background information that other prospective students lack. Working with a professor on a research project, publication, or conference paper is recognized as a step along the path toward an academic career. Similarly, a position on the debating team may indicate strong verbal skills. The résumé is a picture of those parts of your work or college life that are relevant to you as a prospective graduate student.

The personal statement gives the letter writer the overview he or she needs to put together a strong letter, one that shows some knowledge about who you are and makes a convincing case for your admission to graduate school. It also gives you a chance to get feedback from the letter writer. In your personal statement, you should concentrate on assembling information that bears on your ability to go graduate work. Did a junior year abroad program change the way you look at the world? Did a writing assignment engage you in such a powerful way that you produced an A+ paper? If so, what was the basis of the intellectual excitement, what analytic skills did you use, how did it prepare you for more advanced work? Do you have an interest that corresponds to a faculty member's research at the school you want to attend? What would your admission add to the mix at the school you want to attend? What do you expect to get out of your graduate education?

Specific answers to these questions are better than vague ones and might include the following: I wrote a paper on prisons, which got me interested in deterrence, and I would like to work with Professor X, whose work on informal deterrence interests me. I expect to acquire the analytic skills to advance my research in this area. A less desirable set of answers might look like this: I am a hard-working, motivated student, who is interested in crime and hopes to learn about why people commit crimes and to apply what I learn to law enforcement as an FBI agent. Remember, too, that the personal statement is a sample of your work. It tells the admissions committee how well you write and how well you put ideas together. Plan to take it through several drafts, ask professors to read and comment on it, and incorporate their comments into the statement. The writing instructor who drove you crazy in freshman English just might volunteer to review the personal statement.

Many graduate schools give priority to candidates from other institutions, because good professors are those who have been exposed to different educational experiences. This policy means that your current college or university, should it have a graduate school, is not inclined to admit you. In all likelihood, then, the decision to go to graduate school also involves relocation, which has implications for your personal life. Are you single, or are your commitments such that a partner would come with you? Either way, you have to figure out how to finance graduate school, which includes tuition, housing, and living expenses. The more prestigious or well-endowed graduate schools offer financial packages that cover all or part of the tuition and in return expect you provide research and or teaching assistance. Government loans are available, but over time, the debt grows quite large. Part-time work can fit around daytime course work, but if you plan to work full time, be sure to inquire whether you can enroll on a part-time basis and whether you can fulfill your requirements by attending exclusively evening or daytime classes.

Making the Most of Graduate School

Graduate school is an all-consuming experience. The academic work is demanding and proceeds through a series of steps that a student is expected to complete within seven years. Extensions are routinely granted, however. The first step involves course work, required and elective courses designed to give you a theoretical understanding of the field, the tools to conduct independent research, and a specialization in one or more areas. Students may put off the more difficult courses—research methods and data analysis techniques—to the end; but our best advice is to begin with these classes, and take more advanced ones as you go. These are the courses that make you a social scientist. Knowing how to define research problems, to design quantitative and qualitative studies, to conduct ethical research, and to generate valid results is what will carry you through your career.

Graduate students are expected to produce at least one research paper in each graduate class. Unless empirical research is called for, most papers take students through the process of reviewing research studies, monographs, and reports on topics related to course work. If you are unfamiliar with this form of writing, look at the "literature review" section in published research articles, and consult your library for guides and manuals. Both sources help in learning how to write effective reviews. It is also a good idea to use the papers you write for separate courses to progress toward your dissertation. If there is a topic or problem that you find especially interesting, use your papers to explore it systematically. When it comes time to write the proposal for your dissertation work, you will have already completed an exhaustive review of the research.

Even at the graduate school stage of your career, ethical concerns are important. Acknowledging your sources and giving appropriate credit to those whose work you have cited or described is the ethical habit to acquire. Coauthorship, with another student or a professor, has to be carefully negotiated and noted. When citing material in a jointly authored work, all parties are expected to give due credit to all authors, even though the cited material may have been written by one rather than another author. Later, when you are an assistant professor, you will be asked to describe your specific contributions to jointly authored articles. If you have done the majority of work, do not hesitate to claim the position as first author. In all of this, remember that graduate students are expected to embrace the ethical standards of the profession. For this reason, they are held to a higher standard than undergraduates are. Plagiarism and other forms of research misconduct are taken seriously enough to get violators expelled from the university.

Once you have satisfied the course work requirements, you will face qualifying exams of one sort or another. In some programs, a faculty committee poses questions, and the graduate student answers. This is not as awful as it may seem; students may sometimes select the members of the committee or the topic areas. If a student has paid attention in class, discussed ongoing work with faculty, and pumped students who have recently taken qualifying exams, they should have a good idea of what questions they might expect and what kind of answers to give. Mock orals give you a chance to learn how to react on your feet. Other programs organize the qualifying examination around the graduate student's proposal for dissertation research. The student selects the committee members, who pose questions about the proposed research. A student may be asked to refine or rework a section of the proposal; but in the end, the process strengthens the work.

The last step is the dissertation, which demonstrates your ability to use what you have learned in graduate school to conduct independent research. Some students breeze through this last stage, having used prior courses, including methods and statistics, to work out the kinks in the project. Others have more difficulty, either because they have not laid the groundwork for this step and have to start from the beginning, or because unrealistically high expectations paralyze them. The dissertation is finished when your committee says it is completed. Before the committee signs the title page, members may ask for revisions, which are designed to strengthen the dissertation work and which are important to your future. The completed dissertation is the source for your initial publications.

Because graduate education may be all-consuming, you should anticipate its effects on your personal life. That graduate school tends to be hard on prior relationships belongs on the negative side. On the positive side, from your graduate cohort you will find lifelong friends, the kind who understand the job and will tell you the truth. Moreover, the opportunities for political engagement in criminal justice and criminology are abundant. For us, the antiwar movement and feminism connected criminology to the real world. Experiences in the antiwar movement, for example, opened our eyes to the violence of the state—from local police who beat demonstrators to federal agencies that spied on private citizens. A tradition known as critical criminology had its roots in this kind of experience. Therefore, we recommend that you find a way to link your intellectual work to real-life injustices. We now face a new foreign war that ought to challenge aspiring graduate students to draw out its implications for criminology and criminal justice.

Yet graduate school has a way of putting obstacles in your path. The stories of seasoned faculty members attest to the debilitating effects of sexual harassment and other forms of discrimination on the graduate school careers of women and people of color. Because faculty members are in a position of authority vis-à-vis graduate students, quid pro quo arrangements are illegal. Romance may blur the lines some, but faculty retaliation at the end of an affair can be ruinous for a graduate student. In state university systems, faculty members and administrators are required to report disclosures of discrimination or harassment by victims (student or faculty) to a hearing officer, although the victim retains the option to stop the process or to go forward with a formal complaint.

More subtle is the kind of discrimination that promotes people with "central" research interests (e.g., gang violence or deterrence) and marginalizes those with "peripheral" interests (e.g., crime and gender or media studies). Senior faculty may reward students with "central" interests by fellowships, research assignments, teaching assistantships, or coinvestigator status—all of which are vital stepping-stones to other academic and career advancement. One might avoid this kind of marginalization by creating a balanced research profile, that is, by working in both "central" and "peripheral" areas as defined by your graduate program. This sort of balance has advantages in the job market.

Your First Job

We recognize that hiring, promotion, and tenure decisions are further down the road and so less important to undergraduates trying to decide whether to go to graduate school. However, we believe that prospective academics ought to have a sense of the major issues that shape one's career beyond graduate school. In this section, we look at personal, academic, political, and ethical issues shaping academic careers from the first job through tenure. The following are presented as road maps with guideposts about obstacles and strategies that should influence decisions about academic careers. For graduate students interested in more detail about hiring and tenure, we recommend attending career development workshops held at the annual meetings of the American Society of Criminology, American Sociological Association, Academy of Criminal Justice Sciences, Law and Society, and the Society for the Study of Social Problems.

Personal Issues

In all likelihood, your first job will require you to relocate. Most universities stand against "hiring their own." Your choice of places to move to may be unlimited or constricted by personal considerations. When you begin applying for positions, take into account your regional preferences, as well as your inclination for city, suburban, or rural environments. You may in addition have a partner who must be employed along with you, or within commuting distance.

The issue of partner employment for women is often crucial, as men tend to be the breadwinners, so women's jobs follow men's. If you are both academics, finding an institution that has allowances for dual-career hires is necessary. Moreover, universities increasingly recognize the need to develop such policies.

Salary is another salient personal issue, as economics determine so much of our lives. In interviewing for jobs, women tend to avoid talking about money or benefits. We talk about research programs, teaching loads, the community and so forth, but shy away from salary figure discussions. It is part of our socialization, but a detriment to getting a higher salary. You must prepare to negotiate—this is your life.

A further issue may concern leave. The academic calendar is not set up for women. From graduate school, new assistant professors hope to be in a position that carries the possibility of tenure, which places them on the "tenure clock," a highly demanding and stressful time extending over a six- or seven-year stretch. Yet, these pre-tenure years also occur during the general time that women begin—or want to begin—to have families. Many academic women postpone starting a family until it is too late. That women or potential parents sacrifice families for a job is an academic travesty—one that must be recognized. As a result, many of us have begun to ask about maternity leave in job interviews. In some places sick leave may be taken in place of maternity leave. At Caringella's institution, the Women's Caucus provides a safe place for job candidates to ask about maternity leave, sexist culture, and living in town as a single woman. At Humphries's institution, maternity leave has been sandwiched into sabbatical leaves and been used to stop the tenure clock. Maternity leave has not been extended to men, who also take on parental responsibilities. In any event, getting universities to recognize the impact of pregnancy, birth, and newborn care is an essential goal.

Academic Issues

The first issue is to apply for jobs in a timely fashion, but what that means naturally has to be qualified. You need to make the decision about whether or not you want to start your job before you have completed the dissertation. Many places will hire a candidate "ABD" (all but dissertation). There are several advantages and some serious downsides to going out ABD. The major advantage is being immediately employed, without stringing out graduate school and its costs for an extra year. The major disadvantage is being required to move and begin teaching, along with all the other essential involvements, while still having to work on your dissertation. Do not underestimate the double burden; some people never finish the dissertation because of new faculty demands. On the other hand, sometimes it is as easy as the technicality of scheduling a defense.

Giving thought to how you develop your career and reputation should begin early in graduate school. Applying for jobs should be influenced by a vision of who you want to be and how you want to be known. We all cannot realistically aspire to Ivy League schools, but there are wide parameters within which we can craft a plan for our academic future. Having a broader vision can be the key to academic success.

The nature of the institutions you choose to apply to or accept an offer from will matter in developing your career. Research institutions demand high levels of funded research and publication, whereas teaching institutions demand high levels of course preparation and instruction. Virtually all institutions require assistant professors to juggle teaching, research, and service demands. In deciding where you will begin your academic life, you need to find out the formal and informal priorities—for example, most places will count service less than teaching, and oftentimes they value research over classroom performance.

The nature of your research will weigh heavily on your career development. Your choice of topics, methods, theories, and ideological slant will reflect back on you, increasingly, as you develop a body of work. "Women's issues," like rape, domestic violence, sexual harassment, women in prison, women and the family, and feminist sociology, are considered less central than other research areas in criminology. Certain methodologies, specifically, qualitative methodologies, are deemed less scientifically rigorous than quantitative methods. Feminist theory, ideology, and epistemology are sometimes similarly denigrated. The academic and personal choice for many of us is to stay the course, committed to feminist theory and methodology. Others have also opted to add to "mainstream/malestream" areas that demonstrate broader skill sets and abilities. Ironically, male scholars do not seem to receive the same message, nor are they penalized for narrow research agendas (e.g., drug research), nor do they receive the advice to broaden their scope of interests.

In planning your career, you need to be mindful of hierarchies. They exist everywhere. There are not only hierarchies of universities, but of departments, and naturally, of scholars. There are also significant hierarchies of funding agencies, of journals for publications, and of publishing companies for books. It is important to learn where the department you are contemplating a position in stands on such matters, as well as what it expects from you in terms of professional productivity along these lines.

Politics

What we do can reverberate in policy, action, and social change—and this can be progressive or regressive for women, other minorities, victims, offenders, and on and on. As feminists tell us, we are responsible for the product or use of our research. This means we must research, write, and publish in ways that guard against abuses and that serve to empower people, especially women and minorities. Caringella's research on rape reform has been used to devise laws that help to prosecute offenders instead of persecuting rape victims. Humphries's research debunking myths about crack mothers was such that, when a new drug took hold in a particular subculture, it impacted on prosecutors, who shied away from arresting pregnant meth users for causing harm to the fetus.

Other types of political activism bear on our academic life too. In some universities engagement in grassroots, community, local, state, regional, national or international organizations is viewed as part of "service"; in other places it is viewed as radical rabble-rousing. Working with prisoners or prison rights organizations has earned Humphries a dean's reprimand at one institution, faculty praise at another, and a ground swell of hate mail at a third. Being politically active has consequences. This is true for working with colleagues in the university to develop programs, organize demonstrations, or initiate letter-writing campaigns. It is also true for your involvement in high-profile campus or community controversies and in sexual and domestic assault programs. Heightened visibility that results from planning speeches, marches, or protests (like Take Back the Night that Caringella started in her community) may be recognized by your university as valuable service or as troublemaking. Either way, such activism has the capacity to transform individual issues into public causes, which in getting the attention of funding agencies and the media builds toward progressive reform. Deciding whether and how to handle political engagements is part of developing an academic plan.

Departmental politics are pivotal to careers, and trying to get a sense of this is important in choosing the place to begin yours. Tensions over women and feminist work or about criminology and sociology divide many departments. The tensions between sociology, criminal justice, and feminist work were so divisive that Caringella advised a potential hire she recruited to decline the offer of employment. There are also tensions between graduate and undergraduate educations and educators, between the Old Guard and Young Turks, between women's studies and more traditional departments, and so forth. Whether you take a side or attempt to chart a neutral course, your choices can advance your favor, but take care to reflect on how they might also have negative repercussions or backfire.

The relationship between the department, the college, and the university is political too. Needless to say, your active involvement in a faculty union that goes head to head with the college or university over salaries, benefits, and working conditions is not going to endear you to administrators. Just as Caringella started her first job, the faculty union went on strike, presenting hard choices: join the strike and risk revenge at the hands of administrators or cross the picket and become a "scab." Caringella joined the strike, deciding that no job was worth the conditions the administration was trying to implement (vertical and horizontal reassignment of faculty to whatever jobs the administration chose). As a result, she gained the confidence of departmental colleagues, becoming known as the women who risked losing her first job before her first paycheck. As an untenured professor, however, the decision to strike made her vulnerable each time an administrator was involved in reviewing her career.

Ethics

The ethics involved in getting your job are straightforward. You should not apply to places you know you would not accept an offer from under any contingency. Some people accept interviews just for the practice, or because they have another reason to go to a particular place. This wastes valuable time and energy. Furthermore, do not lie to prospective employers about competing offers when only interest has been indicated. You probably do not want to wear your politics on your sleeve, but lying about publications, authorship, or experience is unethical and dishonest.

Ethical considerations as a faculty member overlap with ethical considerations as a student—not taking credit for the work of others, not double-submitting to journals, not presenting something already published—but they surely entail new contemplations as well. Ethics in teaching entails things like responding to student complaints, to plagiarism, and to reports of victimization. In each case, you need to be able to provide complaining or accused students with information about their rights, about procedures, and with referrals to appropriate college offices. Ethical considerations may arise in handling colleagues as well; confidentiality of student complaints against a colleague and due process rights of colleagues are matters that require thoughtful responses, for example. Even when students who disclose harassment or discrimination want to take no further action, faculty are obligated to report the incident. When faced with this situation, Humphries *reported* that an incident had occurred, but *avoided* names, thus honoring the student's decision and protecting an untenured faculty member. However, Caringella has refused even to report in those instances where confidentiality is sought and promised. And she has publicly informed her colleagues about her decision not to report sexual harassment, an act of civil disobedience, in an effort to influence *their* decisions, hoping they might choose to protect the privacy of students as she has done. In the end, we cannot say whether or not this influenced them, but the public discussion was illuminating for many. Caringella has also chosen to help students who decide to go forward with sexual harassment complaints. This is a most difficult decision, as careers can be on the line—theirs—and possibly yours.

Sexual harassment is not going to go away soon. For the generation of scholars that we represent, the pervasiveness of sexual harassment has been more than an unpleasant fact. Some years ago, the Division on Women and Crime of the American Society of Criminology called a last-minute meeting to air this very problem. Every woman who jammed into the meeting room had an experience to share. It was the most powerful session that we had ever experienced.

Obstacles

Discrimination is still with us. Discrimination against women and minorities in the academic world is well established, from hiring to tenure through promotion. Some departments are still slow to hire women and minorities, while others recruit on this basis. Although progress has been made, it is important to remain alert to departmental attitudes toward women, such as disregard of feminist scholarship or hostility toward hiring a female criminologist. Such attitudes may be reason to withdraw your application or reject an offer.

Stereotypes of women academics and "women's work" in criminology operate to devalue our contributions. According to detractors, work on "women's issues" (rape, domestic violence, sexual harassment, feminist theory) and/or work with allegedly less objective or scientific "feminist methodology" (read qualitative versus quantitative) is less important. Because of such diminution of feminist work, research in such areas requires a carefully considered decision. Departments where this type of marginalization can be sensed may not be good homes for scholars who are not willing to broaden or change their agenda.

Strategies

One strategy to overcome discrimination is to decline a job offer from a department that is hostile to women or feminist work. This is a hard choice, especially if no other offers are pending. You can perhaps consider postdoctoral positions, fellowships, or replacement positions. Alternatively, you might decide to broaden your research agenda to better fit in with the job market and/or a particular school. This too is a hard decision. Yet, there are success stories in which women take jobs, albeit in "chilly climates"; do not concede to do "malestream" research; and nevertheless get tenure and go on with successful careers. They perform at top levels and work with less prejudiced and even sympathetic faculty to change the climate or culture of the department over their tenure years. Remember, in the course of six years there can be many personnel changes. This might be a factor to consider in responding to a job offer.

A good strategy for assessing the job market is to take advantage of support networks associated with professional organizations like the American Sociological Association, Society for the Study of Social Problems, Law and Society, and the American Society of Criminology. You can tap into these networks to get experienced advice in deciding about job applications, interviews, negotiations, decisions, and "mapping out your research agenda." A lot of our recent professional activity has been centered on the American Society of Criminology's Division on Women and Crime and Division on People of Color and Crime. In these divisions you meet like-minded people and learn about the places and process of getting your job. In division-sponsored workshops, seasoned experts work with audience members about "Negotiating Your Academic Career," "Seeking Tenure and Redressing Denial," "Networking," and "Mentoring."

Getting Tenure

Personal Issues

Many women build families as they progress through tenure tracks, but the demands of child rearing and an academic career are equivalent to having two full-time jobs. Leave and stopping the tenure clock have improved matters for many women, but they are far from full solutions. Coping with the dual workload is difficult with or without partners. If partners are involved, it is vital to distribute the workload evenly; if single parenthood is the situation, it is important to work out cooperative child-care arrangements and other support beforehand.

Setting priorities is essential to striking a balance inside the academic life as well as the home. Deciding that research is your first priority helps in saying no to less-rewarded tasks of taking on internships, new course preparations, new committee assignments, and the like. The competing demands for teaching, research, and service multiply as opportunities blossom. Time management is an important vehicle for achieving balance and maintaining a personal life in the face of an academic existence.

Being Superwoman is a further personal issue particular to women. We keep thinking we can do it all, or should be able to do it all, all the time. We cannot. This is an unattainable and unfair standard, especially when juxtaposed with the gendered proclivity for women to be less able than men to say no. Trying to do the impossible leads to constant disappointment, and ultimately, to burn out. Learn to say no.

Academic Issues

Your first job is to keep your job. Many of us do not take the time to do the homework on how to get tenure. You must simply learn the rules at your home institution. This means gathering up documents like departmental basic policy statements and faculty union procedures on tenure and promotion. You need to learn the criteria and weighting system and decisional points in the process through the university system. You also want to make a point of learning about the culture, informal norms, expectations, history of tenure cases, and so forth at your home institution. Talk to your colleagues. Start all of this early; do not wait until the tenure year. You usually have annual or biannual evaluations, so you should set goals and make a plan for where you want to be every year or two along the tenure track. How many articles do you plan to have published? How many research proposals do you plan to have funded? How many new courses do you plan to prepare? A plan that answers these questions can empower you to say no to requests that you take on a new course or committee chairpersonship.

Again, in order to do this you need to know the formal and informal norms about teaching, research, and service trade-offs. There are two things for women to watch out for here. First, stereotypes paint women as better at "service" and men as better at "scholarship" or research. Yet, service rarely counts as much as research or teaching. Beware of being overloaded by departmental, college, university, union, student, and community service involvements. Second, be alert for tokenism. Because women and people of color are underrepresented in many departments and universities, we are frequently overburdened with committees. That the university or department needs to demonstrate diversity with women and people of color is less important than your need to complete your research agenda and get tenure.

Your personal statement, your curricula vita and documentation, and external review letters make up the tenure file: each component requires attention. Your personal statement introduces your tenure package, highlighting accomplishments. Here you make your case for a positive evaluation by your colleagues, like a good lawyer. As with letters of recommendation for graduate school, it helps to do the work for the reviewers, providing details you would like to see reflected back in the letters they write on your behalf. Your vita should be clear and easy to follow—and accurate! Moreover, you should be able to document the items on it: journal articles, acceptances, grant proposals. You will also want to keep files to document teaching activities, such as syllabi and evaluations, and service involvements. Most institutions require several letters of evaluation from colleagues at other institutions for your final tenure package. Sometimes you get to suggest people, sometimes the department does, and sometimes it is a mix of the two. The annual meetings of the American Society of Criminology, including the Division on Women and Crime and the Sociologists for Women in Society, a section of the American Sociological Association, provide opportunities for you to meet the scholars who may write on your behalf. You can ask them to read and respond to your work many years ahead of tenure, so that they know you and your work when it comes time for review.

Politics

Many faculty members will not admit that tenure has to do with the question "do they like you?" Meeting college expectations about being a "good colleague" may shift tenure evaluations in your favor. You should know, but not be restricted by this. Principle may be more important. Caringella's continued employment was threatened by a department chair because of some colleagues' complaints and his own disregard for her politics (of feminism, engaging in praxis, etc.) in the department, university, community, and national levels. This may well have reflected the increasing conservatism throughout the country, and the accompanying backlash against civil rights and women's movements, affirmative action, and sexual harassment policies targeting women and people of color who suffer disadvantages in employment and other settings. But it serves to illustrate how chairs and their colleagues fail to separate tenure candidates' political engagement from their scholarship. Forewarned is forearmed.

Being a good colleague also means knowing how to deal with problematic people in the department. Handling them can be a mighty task. Stop. Think. Talk to trusted colleagues about how to react. Rally the troops on campus and off, like the Division on Women and Crime (we have a listserve) and Sociologists for Women to get advice and feedback on how to handle difficult situations. The problems range widely, from inappropriate comments to sexual harassment. Sometimes going public or a lawsuit is the only way; sometimes informal talks are sufficient.

If you have difficulty in your department, are unhappy, and/or fear denial of tenure, it is time to think about relocation. Waiting until you are actually denied tenure is a poor option. Going back out on the job market just before the tenure decision may raise questions about tenure prospects at your home institution, so be prepared to respond to this concern in interviews. In addition, do not wait until the last minute; it can enhance a career to move on, even if there are no tenure difficulties.

Ethics

The first rule of ethics in tenure is having an accurate vita and appropriate documentation. This means, for example, titling, categorizing and crediting authorship precisely. List refereed journals separately from nonrefereed, list book chapters separately from articles, list order of coauthorship as it appears on articles. Padding or exaggerations border on academic dishonesty.

At this point in your career, it is time to think about giving back. There will be many people who have facilitated your career, directly by mentoring and indirectly by promoting research areas or the cause of women and minorities. You benefit from the good will and good work of others, even as a white male, so become a part of it. Give back through mentoring students and more junior colleagues; consider committee work at the departmental and national levels.

Obstacles

Devaluation of feminist topics, methods, theories, and journal outlets as "women's work" or "women's issues" is one set of problems. Another is the marginalization of women in departments, and conversely, our overrepresentation on committees. Never being appointed or elected to any important committee or consulted for any decisions is no different from being the token female or minority on one committee after another. Sexual harassment and other forms of exploitation are a third problem we have discussed and that bears repeating. One noteworthy "other form of exploitation" is not being given credit for your work. Finally, we note the problem of being caught in the "mediator role" because of the gendered tendency to feel responsible for resolving other people's problems.

Strategies

Awareness is the key to prevention. In addition, it is easier than you might think to show how the alleged "women's issues," e.g., rape, domestic violence and feminism, affect men too, and are society-wide issues, with sociological and criminological implications. If you have balanced feminist and mainstream features in some of your work, your task is far easier. Incorporating some mainstream methodology, theory, and/or research in order to respond to sexist devaluation can aid in career success—so that we can grow to be in positions of authority and promote further change to redress such problems!

All universities have sexual harassment offices/officers. This office can help victims in responding to faculty who have harassed or are abusing them. The officers provide information about policy as well as options. Getting your own attorney to sue is another, albeit costly, option.

Agreeing on authorship before writing a joint article is a good strategy to avoid someone else's taking credit for your work. This is true whether you are working with students or with other faculty members. Clear agreement precludes bad feelings that may bear upon tenure.

Dealing with "bad feelings," "personality conflicts," and sexist colleagues is challenging. It can use up all your energies and disadvantage you in a myriad of ways. The strategic way to handle such matters is simply this: choose your battles judiciously.

Our final strategic recommendation is to join the Division on Women and Crime within the American Society of Criminology. This gets you involved and helps you to network with like-minded people, which in turn, can spark collaborative work or new ideas, develop external reviewers, and fight alienation and the sense of marginalization. The DWC also helps you learn about politics, obstacles, and strategies through discussions, the newsletter, the listserve, and a host of workshops on how best to do our jobs. In a survey of members of the DWC, respondents reported that this organization was centrally important in fighting isolation and the sense of being shut out of men's networks in a masculine-dominated field. Besides, it is a home to many of us, where significant friendships evolve and where good parties are thrown!

Conclusion

When we began reflecting on our academic careers to write this article we kept coming back to the workshop on tenure that we give annually at the American Society of Criminology (ASC) meetings for the Division on Women and Crime (DWC) and the Division on People of Color and Crime (DPCC). The workshop has been extremely helpful to graduate students and junior faculty, and we have used audience concerns about their careers to formulate this chapter. Contemplating any career path can be overwhelming, but in thinking about becoming a professor, we want you to bear two things in mind. First, the processes we address cover a long span of time. Typically, it takes at least ten years to move from undergraduate to graduate school and from there to your first job and tenure. Therefore, what you have read may seem like a lot unless you also remember that you will learn a lot over the decade. Second, you might find yourself asking, "Why would I want an academic job?" We answered this question at the outset. The pot of gold at the end of the rainbow is a rewarding career. For us, the pot of gold has meant pursuing a passion for justice. More practically, it breaks down to some attractive features of the job. Academics have autonomy in task and time, and this is coupled with a competitive salary. In addition, we have interesting colleagues from around the world with whom we exchange ideas, share research, and enjoy enduring friendship. A life career of the mind is truly a joy.

Discussion Questions

1. What are the four steps in going from an interested undergraduate to becoming a tenured professor?
2. What are the unique burdens for women or people of color in moving through the four steps?

3. Of the personal, academic, political, and ethical issues that aspiring academics confront, which ones are most meaningful for you? Why?
4. Of the all the obstacles that the chapter describes, which ones would be the most difficult for you to overcome? Why?
5. What strategies do you think would be most effective in overcoming the obstacles that you are concerned about? Can you think of additional strategies?

Chapter 7   Angela Moore Parmley and Jocelyn Fontaine

Diversifying the Research Enterprise

Experiences of African American Women Working
in a Federal Research Agency

How much diversity is enough? What is the ideal amount of diversity in the re-search enterprise? How is progress defined?

As the title suggests, we are writing from a particular vantage point. We are an established female scholar and an emerging female scholar, both African American, working for a federal research agency. And at this critical junction, as women and as minorities, we feel it is important to reflect on the importance of diversity in the research enterprise. By this we are referring to diversity in the people asking the research questions and engaging in research activities. We are not referring to diversity in the populations under study, nor the poten-tial benefactors of research—practitioners and policymakers.

This topic is not new. Scholars have written about the exclusion of African Americans in the criminal justice field (Young and Sulton 1991) and the under-representation of African American scholars in peer-reviewed publications (del Carmen and Bing 2000) and on criminal justice faculty (Gabbidon et al. 2004). Chapters in this volume deal with the unique experiences of women in the overall criminal justice field—as practitioners and as researchers. In light of this, we would like to discuss our personal experiences as African American female scholars and how these identities relate to the overall research field. As with all individuals, our race/ethnicity and gender play an integral role in who we are and how we view our environment. As researchers, our race/ethnicity and gender influence the type of questions we raise in the conduct of inquiry. We

Note: The opinions expressed in this chapter are those of the authors. They do not represent the official position of the National Institute of Justice, Office of Justice Programs or U.S. Department of Justice.

maintain that diversity is critical in the framing, development, and completion of criminal justice research. Therefore, in order for the field to continue to advance, diverse perspectives must be sought vociferously.

As a whole, the criminal justice field has become more diverse, particularly among practitioners. Over the past decade, we have seen more minorities hired as police officers and more women drawn to correctional officer ranks. Certain police departments, such as the Los Angeles Police Department, for example, have employed special initiatives to ensure ethnic and gender diversity in the ranks of their police officers. These hiring practices are fairly intuitive and we believe, right on target. Logic suggests that as the persons being policed are diverse, police departments would do well to accurately reflect the communities they are policing. Proportionate representation establishes legitimacy and builds standing for police departments. Similarly, because individuals within the criminal justice system, victims and offenders, are diverse—so too should be the researchers studying them. This diversity will enhance legitimacy and provide greater standing for the research enterprise. Indeed, long-standing racial tensions that exist in American society are exacerbated when researchers are detached from the population under review (Russell 1998). Likewise, blanket adoption of strictly masculine theories of crime, posited by males, act to reinforce patriarchy when they are generalized to female offenders (Bernat 1995; Chesney-Lind 2006; Henriques 1995).

Historically, criminal justice research was conducted on white males. Though this is correct from a proportional stance, the persons coming through the criminal justice system have become increasingly diverse. Minorities, particularly young African American males, are disproportionately represented as victims and offenders in official criminal justice statistics, although whites numerically outnumber them. Similarly, while female offenders are only a small fraction of the total persons arrested, convicted, and incarcerated, statistics have shown an increase in their proportional representation over the past two decades. Again, we contend that as the populations being served by the criminal justice system have become more diverse, the practitioners serving and the researchers studying these populations must also be diverse. Simply stated, there must be more women and minorities doing the research. Certainly, the field has come to realize that theories about one faction of the population (young white males) are not always generalizable to subpopulations (African American females/males, Hispanic females/males, and so forth).

The classical theories on juvenile delinquency, such as strain or differential association theory, used young white males as the study population.[1] It is not clear that African American females or males engage in crime for similar reasons, because blacks and whites experience vastly different social environments. Specifically, Krivo and Peterson (1996) have found that the disproportionate rate of violence among the African American community is the result of their disproportionate representation in disadvantaged communities. Additionally, most research on female delinquents has found many of the theories on male criminality to be wholly inappropriate and/or inadequate for explaining female criminality or treating women offenders (Chesney-Lind 2006). As Flavin and Desautels (2006:16) state, "violent victimization is not gender nor race nor class neutral." Gender, race, ethnicity, as well as class each play an important role in an individual's decision to engage in criminal activity. And although a simplistic, general theory of crime would be immensely useful for practice and public policy, theories that decontextualize people's experiences as man or woman, minority or majority, and rich or poor certainly lose validity.

We have learned that cultural/ethnic identity plays a significant role in offending and that interventions should take cultural/ethnic identity into account. Research on African American, Hispanic, Asian, and white gangs has found that they vary from each other in significant ways and that female participation in these groups is not always akin to male participation. Therefore, it is important to have diverse theories of crime and criminality and to ensure that these theories receive proper attention. Diversity in research, such as in theory building and testing, sample issues, and analytical methods, highlights alternative ways of thinking, which influence policy and practice.

Recently, scholars have suggested that an intersectional, integrative model is necessary for studying criminal phenomena. Arguing for a multiracial feminist perspective, Burgess-Proctor (2006) suggests that the intersections of race, class, and gender are important in criminological inquiry. Although her discussion is specific to feminist criminology, her arguments apply generally. She suggests, and we concur, that it is important for research to highlight the ways in which race, class, and gender interact to shape behavior. Power and dominance, as well as inequality and oppression, are integral to understanding criminological behavior—for men and women, whites and minorities. Without each of these perspectives represented in the criminological discussion, we are missing the ways in which people's lives are framed over the life course. One only needs to reflect on any one of their behaviors over their lifetime to see that race/ethnicity, class, and gender collectively and independently shape our actions, whether that behavior is criminal or not.

This is not to say there are no commonalities across gender and race, but only that the extant research has focused on many differences. Minorities and whites occupy different social environments, and men and women are not similarly socialized in American society. Are there enough women and minorities in the research enterprise to continue to highlight, explore, and provide recommendations on how policy and practice should respond to those differences in race/ethnicity, gender, and class? Is there a group of diverse people asking the questions?

How Much Diversity?

As implied by the first two questions that introduce this essay, it would be difficult to determine an ideal number or percentage of minorities/women in the criminal justice research enterprise. Should it be proportionate to the number of researchers in general, or should the number be proportionate to the populations being studied? That question goes beyond the scope of this chapter and is perhaps more philosophical than necessary. Still, we argue that the criminal justice field would be well served to have more diversity in the research enterprise. Advancements have been made, but certainly more can be done. If we think that researchers are in the position to influence policy and practice, then it is important to continue to push for diversity in the research enterprise.

As African American women working for the National Institute of Justice (NIJ), we immediately noticed that we were in the minority. NIJ is dedicated to researching crime and justice—with the goal of creating knowledge to enhance the administration of justice and public safety. The emphasis is on building knowledge with practical and policy implications. The staff of NIJ is composed of highly educated people: sociologists, economists, social workers, psychologists, and criminologists. Many have worked in the field as criminal justice practitioners for a number of years, while others have devoted their lives to being civil servants. The overwhelming majority of social science analysts and policy advisers in the agency have advanced degrees. Although there is about an equal percentage of men and women working at NIJ, there are very few African Americans (or Hispanics) working in the agency.

To be clear, the working environment at NIJ is in stark contrast to the Department of Justice overall, where nearly 30 percent of the workforce is minority (Office of Personnel and Management 2004). The environment also contrasts with the minority representation within the Office of Justice Programs (NIJ's umbrella agency), where there are many minorities in both support and administrative positions. On reflection about the underrepresentation of minorities at NIJ, it becomes obvious that the minority representation reflects the wider pool of criminal justice researchers. Simply, there are not enough minorities in the business of research. Not only is there a limited number of people of diverse cultural backgrounds working at NIJ, but there are only a small portion of people from diverse cultures who serve as consultants and principal investigators on research projects. Although an increasing number of minority scholars have been entering the criminal justice field, the overwhelming majority of scholars continues to be white.

Data from the most recent decennial U.S. census confirm what we experience anecdotally. Less than 1 percent of the population over age twenty-five has a doctoral degree. Furthermore, when that percentage is disaggregated by gender and race, we can see that NIJ reflects the larger group of researchers. The majority of persons who have a doctoral degree are white and male. Fully 68 percent of those with doctoral degrees are male. Less than one-third are female. Although the census does not disaggregate doctoral degrees by race, statistics on those persons with a graduate/professional degree reveal the dominance of whites, particularly white males. In 2000, there were more than seven million white males with a graduate/professional degree (which includes master's, law degrees, medical degrees, etc.). The number was slightly more than six million for white females. Compare these figures with 380,000 and 560,000 for African American males and females, respectively. Without looking at proportions or asking what proportion of black/white professionals is ideal, it is clear from the raw numbers that the field is largely white. It is noteworthy that African American females are doing much better than their male counterparts, whom they outnumber in undergraduate and graduate degrees—a trend that is opposite those found for white females (U.S. Bureau of the Census 2000).

Comparisons of white, African American, and Hispanic statistics cannot be made easily with existing census data on educational attainment. Hispanics can be of any race—white, African American, or other; therefore, comparisons made between the three populations could result in double-counting. For this reason, we focus our discussion here on whites and African Americans. Notwithstanding, an examination of the data solely on Hispanics indicates that there are fewer Hispanics over age twenty-five with graduate/professional degrees than African Americans or whites. Approximately 350,000 Hispanic males and 340,000 Hispanic females have graduate/professional degrees. Interestingly, this data shows that Hispanic males and females are more equally matched than their African American or white counterparts. There does not appear to be a similar effect of gender on educational attainment within the Hispanic ethnicity.

Although there have been significant advancements in the educational attainment of minorities, the gap between whites and minorities persists. The differential between African American and white women is smaller than that for African American and white men, but white females still outnumber their African American counterparts eleven to one. These gaps are significant, yet recent education statistics provide a reason to be hopeful. Statistics show that women have outnumbered men since the mid-1980s and the number of full-time female graduate students has increased by 61 percent compared with only 20 percent for full-time male students since the early 1990s. In addition, minority representation has also increased to 29 percent, which is up from roughly 15 percent in the late 1970s (*Digest 2004*, 2005). These statistics demonstrate the advancements, but certainly more can be achieved.

Some have suggested that only limited opportunities for minorities, particularly African Americans, exist in the criminal justice field. Young and Sulton

(1991) published a bleak assessment of the discipline as it relates to African American researchers. In their opinion, the contributions of African American scholars had been systematically ignored. The authors provided a road map to inclusion that proposed having more African American perspectives incorporated into criminal justice theories and more funding distributed to African American researchers. Gabbidon et al. (2004) reexamined Young and Sulton's claims about the exclusion of African Americans scholars and scholarship in the discipline. They found progress in certain areas, such as representation in leadership roles in criminal justice degree programs and in criminal justice professional associations. They concluded that there have been moderate improvements in the inclusion of African Americans over the past decade and that the contributions of African Americans must be acknowledged.

Why Diversity Matters

By the majority of accounts, including our own, progress has certainly been made. We could argue over whether the advancements have been substantial, moderate, or insignificant and how much more needs to be done. Without a benchmark for an acceptable level of diversity, this would be difficult to determine. How is or can progress be defined? Rather than focusing our attention on this question, we emphasize the goal of continual pursuit of diversity in the criminal justice research enterprise. We would like to see the increasing number of African Americans and women enrolled in graduate school translate into more criminal justice researchers in the field. Research has suggested that the academic environment has become increasingly more receptive to African American (men and women) faculty members (Edwards et al. 1998). African American women, however, seem to have a better relationship with their students than their colleagues (Gilbert and Tatum 1999).

Diversity in research is important because gender and ethnicity undoubtedly influence the types of questions asked. Females are naturally more inclined to ask questions related to gender and minorities are more inclined to ask questions related to race/ethnicity. As we have suggested earlier, this is because the intersection of race/ethnicity, gender, and class influence the ways in which people view their environment and behave within it. Although this may go unnoticed in certain aspects of life, each person is shaped by his or her race, gender, and class. These constructs, socially developed or not, are inextricably linked to who we are and what we do.

Our professional choices, such as which career to pursue, are impacted by our race, gender, and class. As researchers, our decisions as to which behavioral phenomena are worthy of examination are also affected by our race, gender, and class. This is because our experiences within the world, funneled through our social identity, come to shape what we think is important and worth studying. This is not to say that researchers are only equipped to research phenomena that are related to or bear on their particular gender, race/ethnicity, or class. In fact, some researchers may not possess the cultural identity to examine and understand the experiences of individuals of their own particular gender, race/ethnicity, or class. Notwithstanding, we insist that different questions, approaches, and people are necessary to fully exploring social and behavioral phenomena.

Extant research suggests that interviewers' race/ethnicity and gender have an effect on study participants' responses. In general, people tend to be more responsive to female interviewers than their male counterparts. Individuals tend to disclose more information to women than men, presumably because women have better interpersonal skills: they seem to be more understanding, they make better eye contact, and they offer more encouragement (see Lamb and Garretson 2003 for review). It also appears that whites and African Americans respond differently when the interviewer is of the opposite race when dealing with issues concerning race and ethnicity (Krysan and Couper 2003). This is not unexpected in light of our society's history of racial tension, but it is also illustrative given the array of questions that arise in criminal justice research.

Issues that deal with race/ethnicity and gender are an integral part in understanding criminal phenomena. The research highlighted in the paragraph above suggests that women and African Americans must be part of the research process in order to yield more inclusive data. Again, as our identities are shaped by race/ethnicity and gender, it follows that our interactions with people similar to us aids in contextualizing our experiences. Thus an African American female interviewer may be better able to build rapport and contextualize the world of a battered African American woman than a white male.

It is not enough to have minorities and women doing the fieldwork, however. Minorities and women must also conceptualize, develop, implement, and disseminate criminal justice research. Racial/ethnic identity, as well as gender, shape the way research is executed, as well as how it is originally conceived and the subsequent findings interpreted (Best 2003). Sticking with the example above, the African American female scholar studying the battered woman might have a different interpretation of her findings than a white male. By building rapport through their common identity as African American females, the African American scholar might have more culturally relevant information to disseminate to practitioners and policymakers as well as the public. Research is more effective if it is culturally relevant and gender sensitive. Yet again, as our identities shape our experiences and our worldview, minorities and females are needed in the research enterprise to fully uncover the complexities in criminal phenomena among diverse populations.

A variety of measures can be employed to increase the number of minorities and women engaged in criminal justice research. Below we reflect on our own academic/professional careers as African American women working within a federal research agency and explain why we do not think increased diversity in the research enterprise has to be a lofty goal. Mentoring is crucial.

How to Diversify

As echoed in several articles on graduate education, mentoring is important. Mentoring not only has implications for academic productivity after graduation but also influences how graduate students view their overall academic experience (Berg and Bing 1990; Bing et al. 1995; Long and McGinnis 1985). Heard and Bing (1993) found that more than 35 percent of African American criminologists did not have a mentor during their graduate studies, and McElrath (1990) found that more than 25 percent of females reported no mentor. Outside of the things learned in the classroom, mentoring and collaboration are the foundation of graduate study. The lack of diversity in available mentors could translate into smaller numbers of African Americans and women in the research field. It also has consequences for how much these groups are able to contribute to criminal justice literature and criminal justice policy.

Gabbidon et al. (2004) highlighted a real shortage in the number of African American faculty in Ph.D. programs in 2002. Although two-thirds of the doctoral granting institutions with a criminology/criminal justice program had at least one African American faculty member, that percentage roughly translates into only twenty scholars. According to recent statistics from the Department of Education (*Digest 2004*, 2005), roughly 15 percent of the faculty members at American colleges and universities are minority—only 6 percent of which are African American. Nearly half of college faculty are white males (more than 45 percent), and 36 percent are white females. These figures demonstrate the relative lack of mentorship opportunities with African American faculty—both men and women. To be clear, this does not assume that African American students should or only want to study under African American faculty, but rather that some portion of African American students are likely to be deterred if they do not see people similar to them finding success in that career.

Thoughts from an Emerging Graduate Student

Ultimately, there is a strong need for all faculty—white, African American, Asian, and Hispanic—to reach out to minority graduate students. As a master's student, I (Jocelyn Fontaine) was encouraged by several white professors to consider pursuing my Ph.D. At the time I was reluctant simply because I was unsure of what would be required and where the degree would lead. I was always interested in criminal justice research but uncertain about exactly how that translated into an actual career. Like many students, I was intrigued by the crime issues portrayed on popular television, but I had only a vague idea what criminal justice professionals actually did. The fashionable careers, such as those of forensic investigators and federal agents, are what initially piqued my interest. I thought those occupational paths were the ways to uncover the criminal mastermind.

Looking back, I was always interested in questions like "What makes criminals tick?" "What is their underlying motivation?" and "How/why do people turn to lives of crime?" My naïveté thought it was evil at play, so initially I wanted to discover what individual pathologies made people evil and criminal. These days, however, my interests have morphed into exploring the underlying environmental/neighborhood mechanisms that induce groups/people to engage in crime. I now understand that criminals are not necessarily evil and calculating, though they are frequently portrayed that way on television, but they are often constrained by social structural factors and barriers. On reflection, I have always been interested in research and understanding social phenomena. I asked questions and wanted to understand the "how" and "why" things happen, rather than wanting to combat, detect, or uncover crime. I thank my mentors for helping me realize that I was better suited as a researcher than a federal agent or forensic investigator.

Not coming from a family of academics, like most students unfamiliar with postgraduate education, a Ph.D. degree initially seemed a bit elusive. I have been fortunate to have supportive faculty throughout my postsecondary education, undergraduate and master's level, who believed in my ability, stoked my intellectual curiosity, and helped me strive for the doctoral degree. My internship and subsequent assistantship at the National Institute of Justice pushed me even further. To be among so many educated people is initially startling and overwhelming. Over time, it has become empowering. The learning experience as a young, emerging scholar has been invaluable. As mentioned earlier, there are a small number of African American analysts at NIJ. This could be disarming, but I was fortunate enough to be placed under the supervision of an African American female Ph.D., my coauthor here. Although she did indeed take some of the mystery out of the avenue toward the degree, more important, she has served as my mentor.

Having a mentor both within and outside an academic setting offers a glimpse of the array of career opportunities that lay ahead. It is unclear whether I would be in a different field had I not initially interned for NIJ, but I remain convinced that my professional and academic career has been enriched because of the agency and my mentor. Since the very beginning of my graduate studies, I have been encouraged to pursue excellence in the field. My mentors have facilitated my growth through the program. I would have a different assessment of my graduate studies without their guidance and support. There are not many doctoral students who understand the specific challenges and nuances of the degree. As the census figures illustrate, there are not a lot of people going through Ph.D. programs, which leaves a small pool of potential mentors. It is important to have the support of those who have been through the program in order to guide students during their studies.

My mentors, both at NIJ and also at the American University, have provided consistent encouragement to write papers for publication that could be initially presented at national criminal justice/criminology conferences in order for me to be exposed to professional societies. Certainly, it is not enough for young scholars to simply be taught quantitative and qualitative methods within the classroom; they must be given the opportunity to apply those skills in the field. For academics, presenting our work at national conferences and writing peer-reviewed publications are the avenues to illustrate what we have learned. Additionally, publications and presentations are the Ph.D.'s contribution to the field. Encouragement from my mentors also facilitated my growth outside of the classroom in venues such as the annual Academy of Criminal Justice Sciences conference as well as the annual American Society of Criminology conference. As a young scholar, it can be difficult, if not impossible, to venture out to conferences without the backing of one's mentors. This kind of support cannot be obtained simply through peer associations.

Thoughts from an Established Employee/Scholar

In the fall of 1994, I (Angela Moore Parmley) declared, "I need a job!" I realized that I could no longer subsist on my graduate student stipend. I had been afforded the opportunity to work on a research project for two years while pursuing my doctoral degree, and that was an invaluable experience. Prior to this research experience, I existed on a minority fellowship. I learned during my matriculation that a considerable number of minority students would be offered these fellowships, which presented a catch-22 situation. On the one hand, they did not require you to do any work beyond your graduate studies so you could focus solely on your academics. On the other hand, however, they did not provide the opportunity to gain valuable research experience and mentorship through working with a faculty member. Although serving as a project manager on a research study was enlightening and taught me a lot regarding the challenges of conducting criminal justice research, I was ready to move on. Moreover, at that time I needed to enhance my cash flow.

At the same time that I realized I needed a "real job" I attended the annual American Society of Criminology conference, the largest professional organization in the criminology discipline. During a meeting of the Division on People of Color and Crime, the chair indicated that the "National Institute of Justice is hiring; call the director." I was familiar with the exemplary work of NIJ as a result of my graduate studies. The institute had funded many of the research efforts that I read about, and I had been informed that it was "the" federal criminal justice research agency. Full of faith, I did exactly as was recommended—I called the director of NIJ. And the rest is history.

When I began my tenure at NIJ in 1995, I was at a tenuous juncture in my academic career. I took on a full-time job when I was ABD (meaning, "all but dissertation," a common phrase to indicate all coursework and comprehensive examinations are completed). Many advised against this move and clearly stated that I would "never finish" the dissertation. In addition, I left my graduate program for a nonacademic position. This also was frowned on because part of graduate training focused on teaching and ultimately attaining an academic position at a college or university. Yet I knew that the only person that I was accountable to for my decisions was me.

Not long after I began working at NIJ, I learned that there were two classes of employees: technical and administrative. This was a classification essentially imposed by the federal government, and not necessarily by the agency. What I saw at NIJ was that the vast majority of technical employees were white males, and the administrative staff were black females. There was one black female among the technical employees, who also worked in NIJ's Office of Research and Evaluation.

The staff was growing by leaps and bounds during this time with the passage of the Violent Crime Control and Law Enforcement Act in 1994. Many relatively young Ph.D.s or ABDs, including myself, had been hired. A few of these were black males, and there were several other minorities. There was considerable opportunity for advancement, yet the two categories of employees remained the same for the most part. The technical employees were overwhelmingly white males (and, increasingly, white females), and the administrative and support staff were black females. It was disheartening for me to not see any advanced women of color in leadership positions, who could mentor me during this transition.

So, I began my career at NIJ balancing many roles: I worked long hours to master my new job as a federal research grant manager while I tried to complete my dissertation and Ph.D. degree. Simultaneously, I learned that most of the research funded by NIJ was conducted by white researchers, primarily men, and it was primarily quantitative research. There was limited diversity in who received research funds, and the research methods employed to conduct those studies. NIJ did offer graduate research fellowships to master's-level students at historically black colleges and universities, but the response to our announcements of these fellows was dismal. That program was subsequently discontinued. In addition, the institute provides dissertation fellowships to students at universities throughout the country, but given the relatively low numbers of Ph.D. students in general, and minorities in particular, this program is not a major vehicle for attracting minority scholars to the field of criminal justice research.

Ten years later, I can say that there have been substantial changes in the way NIJ operates. Fortunately, I have been able to participate in these changes and have been a part of the solution. Through hard work, perseverance, tenacity, and persistence, I am the first African American to permanently head a research division within NIJ. In this position, I am able to shape the criminal justice research that we fund. Given the nature of the topics we address within this division, research that employs both quantitative and qualitative methods is encouraged and supported. Further, we have increased the pool of researchers and consultants to include more minorities and women. In addition, during this decade, NIJ created the W.E.B. DuBois Fellowship program. This program seeks to advance the field of knowledge regarding the confluence of crime, justice, and culture in diverse societal contexts.

It is still the case that the overwhelming majority of administrative staff at NIJ are black females. But several of these women have been promoted to the highest level within their occupational series. In addition, there have been a few instances in which some of these women have moved from administrative to technical positions. I am delighted to have been able to assist them in their professional endeavors. Currently, there are several African American analysts within NIJ, and three African American supervisors.

My experience at the agency, though challenging, has been extremely rewarding. I have and continue to work with some of the smartest, energetic, and wonderful people in the federal government. I have been exposed to top-notch research and have networked with the best and the brightest in the criminal justice field. My position affords me the opportunity to develop and implement criminal justice research programs, while enhancing my organizational and managerial skills.

Perhaps the greatest reward for what is no longer a job, but rather my career, is the opportunity to influence the next generation of criminal justice scholars. My goal is to pass along to my staff, especially our research assistants, all the substantive knowledge gleaned from my predecessors and current colleagues, as well as knowledge acquired through trial-and-error. I want them to realize that attaining their doctorate is a worthwhile goal. There are diverse opportunities for Ph.D.s, even outside of academia. Our work can be meaningful and have an impact on the field, although we are not on the front lines collecting data or conducting interviews. We can contribute to research scholarship even though the bulk of our time is spent managing others' research.

Serving as a mentor to our research assistants is one way that I can contribute to expanding the field of criminal justice scholars. With our current research assistants, I am also able to enhance diversity within the field. I not only encourage our assistants, such as my coauthor here, to attend professional conferences, present research, and publish, but I also engage in these activities with them. I recognize the importance of mentoring, especially as I did not have a mentor while matriculating, and have not had one while at NIJ, although many of my colleagues were highly supportive as I completed my doctoral degree and when I transitioned into management in 2001. Serving as a mentor benefits the students I work with by providing them greater access and exposure to the criminal justice discipline. I benefit because I am learning from budding scholars. We are all profiting from these professional relationships.

Concluding Comments

The National Institute of Justice is the research, development, and evaluation agency of the United States Department of Justice. It is the only agency within the federal government solely dedicated to funding criminal justice research. With this distinction, NIJ is in a key position to influence public policy and practice. Given this pivotal role, it is critical for NIJ's work to reflect the diversity of individuals who come in contact with the criminal justice system on a daily basis, whether they be offenders, victims, practitioners, policymakers, or researchers.

Undoubtedly, the types of questions asked by criminal justice researchers are shaped by ethnicity and gender (among a range of other things, such as social class, political orientation, and so forth). In our short (and relatively long) careers, we have been interested in the intersection of race and gender and their relationship to crime owing to the influences of race and gender in our own lives. Our voice is important in the dialogue, as are others from various cultural, social, and political backgrounds. Women and minorities provide alternative perspectives that should not be excluded.

The ongoing challenge is for criminal justice scholars to view increased minority and female recruitment as a worthwhile goal. As the number of minorities and women continues to increase in official education statistics, criminal justice researchers should continue to see that those numbers translate into greater diversity in the pool of people engaging in research activities. We have seen considerable changes during our tenure at NIJ and in the criminal justice discipline. Therefore, we remain confident that greater advancements lie ahead. Paving the way for the next generation of minority scholars is an important step in enhancing the criminal justice research enterprise. We hope our stories have provided encouragement that success is possible for women and minorities in the field of criminal justice research.

Discussion Questions

1. How much diversity is enough? Is diversity quantifiable?
2. Do you think African Americans are better at studying African Americans, Hispanics are better equipped to study Hispanics, etc.? Do you think the same for women and men? Explain.
3. Do you think that criminal justice research needs to be more diverse? Why or why not?
4. Does who asks research questions matter? Why or why not?
5. Would increasing diversity in the criminal justice research enterprise enhance the quality of the research?
6. How can we diversify criminal justice research?
7. Should we encourage more minorities to pursue graduate degrees, and/or engage in scholarly research? Why?

Note

1. See Akers and Sellers (2004) for theory review.

References

Akers, R. L., and C. S. Sellers. 2004. *Criminological theories: Introduction, evaluation, and application.* 4th ed. Los Angeles: Roxbury.

Berg, B., and R. L. Bing III. 1990. Mentoring members of minorities: Sponsorship and the gift. *Journal of Criminal Justice Education* 1:153–65.

Bernat, F. P. 1995. Opening the dialogue: Women's culture and the criminal justice system. *Women and Criminal Justice* 7:1–8.

Best, A. L. 2003. Doing race in the context of feminist interviewing: Constructing whiteness through talk. *Qualitative Inquiry* 9:895–914.

Bing, R. L., III, C. A. Heard, and E. Gilbert. 1995. The experiences of African Americans and whites in criminal justice education: Do race and gender differences exist? *Journal of Criminal Justice Education* 6:123–45.

Burgess-Proctor, A. 2006. Intersections of race, class, gender, and crime: Future directions for feminist criminology. *Feminist Criminology* 1:27–47.

Chesney-Lind, M. 2006. Patriarchy, crime, and justice: Feminist criminology in an era of backlash. *Feminist Criminology* 1:6–26.

del Carmen, A., and R. L. Bing. 2000. Academic productivity of African-Americans in criminology and criminal justice. *Journal of Criminal Justice Education* 11:237–49.

Digest of education statistics, 2004. 2005. Washington, D.C.: National Center for Education Statistics, U.S. Department of Education.

Edwards, W. J., N. White, I. Bennett, and F. Pezzella. 1998. Who has come out of the pipeline? African Americans in criminology and criminal justice. *Journal of Criminal Justice Education* 9:249-65.

Flavin, J., and A. Desautels. 2006. Feminism and crime. In C. M. Renzetti, L. Goodstein, and S. L. Miller, eds., *Rethinking gender, crime, and justice: Feminist readings,* 11-28. Los Angeles: Roxbury.

Gabbidon, S. L., H. T. Greene, and K. Wilder. 2004. Still excluded? An update on the status of African American scholars in the discipline of criminology and criminal justice. *Journal of Research on Crime and Delinquency* 41:384-406.

Gilbert, E., and B. L. Tatum. 1999. African American women in the criminal justice academy: Characteristics, perceptions and coping strategies. *Journal of Criminal Justice Education* 10:231-46.

Heard, C., and R. Bing. 1993. African American faculty and students on predominately white university campuses. *Journal of Criminal Justice Education* 4:1-13.

Henriques, Z. W. 1995. African American women: The oppressive intersection of gender, race, and class. *Women and Criminal Justice* 7:67-80.

Krivo, L. J., and R. D. Peterson. 1996. Extremely disadvantaged neighborhoods and urban crime. *Social Forces* 75:619-50.

Krysan, M., and M. P. Couper. 2003. Race in the live and the virtual interview: Racial deference, social desirability, and activation effects in attitude surveys. *Social Psychology Quarterly* 66:364-83.

Lamb, M. E. and M. E. Garretson. 2003. The effects of interviewer gender and child gender on the informativeness of alleged child sexual abuse victims in forensic interviews. *Law and Human Behavior* 27:157-71.

Long, J. S., and R. McGinnis. 1985. The effects of the mentor on the academic career. *Sociometrics* 7:255-80.

McElrath, K. 1990. Standing in the shadows: Academic mentoring in criminology. *Journal of Criminal Justice Education* 1:135-51.

Office of Personnel and Management. 2004. Demographic profile of the federal workforce. Washington, D.C.: From http://www.opm.gov/feddata/demograp/demograp.asp#RNOData.

Russell, K. K. 1998. *The color of crime: Racial hoaxes, white fear, black protectionism, police harassment, and other macro-aggressions.* New York: New York University Press.

U.S. Bureau of the Census. 2000. 2000 U.S. Census.Washington, D.C. From http://factfinder.census.gov.

Young, V., and A. T. Sulton. 1991. Excluded: The current status of African-American scholars in the field of criminology and criminal justice. *Journal of Research in Crime and Delinquency* 28:101-16.

III

Sites of Inquiry

Topics and Samples

Chapter 8

Changing My Life, among Others

Reflections on the Life and Work of a Feminist Man

> *It is by men coming to personally own the problem (and the solutions) that they become engaged to take personal action.*
>
> —Funk 2006, xvi

In early fall of 2006, shortly after Susan Miller invited me to contribute a chapter to this book, I met with my fourteen-year-old daughter's principal, Pamela McInroy, to discuss developing woman abuse prevention and awareness workshops at her all-female school. At the start of our conversation, she asked me, "So, how did you come to do work on violence against women?" I expected to hear this, given that many other women I meet on planes, in restaurants, at parties, and in other public places ask me the same question after they discover what I do for a living. Like Ms. McInroy, a large number of people are taken aback that a man would study and struggle to end a major social problem deemed by thousands, if not millions, of North Americans to be primarily a woman's issue. As Jackson Katz (2006, 5) reminds us: "Most people think violence against women is a women's issue. And why wouldn't they? Just about every woman in this society thinks about it every day. If they are not getting harassed on the street, living in an abusive relationship, recovering from rape, or in therapy to deal with the sexual abuse they suffered as children, they are ordering their daily lives around the *threat* of male violence."

Most men, however, are surprised by my research, attitudes, and beliefs because they neither embrace feminism nor see woman abuse as a significant issue and thus find it difficult to accept that I am distinct from them. Unfortunately, there is ample evidence showing that it is men who *do not* engage in or who *do not* directly or indirectly support woman abuse who are the deviants in North American society and whose bond to the dominant patriarchal social order is weak or broken (Godenzi, Schwartz, and DeKeseredy 2001). Sadly, despite major efforts to curb sexual harassment, rape, wife beating, and other crimes of violence disproportionately targeting girls and women, "in the United States, we continue to produce hundreds of thousands of physically and emotionally abusive—and sexually dangerous—boys and men each year. Millions more men participate in sexist behaviors on a continuum that ranges from mildly objectifying women to literally enslaving them in human trafficking syndicates" (Katz 2006, 7).

So, let's rephrase Ms. McInroy's question: "How did you come to be a deviant man?" Here, deviance is defined as behaviors, attitudes, and beliefs that support ending all forms of male violence and the transition to a society based on gender, race, and class equality. I publicly identify myself as a feminist man, and the key objective of this chapter is to describe how I became one and how I do my empirical, theoretical, and political work on woman abuse.

The Ongoing Journey

The Start of the Journey

I am the son of parents who experienced a substantial amount of male violence. For example, my father was born and grew up in Hungary, was frequently hit by his father, survived the Great Depression that lasted through most of the 1930s, served in the Hungarian military during World War II, and fled his homeland during the 1956 Hungarian Revolution along with two hundred thousand other refugees. Born and raised in Berlin, Germany, my mother also experienced much pain and suffering caused by the Great Depression and World War II, including being gang raped by some Russian soldiers during the postwar occupation of Germany. In the mid 1950s, she moved to Canada, where she was considered by some men, including her landlord and her boss at a movie theater, to be a "worthy object" of sexual harassment and other forms of sexual assault because she came from "an enemy country." In 1956, my father also came to Canada and experienced much racism, spawned in part by the "red scare" generated by Senator Joseph McCarthy and those who supported his claims about communist infiltration in North America.

My parents met and got married in Calgary, Alberta, and I was born in Vancouver, British Columbia, in 1959. A few years later, we moved to Oakville, Ontario, and then to a small town outside Montreal, Quebec, in the mid 1960s. In 1967, we moved back to Oakville because my parents were deeply afraid of violence stemming from the separatist movement in Quebec. Like many other children, I was first exposed to violence through my parents' spanking me, which still, to this day, is seen by the vast majority of North Americans as "necessary, normal, and good" (DeKeseredy 2005; Straus,

Gelles, and Steinmetz 1981). However, on the whole, my parents were gentle and worked hard to ensure that I thrived and led a healthy lifestyle.

Although the spankings deeply hurt me, they paled in comparison to the abuse I endured at the hands of some of my male classmates at Oakville's Brantwood Elementary School and New Central Public School during grades 3 to 7. Because I was overweight, some of the boys at these schools, with the help of some girls, "socially constructed me as the 'other'" because my "inferior body . . . did not live up to their contextual masculine expectations" (Messerschmidt 2000, 93). I experienced what Kindlon and Thompson (1999, 72–73) refer to as the "culture of cruelty," which involved being frequently beaten up after school just because of my physical size. Certainly, at schools like those I attended during the late 1960s and early 1970s, "anything a boy says or does that's different can and will be used against him" (73). Unfortunately, this is still the case today (Katz 2006; Messerschmidt 2004)

I was not able or willing to fight back, and the teachers I turned to for social support offered me little, if any, assistance. In fact, in 1970, when I talked to my fifth-grade teacher about one of the brutal beatings I endured, she told me to "be a man and fight back." Hence, well before reading the writings of masculinities theorists such as James Messerschmidt, I received many lessons on the painful consequences of rejecting and/or not being able to live up to the principles of hegemonic masculinity (Connell 1995). The basic components of this type of masculinity are to avoid all things feminine, restrict one's emotions severely, show toughness and aggression, strive for achievement and status, exhibit nonrelational attitudes toward sexuality, "measure up to the school view of the ideal masculine body," and actively engage in homophobia (Levant 1994; Messerschmidt 2000, 93).

Things radically changed for me in the summer of 1972 prior to starting the eighth grade. My body went through a rapid transition. I increased in height and lost approximately twenty pounds. Then, people treated me differently. I was no longer the target of schoolyard beatings, and girls frequently spoke to me in a friendly fashion. At first, I could not understand the radically different societal reaction. However, after my first month in school that year, a classmate told me, "You are okay now. You lost weight." I replied, "But I am the same person I was a year ago." For most of my classmates, this was irrelevant. The most important thing to them was that I conform to their masculine body norms.

Moving on to high school in 1973, I learned more lessons about sexism, homophobia, and hegemonic masculinity. I played competitive, male-dominated sports and garnered much respect for my goaltending and lacrosse skills, but I was deeply drawn to bicycle racing in the spring of that year. Owing in large part to Lance Armstrong's amazing Tour de France victories, this sport is now held in high regard, but when I was a teenager, most boys and girls labeled it a "girls' sport." Moreover, that I shaved my legs and wore tights in the fall, winter, and spring led many of my peers to believe that I was gay. When I told people that I shaved my legs so that it would be less painful to remove bandages required after crashing in a race and that I wore tights to keep warm and decrease wind resistance, the typical response was, "What's wrong with you? Are you some type of fag?" Note, too, that I never had a steady girlfriend until grade 13,[1] and she went to a private girl's school. I soon found out that her interest in me was heavily influenced by her female peers' constantly ridiculing her for not having a boyfriend. Hence, two people victimized by heterosexism and with low self-esteem developed a long-term relationship based on survival and convenience. I suppose we were together to prove that we could "fit in."

Although I could not name it at the time, I was becoming politicized, and one of the most important events in my life was deciding to attend York University in 1978. Located in north Toronto, York is one of the most multicultural North American universities and is famous for offering programs aimed at challenging various types of structured social inequality. During my undergraduate career there, instead of being punished for not adhering to the principles of hegemonic masculinity, my professors encouraged me to think critically about many injurious microsocial relations and broader social forces. However, it was not until I started working on my doctoral dissertation that I pursued a feminist education and a deep rooted desire to study and end woman abuse.

The Early Ph.D. Experience

This will not surprise many female academics, but during my entire undergraduate career (1978–82), I barely heard about feminism in any of my classes. This was owing in large part to the fact that the bulk of mainstream sociology and criminology was "gender-blind" (Gelsthorpe and Morris 1988). In other words, most of the empirical and theoretical contributions people were exposed to at that time focused on the work of men and male experiences. Further, until the mid 1980s, the male faculty in York University's sociology department greatly outnumbered female professors. Certainly, when gender was discussed at all in my undergraduate classes, it was typically reduced to an afterthought or to a control variable in a regression statistical equation.

Things, however, changed in 1985. I was a graduate student affiliated with York University's LaMarsh Research Centre on Violence and Conflict Resolution, and I helped the late Michael (Mike) Smith organize a seminar series. One of the speakers was York University's Alice Propper, and she presented an overview of North American sociological research on wife beating and other forms of violence in family/household settings. Today, I cannot believe I was that naive or ignorant, but I was shocked by the alarming statistics she presented to the audience. Moreover, her presentation prompted me to read literature about violence against women. Still, my reading was primarily restricted to mainstream research devoid of feminist analysis. Although I obviously had direct experience with the harmful consequences of patriarchy and have a mother who was savagely abused by men, the lessons of "hard, objective" science I learned as an undergraduate still primarily informed my intellectual work. I was by no means an antifeminist and was slowly developing an interest in feminist inquiry, but it was not until 1986 that I radically altered my intellectual, personal, and political journey.

The Beginning of My Liberation

In the mid-1980s, critical criminology was beginning to move from the margins to the center of criminological thought. Although various definitions of critical criminology have been proposed, there is no widely accepted precise formation.[2] For the purpose of this chapter, however, critical criminology is defined as a perspective that views the major sources of crime as the class, race/ethnic, and patriarchal relations that control our society. It is also a perspective that rejects as solutions to crime short-term measures such as tougher laws, increased incarceration, counseling therapy, and the like. Rather, it regards major structural and cultural changes within society as essential steps to reducing criminality.[3]

Starting in 1985, as a result of the fact that growing numbers of criminology professors and students across North America were seriously engaging with critical criminological contributions (which also included some feminist work) and of my own intellectual curiosity, I simultaneously read materials on woman abuse and on critical criminology and was starting to make some important connections. Still, it was not until November 1986 that I really started to "see the light." Together with York University professors Desmond (Des) Ellis and Mike Smith (who were members of my Ph.D. supervisory committee), I attended the annual meetings of the American Society of Criminology in Atlanta. We went to sessions featuring prominent feminist scholars such as Meda Chesney-Lind, Kathleen Daly, Susan Caringella, Dorie Klein, Betsy Stanko, Russell and Rebecca Dobash, and Claire Renzetti. The three of us, especially me, were deeply moved by their passion, research, and critiques of "malestream" criminology. They offered us alternative ways of understanding the social world and motivated us to think outside what Tony Porter (2006a), cofounder of A Call to Men: National Association of Men and Women Committed to Ending Violence against Women, calls the "man box."

Although these scholars' presentations were in and of themselves important to me, what also sent me along my current path is a long conversation I had with Kathleen Daly, Meda Chesney-Lind, Dorie Klein, and Betsy Stanko in a bar located in the conference hotel. They were patient with my unsophisticated understanding of the extant feminist literature on crime and strongly encouraged me to pursue my inner desire to engage in feminist inquiry. I will always remember that conversation, and I am deeply grateful for their kindness, collegiality, and compassion.

I returned to Toronto after the conference with much energy and a commitment to find an exciting and useful dissertation topic that would be heavily informed by feminist analyses. Mike was developing a Toronto survey of woman abuse in marital/cohabiting relationships. Eager to fill another Canadian research gap, Des started studying violence against women after separation/divorce, and I, too, wanted to conduct an original Canadian study, which brought me to the topic of woman abuse in dating.

Based on my own personal experiences with men and as a man, I wanted to gather data from men to enhance a sociological understanding of a major variant of woman abuse. This was both theoretically and empirically important, given that during the mid-1980s, most of the woman abuse studies gathered data from women. There were, and still are, other reasons for why I wanted to study and continue to focus on men. For example, looking only at survivors' characteristics rather than those of perpetrators can be interpreted as blaming women for their assaults (Mahoney, Williams, and West 2001). Research that examines how survivors differ from those who are not victimized suggest that there is something "wrong" with those who are abused by men (Bograd 1988). Certainly, what would it tell us if we happened to find that abused women are less intelligent than their partners? Do less intelligent or more intelligent women deserve to be beaten, psychologically abused, sexually assaulted, or victimized by men in other ways?

Another reason to study men is that the sources of woman abuse can be best understood by examining the characteristics of men rather than women (DeKeseredy, Rogness, and Schwartz 2004; Mahoney, Williams, and West 2001). Note that previous research on woman abuse and in-depth reviews of the extant literature reveal that focusing on survivors' characteristics is futile. For example, Hotaling and Sugarman (1986) found only one variable out of forty-two characteristics allegedly related to wife-victims that consistently discriminated between abused and nonabused women. This finding is consistent with the argument that any woman is a possible object of violence or other forms of abuse. What differs is not the woman, but the man. If the man is abusive, he will victimize any woman with whom he lives or has lived (DeKeseredy and Schwartz 1998).

I strongly assert that research on men is required because, as Scully (1990, 4) states, women cannot accurately reveal the reasons why men rape them because "they don't share the reality of sexually violent men. Such insight is acquired through invading and critically examining the social construction of men who rape." The same can be said about men who engage in other forms of woman abuse. Moreover, the farther one is from the source of harm, such as sexual assault, the more likely the information is to be biased (Mahoney and Williams 1998). Consider, too, that men's abuse of women is male behavior and thus "more fruitful efforts" to explain it should focus on men (Hotaling and Sugarman 1986).

This is not to say, though, that we cannot learn much about the risk factors associated with woman abuse by asking women questions about the men who harmed them. In fact, all of the marital rape research conducted so far has elicited data from victims on the characteristics of perpetrators, and this approach has identified key risk factors such as men's adherence to the ideology of familial patriarchy (e.g., male domination and control in intimate settings).[4] The forty-three women who participated in my recent qualitative study of separation/divorce sexual assault in rural Ohio offered very rich information on the key factors that they perceived as motivating their estranged partners to hurt them and their children.[5]

The Dissertation

My Ph.D. dissertation presents the results of the first Canadian survey of woman abuse in university dating. Nevertheless, this study was much more than an attempt to gather new data. My project also included an original theoretical framework that I constructed and tested, and which is referred to as the male peer support model (see DeKeseredy 1988a, 1988b). Briefly, I argued that many men experience various types of stress in intimate heterosexual relationships, ranging from sexual problems to threats to the kind of authority that a patriarchal culture has led them to expect to be their right by virtue of being male. Some men try to deal with these problems themselves, while others turn to male friends for guidance, advice, and various other kinds of social support. The key point here is that the resources provided by male peers may under certain conditions encourage and justify the physical, psychological, and sexual abuse of women. I also argued that men do not absolutely require a condition of stress in order to justify the abuse of women. Male peer support in particular can also influence men to victimize their current or estranged partners regardless of whether or not they are currently experiencing stress.

My survey provides some empirical support for this model and encouraged me to further study how all-male sexist peer groups contribute to woman abuse. Most of the encouragement to carry on my work in this area came from Mike, Des, and my female feminist colleagues, such as Susan Miller. She and I were simultaneously working on our dissertations in the late 1980s and would support each other at conferences, such as the 1987 Academy of Criminal Justice Sciences conference in St. Louis. However, meeting Ohio University sociologist Martin D. Schwartz (Marty) at the 1987 American Society of

Criminology (ASC) conference in Montreal was one of the most significant moments in my journey toward becoming a feminist man.

Enter Marty Schwartz

I accidentally met Marty at the ASC conference book exhibit. At one of the displays he overheard me criticizing a colleague's textbook for "only paying lip service" to critical criminological theories such as those developed by feminist scholars. He turned to me and said, "Why don't you write the author?" Then he looked at my name tag and enthusiastically said, "I need to talk to you!" I had applied for a job in Ohio University's sociology and anthropology department, and he read my application file, which included a paper describing my male peer support model. We went for a coffee, and he told me that although he was impressed by my application file, my chances of getting the job were slim because his department was committed to increasing the number of female faculty. I fully supported his department's position, and regardless of whether I got the job, I still wanted to exchange ideas with Marty, given that he was, at that time, one of the few men deeply committed to feminist principles of scholarship and praxis. We went on to establish a strong friendship and working relationship that is still going strong.

Since publishing our first coauthored piece (Schwartz and DeKeseredy 1988), we revised my original male peer support model in several ways, including addressing the role of broader patriarchal forces, economic and social exclusion, and the influence of living in rural communities.[6] Moreover, we were the first North American scholars to publish feminist critiques of left realism, a critical criminological school of thought that garnered much attention in the mid-1980s and early 1990s.[7] Our other projects included studying woman abuse in Canadian public housing (DeKeseredy et al. 2003), jointly responding to the neoconservative backlash against feminist studies of woman abuse (DeKeseredy and Schwartz 2002; Schwartz and DeKeseredy 1993), studying separation/divorce in rural communities (DeKeseredy et al. 2006; DeKeseredy and Schwartz in press), and collaborating on a Canadian national representative survey of woman abuse in university/college dating (DeKeseredy and Schwartz 1998; Schwartz and DeKeseredy 1997; Schwartz et al. 2001).

Marty and I were, and still are, deeply moved by work being done by members of the feminist men's movement, such as Rus Funk (1993, 2006), Jackson Katz (2006), and Tony Porter (2006a, 2006b). These and other feminist men (together with feminist women) have helped me change my life, among others, including that of my dear friend and colleague Shahid Alvi. Although there are variations in the feminist men's movement, a general point of agreement is that men must take an active role in stopping woman abuse and eliminating other forms of patriarchal control and domination throughout society (DeKeseredy,

Schwartz, and Alvi 2000). Furthermore, feminist men place the responsibility for woman abuse squarely on abusive men. A widely cited assertion is that "since it is men who are the offenders, it should be men—not women—who change their behavior" (Thorne-Finch 1992, 236).

Feminist men like me are involved in an ongoing process of self-examination, self-discovery, and change themselves (Funk 1993), with the ultimate goal of shedding their "patriarchal baggage" (Thorne-Finch 1992). This is, what Katz (2006, 260) refers to as "similar to the sort of introspection required of anti-racist whites." Am I truly there yet? Well, it is ultimately up to others, especially my female colleagues, friends, and relatives to decide, but I have definitely taken great strides in my research and day-to-day life to escape entirely from the "man box," and I have definitely moved from being simply a "well-meaning man" to becoming a feminist man. Again, the "man box" is a term created by Tony Porter (2006a), and in this box are the elements of hegemonic masculinity described in a previous section of this chapter. According to Porter (2006b, 1), a well-meaning man is "a man who believes women should be respected. A well-meaning man would not assault a woman. A well-meaning man, on the surface, at least, believes in equality for women, a well-meaning man believes in women's rights. A well-meaning man honors the women in his life. A well-meaning man, for all practical purposes, is a nice guy, a good guy." However, well-meaning men also directly or indirectly collude with abusive men by remaining silent. As Ted Bunch (2006) correctly points out, "When we remain by-standers we are making a choice to support the abuse. The abusive behavior by any man reflects and therefore reinforces the established status and privileges of all men."

I am, together with Marty, Shahid, and others, very vocal about ending male privilege, woman abuse, and other highly injurious symptoms of patriarchy. Further, like other feminist men, I work individually and collectively to change men by criticizing and challenging through other means the broader social and economic structure and institutions like the pornography industry, the military, the media, professional sports, and the justice system (Kimmel and Mosmiller 1992; Thorne-Finch, 1992). Still, I accept that having been socialized in a patriarchal, racist, and class-based society, my reeducation process will not end until I die. For example, on November 21, 2006, Tony Porter made a public presentation about the work he and his partners associated with "A Call to Men" do to curb woman abuse at the University of Ontario Institute of Technology. He asked several men in the audience, including me, what they would do if a man approached them during a public, nonviolent argument they were having with an intimate female partner to see if she was safe. My response to Tony's question was, "I would let my partner speak first." He then responded, "Walter, you would *let her speak?*" Obviously, then, the process of changing myself is not over, as it is not for Tony and other men who share our politics.

My Work on Woman Abuse

Some of the work I do has already been described. Some of the other things I do are as follows. First, my research is consistently dedicated to opening new lines of discovery. For example, I constantly try to gather data on topics that have not been studied or that have received little attention. Of course, there is nothing decidedly feminist about this approach. Still, rather than simply add a new variable to studies similar to those done in the past, I gather original data that can be used for policy purposes. For example, to the best of my knowledge, together with a team of other researchers, I conducted the first study of separation/divorce sexual assault in rural communities. Currently, Barbara Perry and I are administering the first Canadian survey of hate crime on Canadian university/college campuses, a project that examines how the intersections of race, class, sexual orientation, and gender contribute to much pain, suffering, and fear in institutions of higher learning.

Second, regardless of what I study, gender is at the forefront of my analysis, and I devote special attention to how it shapes male behaviors, attitudes, and beliefs. It is important to emphasize that gender is not the same as sex. Rather, gender refers to "the sociocultural shaping, patterning, and evaluating of female and male behavior" (Schur 1984, 10).

Third, I use a variety of methods to gather data, and my decision to use any particular technique is based on the topic I am studying. For example, to determine the extent, distribution, sources, and outcomes of woman abuse in Canadian university/college dating relationships, my colleagues and I used a representative sample survey that included both closed-ended and open-ended questions (see DeKeseredy and Schwartz 1998). On the other hand, it is extremely difficult, if not impossible to conduct a survey of any form of woman abuse in rural communities characterized by geographic and social isolation (Dutton et al. 2002; Krishnan, Hilbert, and VanLeeuwen 2001; Websdale and Johnson 2005), inadequate (if any) public transportation (Lewis 2003), the existence of a powerful "ol' boys network" consisting of patriarchal criminal justice officials and some abusive men, and relatively low telephone subscription rates (Websdale 1998). To make matters worse, many rural women have abusive current or former partners who "feed off" women's isolation and poverty to magnify their isolation. And, they often use tactics such as disabling cars for forbidding women to leave the house (DeKeseredy in press; Websdale 1998).

Thus, to gather data on separation/divorce sexual assault in three rural Ohio communities, I conducted semistructured interviews with forty-three women, and they were recruited using multiple methods. For example, an advertisement about the study was placed once a week during two different six-week periods in a free newspaper available throughout Athens County, Ohio. Also, posters about the study were pinned up in public places, such as courthouses, and were given to social service providers who come into contact with abused women. In addition,

- Two local newspapers gave considerable coverage to the project.
- Ohio University sent out a press release to newspapers and other Ohio-based media.
- Three local radio stations and Ohio University's television station carried public service announcements about the study.
- The director of the local shelter and I appeared on a local television news show to discuss this project and broader issues related to it.
- The Ohio Domestic Violence Network and other agencies told interested parties (e.g., rural shelter workers) about the study and helped to recruit participants.
- Local shelter staff, a police department social worker, employees of the county sheriff's department, Planned Parenthood, Women's Center staff at a local two-year college, and employees of the local Sexual Assault Survivor Advocate Program informed possible respondents about the study.
- Ohio University sociologist Judith Grant told women who participated in her addiction study about the research.[8]
- Indexlike cards with the information provided in the recruiting poster were routinely placed on top of newspaper boxes inside stores and on sidewalks in Athens, Ohio.

My view of any method, regardless of whether it is used by feminists or mainstream criminologists, is that it is simply a tool. Even so, tools can be used in positive or negative ways. Consider a shovel. It can help build a battered women's shelter or a pornographic billboard. My methodological tools are always used in ways to enhance women's safety and to reduce male violence.

Theoretically, I am still very much interested in male peer support theory. However, lately, and always with Marty Schwartz, I am working on constructing integrated theories that include male peer support as well as elements of other theories, such as feminist perspectives, Hirschi's (1969) social bond theory, critical perspectives on urban poverty and unemployment, and left realism. Consider, too, that rural issues are now heavily at the forefront of my mind. For example, as my colleagues and I point out elsewhere (DeKeseredy et al. 2006), since the birth of the discipline in the early 1970s, rural crime has ranked among the least-studied social problems in critical criminology. Of course, the neglect of rural can just as easily be said about criminology in general throughout the twentieth century (Donnermeyer, Jobes, and Barclay 2006). Since the 1990s, a growing number of international scholars have expanded rural crime research (e.g., Aust and Simmons 2002; Weisheit, Falcone, and Wells 2006; Wood and Griffiths 1996), but the bulk of their theoretical and empirical work is still not guided by any variant of feminism or other types of critical criminological thought.

Certainly, rural crime research has yet to develop a critical theoretical framework that can synthesize current scholarship on what Hogg and Carrington (2006, 171) refer to as "gendered violence and the architecture of rural life." Further, the limited theoretical work that does exist on this topic ignores separation/divorce sexual assault. Thus, to help fill the above gaps in the rural crime literature, my colleagues and I offer an empirically informed theory that allows for a simultaneous consideration of microlevel gender relations and broader social and economic structural changes that over the decades have transformed rural communities and that today account for persistently high levels of unemployment and poverty within them (Duncan 1999; Johnson 2006). Referred to as a rural masculinity crisis/male peer support model of separation/divorce sexual assault, the theory developed by me, Joe Donnermeyer, Marty Schwartz, Ken Tunnell, and Mandy Hall (2006) is guided in part by the feminist/male peer support model of separation/divorce sexual assault constructed by me, MacKenzie Rogness, and Marty Schwartz (2004). Although this offering is heavily influenced by feminism and male peer support theory, it does not address key rural problems, such as the disappearance of work and the loss of family farms. Therefore, Joe, Marty, Ken, Mandy, and I build on the feminist/male peer support model by focusing on these and other factors that enhance a sociological understanding of separation/divorce sexual assault, masculinities, and the U.S. rural gender order.

My policy work, which is fundamentally opposed to promoting and supporting conservative, draconian means of curbing crime (e.g., harsh prison sentences), focuses heavily on prevention and "chipping away" at broader patriarchal, capitalist forces that contribute to crime and its control (Messerschmidt 1986). For example, informed by the work of feminist male educators such as Funk (1993), Thorne-Finch (1992), Katz (2006), and Porter (2006), I publicly protest against pornography and war, and I confront men who engage in sexist behaviors. I also work with progressive all-male collectives around North America to encourage men to break out of the "man box" and to lead peaceful lives dedicated to ending sexism, racism, and other forms of inequality.

On November 21, 2006, in a guest lecture to students enrolled in my violence against women class, Tony Porter stated that one cannot eliminate one form of inequality by promoting another. Certainly, this is true, and often woman abuse is simultaneously a function of economic, racial, and class inequality. Thus, with colleagues such as Marty Schwartz and Shahid Alvi, I consistently call for a higher minimum wage, state-sponsored child care, and an antiracist curriculum, among other initiatives. Further, I pressure politicians with letters and telephone calls that strongly encourage them to address these concerns. Voicing my thoughts and views in the mass media is another technique I often use, which is what critical criminologist Gregg Barak (1988) defines as "newsmaking criminology."

I am obviously not the only person to promote and do such progressive work. In fact, I learned about these initiatives from engaging with my peers, including many of the people cited in this chapter. They helped change my life, and I am trying to do the same for others. Still, the feminist work I do often elicits angry and hateful responses from groups of right-wing men and women. For example, in 1993 I was a professor of sociology at Carleton University in Ottawa, Canada. In February of that year, shortly after a colleague and I released some data generated by the Canadian national survey of woman abuse in university/college dating to the press, I received hate letters, some of which included pictures of aborted fetuses, and harassing phone calls from anonymous "men's rights" advocates. At the same time, the all-female support staff in Carleton's sociology and anthropology department received so many harassing calls that a male student was hired to answer the phone in the department's main office over the next week or so.

Certainly, I was scared. It is only in retrospect that a frightening phone call or letter can be designated as insignificant (Kelly and Radford 1987). For example, immediately after I got my first harassing phone call about the national survey, I, like many female survivors of obscene phone calls, thought the perpetrator was going to act on his abusive threats. This is not an irrational perception, as some violent men follow up their phone calls with assaults (DeKeseredy 1999; Stanko 1990). What made matters worse was that several prominent people at Carleton University, including some high-ranking administrators, did not take my fears seriously. For instance, after I told an administrator about a spiteful letter that was sent to me, he said, "You shouldn't be surprised. This is what happens when you do that type of research. It goes with the territory." Obviously, what he did not understand is that there is no antifeminist or harassment gene in human beings and that harassment, woman abuse, and sexism are not immutable behaviors. They can be eliminated if people take the time and effort to do so (Stark-Adamec 1996).

The tactics of the antifeminist backlash described here and in other sources are widespread and highly injurious (DeKeseredy 1996, 1999; Doob 1995; Faludi 1991; Katz 2006; Renzetti 1994). In my own case, social support enables me to muster up energy and resources to challenge and resist the backlash. I have developed strong ties with feminist scholars and collectives, and I share my personal and emotional reactions. Further, I provide others who are struggling to end woman abuse and other forms of structured social inequality with social support. Indeed, "building alliances for social support and social change is one way to combat the feelings of isolation and frustration many of us working in the field . . . inevitably feel" (Stanko 1997, 84).

Conclusion

Feminist empirical, theoretical, and political work excites me, and while I publicly identify myself as a feminist man, my transition is not over. Fortunately, we are witnessing more men becoming "deviant" like me or who are seriously considering "crossing over to the dark side." Katz (2006, 255) is another progressive man who sees the same transition:

> I am convinced that millions of men in our society are deeply concerned about the abuse, harassment and violence we see—and fear—in the lives of our daughters, mothers, sisters, and lovers. In fact, a recent poll conducted for Lifetime Television found that 57 percent of men aged sixteen to twenty-four believe gender violence is an "extremely serious" problem. A 2000 poll conducted by the Family Violence Prevention Fund found that one-quarter of men would do more about the issue if they were asked. And some compelling social norms research on college campuses suggests that one of the most significant factors in a man's decision to intervene in an incident is his perception of how other men would act in a similar situation. Clearly, a lot of men are uncomfortable with other men's abusive behaviors.

These signs of progressive change are important and generate much hope, but caution is still required. After all, as many feminist scholars, activists, and practitioners have repeatedly experienced, some men who work with women to challenge patriarchy, racism, and class inequality often refuse to accept female leadership. As noted by Canadian feminist scholar Meg Luxton (1993, 352), "Ironically, many feminists have participated in discussions where men, while talking about the problems of male dominance and patriarchy, hog the conversational space and silence the women as they do so." Further, some progressive men focus only on challenging sexism and ignore the harms generated by racism and other forms of inequality that also directly or indirectly contribute to woman abuse.

I and others are aware of these and other obstacles, and we are prepared for the long haul. Regardless of how long it takes to get there, the long, hard journey toward a truly egalitarian social order is worth it, and I encourage all men to become fellow travelers and allies with women. However, as Funk (2006, 207) points out, always keep in mind that being allies with women is as much about "liberating men from the constraints of masculinity" as it is about helping to save women's lives and supporting their inherent right to live in peace.

Discussion Questions

1. After reading this chapter, what do you make of woman abuse and the role men can play in the struggle to end it?

2. What is missing for you?
3. What did you struggle with?
4. Did this chapter influence you to rethink your own position on woman abuse?
5. What will *you* do to challenge the broader social forces that contribute to sexual harassment, sexual assault, beatings, and the like?

Acknowledgments

The title of this chapter echoes that of the late Dr. Timothy Leary's (1982) book *Changing My Mind, among Others: Lifetime Writings, Selected and Introduced by the Author.* I would also like to thank Shahid Alvi, Susan L. Miller, Claire M. Renzetti, and Martin D. Schwartz for their advice and guidance.

Notes

1. Grade 13 was abolished by the Province of Ontario a few years ago.
2. See DeKeseredy and Perry (2006); DeKeseredy and Schwartz (1996); Lynch, Michalowski, and Groves (2000); and Maclean and Milovanovic (1991) for various definitions of critical criminology.
3. This is a modified version of Young's (1988) definition of radical criminology.
4. See Bergen (1996, 2006); DeKeseredy (in press); and DeKeseredy, Rogness, and Schwartz (2004) for reviews of research on sexual assaults in marriage and during and after separation/divorce.
5. See DeKeseredy (in press); DeKeseredy and Joseph (2006); and DeKeseredy et al. (2006) for more information on this study and the data generated by it.
6. See DeKeseredy and Schwartz (1993, 2002); DeKeseredy et al. (2006); Godenzi, Schwartz, and DeKeseredy (2001); and Schwartz and DeKeseredy (1997).
7. See DeKeseredy and Schwartz (1991); and Schwartz and DeKeseredy (1991).
8. At the time of writing this chapter, Judith Grant was based at Missouri State University.

References

Aust, R., and J. Simmons. 2002. *Rural crime in England and Wales.* London: Home Office.
Barak, G. 1988. Newsmaking criminology: Reflections on the media, intellectuals, and crime. *Justice Quarterly* 5:565–88.
Bergen, R. K. 1996. *Wife rape: Understanding the response of survivors and service providers.* Thousand Oaks, Calif.: Sage.

———. 2006. Marital rape: New research and directions. *VAWnet*, February:1–13.

Bograd, M. 1988. Feminist perspectives on wife abuse: An introduction. In *Feminist perspectives on wife abuse*, ed. K. Yllo and M. Bograd, 11–27. Newbury Park, Calif.: Sage.

Bunch, T. 2006. Ending men's violence against women. A Call to Men: National Association of Men and Women Committed to Ending Violence against Women. http://www.acalltomen.com/page.php?id=52.

Connell, R. W. 1995. *Masculinities*. Berkeley, Calif.: University of California Press.

DeKeseredy, W. S. 1988a. Woman abuse in dating relationships: The relevance of social support theory. *Journal of Family Violence* 3:1–13.

———. 1988b. *Woman abuse in dating relationships: The role of male peer support.* Toronto: Canadian Scholars' Press.

———. 1996. The Canadian national survey on woman abuse in university/college dating: Biofeminist panic transmission or critical inquiry? *Canadian Journal of Criminology* 38:81–104.

———. 1999. Tactics of the antifeminist backlash against Canadian national woman abuse surveys. *Violence against Women* 5:1258–76.

———. 2005. Patterns of family violence. In *Families: Changing trends in Canada*, ed. M. Baker, 229–57. Whitby, Ont. McGraw-Hill Ryerson.

———. In press. *Sexual assault during and after separation/divorce: An exploratory study*. Washington, D.C.: U.S. Department of Justice.

DeKeseredy, W. S., S. Alvi, M. D. Schwartz, and E. A. Tomaszewski. 2003. *Under siege: Poverty and crime in a public housing community*. Lanham, Md.: Lexington Books.

DeKeseredy, W. S., J. Donnermeyer, M. D. Schwartz, K. Tunnell, and M. Hall. 2006. Thinking critically about rural gender relations: Toward a rural masculinity crisis/male peer support model of separation/divorce sexual assault. Paper presented at the annual meetings of the American Society of Criminology, Los Angeles.

DeKeseredy, W. S., and C. Joseph. 2006. Separation/divorce sexual assault in rural Ohio: Preliminary results of an exploratory study. *Violence against Women* 12:301–11.

DeKeseredy, W. S., and B. Perry, eds. 2006. *Advancing critical criminology: Theory and application*. Lanham, Md.: Lexington Books.

DeKeseredy, W. S., M. Rogness, and M. D. Schwartz. 2004. Separation/divorce sexual assault: The current state of social scientific knowledge. *Aggression and Violent Behavior* 9:675–91.

DeKeseredy, W. S., and M. D. Schwartz. 1991. British left realism on the abuse of women: A critical appraisal. In *Criminology as peacemaking*, ed. H. Pepinsky and R. Quinney, 154–71. Bloomington: Indiana University Press.

———. 1993. Male peer support and woman abuse: An expansion of DeKeseredy's model. *Sociological Spectrum* 13:393–413.

———. 1996. *Contemporary Criminology*. Belmont, Calif.: Wadsworth.

———. 1998. *Woman abuse on campus: Results from the Canadian national survey*. Thousand Oaks, Calif.: Sage.

———. 2002. Theorizing public housing woman abuse as a function of economic exclusion and male peer support. *Women's Health and Urban Life* 1:26–45.

————. 2003. Backlash and whiplash: A critique of Statistics Canada's 1999 General Social Survey on Victimization. *Online Journal of Justice Studies.* http://www .ojjs.icaap.org.

————. In press. *Exiting dangerous relationships: The abuse of women in rural America.* New Brunswick, N.J.: Rutgers University Press.

DeKeseredy, W. S., M. D. Schwartz, and S. Alvi. 2000. The role of profeminist men in dealing with woman abuse on the Canadian college campus. *Violence against Women* 9:918–35.

DeKeseredy, W. S., M. D. Schwartz, D. Fagen, and M. Hall. 2006. Separation/divorce sexual assault: The contribution of male peer support. *Feminist Criminology* 1:228–50.

Donnermeyer, J., P. Jobes, and E. Barclay. 2006. Rural crime, poverty, and community. In *Advancing critical criminology: Theory and application,* ed. W. S. DeKeseredy and B. Perry, 199–218. Lanham, Md.: Lexington Books.

Doob, A. 1995. Understanding the attacks on Statistics Canada's Violence against Women Survey. In *Wife assault and the Canadian criminal justice system,* ed. M. Valverde, L. MacLeod, and K. Johnson, 157–65. Toronto: Centre of Criminology, University of Toronto.

Duncan, C. M. 1999. *Worlds apart: Why poverty persists in rural America.* New Haven, Conn.: Yale University Press.

Dutton, M. A., A. Worrell, D. Terrell, S. Denaro, and R. Thompson. 2002. *National evaluation of the rural domestic violence and child victimization enforcement grant program: Final report, volume 1.* Washington, D.C.: National Institute of Justice.

Faludi, S. 1991. *Backlash: The undeclared war against American women.* New York: Crown.

Funk, R. E. 1993. *Stopping rape: A challenge for men.* Philadelphia: New Society Publishers.

————. 2006. *Reaching men: Strategies for preventing sexist attitudes, behaviors, and violence.* Indianapolis: JIST Life.

Gelsthorpe, L., and A. Morris. 1988. Feminism and criminology in Britain. *British Journal of Criminology* 28:93–110.

Godenzi, A., M. D. Schwartz, and W. S. DeKeseredy. 2001. Toward a gendered social bond/male peer support theory of university woman abuse. *Critical Criminology* 10:1–16.

Hirschi, T. 1969. *Causes of delinquency.* Berkeley: University of California Press.

Hogg, R., and C. Carrington. 2006. *Policing the rural crisis.* Sydney, Australia: Federation Press.

Hotaling, G., and D. Sugarman. 1986. An analysis of risk markers and husband-to-wife violence: The current state of knowledge. *Violence and Victims* 1:102–24.

Johnson, K. 2006. *Demographic trends in rural and small town America.* Durham: University of New Hampshire, Carsey Institute.

Katz, J. 2006. *The macho paradox: Why some men hurt women and how all men can help.* Naperville, Ill.: Sourcebooks.

Kelly, L., and J. Radford. 1987. The problem of men: Feminist perspectives on sexual violence. In *Law, order and the authoritarian state,* ed. P. Scraton, 237–53. Philadelphia: Open University Press.

Kimmel, M. S., and T. E. Mosmiller. 1992. Introduction. In *Against the tide: Profeminist men in the United States, 1776–1990,* ed. M. S. Kimmel and T. E. Mosmiller, 1–46. Boston: Beacon Press.

Kindlon, D., and M. Thompson. 1999. *Raising Cain: Protecting the emotional life of boys.* New York: Ballantine.

Krishnan, S. P., J. C. Hilbert, and D. VanLeeuwen. 2001. Domestic violence and help-seeking behaviors among rural women: Results from a shelter-based study. *Family Community Health* 24:28–38.

Leary, T. 1982. *Changing my mind, among others: Lifetime writings, selected and introduced by the author.* Englewood Cliffs, N.J.: Prentice-Hall.

Levant, R. 1994. Male violence against female partners: Roots in male socialization and development. Paper presented at the American Psychological Association meetings, Los Angeles.

Lewis, S. H. 2003. *Unspoken crimes: Sexual assault in rural America.* Enola, Pa.: National Sexual Violence Resource Center.

Luxton, M. 1993. Dreams and dilemmas: Feminist musings on "the man question." In *Men and masculinities: A critical anthology,* ed. T. Haddad, 347–74. Toronto: Canadian Scholars' Press.

Lynch, M., R. Michalowski, and W. B. Groves. 2000. *The new primer in radical criminology: Critical perspectives on crime, power and identity.* Monsey, N.J.: Criminal Justice Press.

MacLean, B. D., and D. Milovanovic. 1991. On critical criminology. In *New directions in critical criminology,* ed. B. D. MacLean and D. Milovanovic, 1–8. Vancouver: Collective Press.

Mahoney, P., and L. M. Williams. 1998. Sexual assault in marriage: Prevalence, consequences, and treatment of wife rape. In *Partner violence: A comprehensive review of 20 years of research,* ed. J. L. Jasinski and L. M. Williams, 113–62. Thousand Oaks, Calif.: Sage.

Mahoney, P., L. M. Williams, and C. M. West. 2001. Violence against women by intimate relationship partners. In *Sourcebook on violence against women,* ed. C. M. Renzetti, J. L. Edleson, and R. K. Bergen, 143–78. Thousand Oaks, Calif.: Sage.

Messerschmidt, J. W. 1986. *Capitalism, patriarchy, and crime: Toward a socialist feminist criminology.* Totowa, N.J.: Rowman and Littlefield.

———. 2000. *Nine lives: Adolescent masculinities, the body, and violence.* Boulder, Colo.: Westview.

———. 2004. *Flesh and blood: Adolescent gender diversity and violence.* Lanham, Md.: Rowman and Littlefield.

Porter, T. 2006a. *Well meaning men: Breaking out of the man box.* Charlotte, N.C.: A Call to Men: National Association of Men and Women Committed to Ending Violence against Women. http://www.acalltomen.com/page.php?id=53.

———. 2006b. Becoming part of the solution. A Call to Men: National Association of Men and Women Committed to Ending Violence against Women. http://www.acalltomen.com/page.php?id=53.

Renzetti, C. M. 1994. On dancing with a bear: Reflections on some of the current debates among domestic violence theorists. *Violence and Victims* 9:195–200.

Schur, E. 1984. *Labeling women deviant: Gender, stigma and social control.* Philadelphia: Temple University Press.

Schwartz, M. D., and W. S. DeKeseredy. 1988. Liberal feminism on violence against women. *Social Justice* 15:213–21.

———. 1991. Left realist criminology: Strengths, weaknesses and the feminist critique. *Crime, Law and Social Change* 15:51–72.

———. 1993. The return of the battered husband syndrome through the typification of women as violent. *Crime, Law and Social Change* 20:249–65.

———. 1997. *Sexual assault on the college campus: The role of male peer support.* Thousand Oaks, Calif.: Sage.

Schwartz, M. D., W. S. DeKeseredy, D. Tait, and S. Alvi. 2001. Male peer support and a feminist routine activities theory: Understanding sexual assault on the college campus. *Justice Quarterly* 18:623–49.

Scully, D. 1990. *Understanding sexual violence: A study of convicted rapists.* Boston: Unwin Hyman.

Stanko, E. A. 1990. *Everyday violence: How women and men experience sexual and physical danger.* London: Pandora.

———. 1997. "I second that emotion": Reflections on feminism, emotionality, and research on sexual violence. In *Researching sexual violence against women: Methodological and personal perspectives,* ed. M. D. Schwartz, 74–85. Thousand Oaks, Calif.: Sage.

Stark-Adamec, C. 1996. Psychological violence in academia. In *Violence: A collective responsibility,* ed. C. Stark-Adamec, 21–30. Ottawa: Social Science Federation of Canada.

Straus, M. A., R. J. Gelles, and S. Steinmetz. 1981. *Behind closed doors: Violence in the American family.* Newbury Park, Calif.: Sage.

Thorne-Finch, R. 1992. *Ending the silence: The origins and treatment of violence against women.* Toronto: University of Toronto Press.

Websdale, N. 1998. *Rural woman battering and the justice system: An ethnography.* Thousand Oaks, Calif.: Sage.

Websdale, N., and B. Johnson. 2005. Reducing woman battering: The role of structural approaches. In *Domestic violence at the margins: Readings on race, class, gender, and culture,* ed. N. J. Sokoloff, 389–415. New Brunswick, N.J.: Rutgers University Press.

Weisheit, R. A., D. N. Falcone, and L. E. Wells. 2006. *Crime and policing in rural and small-town America.* Long Grove, Ill.: Waveland.

Wood, D. S, and C. T. Griffiths. 1996. Patterns of aboriginal crime. In *Crime in Canadian society,* ed. R. A. Silverman, J. Teevan, and V. F. Sacco, 222–33. Toronto: Harcourt Brace.

Young, J. 1988. Radical criminology in Britain: The emergence of a competing paradigm. *British Journal of Criminology* 28:159–83.

Chapter 9   Michelle L. Meloy

Managing a Man's World

The Experiences of a Female Probation Officer in a

Sex Offender Supervision Unit

Sex offenders, especially unknown assailants who victimize children, are universally despised and feared. High-profile cases involving long-time sex offenders like the 1993 abduction and murder in California of twelve-year-year old Polly Klass and the 1994 murder and rape in New Jersey of seven-year-old Megan Kanka, have helped pave the way for targeted state and federal laws such as sex offender registration with community notification (often referred to as "Megan's Law," named after the New Jersey victim), and involuntary civil commitment. More recently, the unrelated kidnappings and murder of two young girls in Florida, victims Jessica Lundsford (age nine) and Sarah Lunde (age thirteen), by two different convicted sex offenders resulted in new sex offender laws at the state and municipal level, as well as appeals for additional federal sex offender legislation (named after the Florida victims) that would create "predator-free" child molester zones, a national sex offender registry, and a sentencing guideline mandating that child molesters serve life sentences or twenty-five-year prison terms, followed by lifetime community supervision.[1] Probation is the most popular form of community-based supervision (Glaze and Palla 2005). Yet, compared to other areas of correction, we know relatively little about the history, purpose, theoretical rationale, role of its officers, and probation's efficacy for sex offenders. One of the reasons probation has received limited scholarly attention is due to the impression that it serves primarily non-serious offenders (Petersilia 1998a), and although historically this was the case, today's probation client is likely to be a convicted felon (Glaze and Palla 2005). Despite the possible controversy, the use of probation as a sentencing alternative for convicted sex offenders is increasingly common and, as such, is the focus of this chapter.

I approach this topic from a dual perspective, as a researcher and as a practitioner. My scholarly interest in sexual violence was born out of my years of working as a probation officer in a sex offender supervision unit. This unique vantage point allows me to speak to the larger body of research, my own empirical work on these offenders, as well as sharing my experiences as a female probation officer of sexually violent offenders. Therefore, the following pages will highlight the history and goals of probation as a general sanctioning option, the contemporary population shifts and specific techniques of supervising sex offenders in the community, and my own work and experiences with this convicted population.

History of Probation and Probation Officers

John Augustus, a Boston shoemaker and religious man, is recognized as the first (unofficial) probation officer after he bailed out a man—charged with public drunkenness—in 1841 from the Boston Police Court (Dressler 1962). When the defendant appeared before a judge a few weeks later, Augustus requested a deferred criminal sentence so that he could rehabilitate the man, promising to personally supervise the man during the deferral period. After a trouble-free stint in the community, the defendant convinced the judge of his reformed ways and was released with a small monetary fine. Augustus did this for thousands of small-time criminals, with success after success. This activity marked the beginning of probation. In 1878, Massachusetts was the first to introduce a statewide probation system (for juveniles), and in 1901 New York State authorized the first official adult probation system for convicted offenders (Petersilia 1998b). The early probation officers were volunteers, like Augustus, but with increases in crime and the probation practice gaining mainstream appeal, the positions were transformed from volunteer posts to paid positions (Dressler 1962).

The first professional probation officers were retired law enforcement personnel who were hired to report to the court on the defendant's probation status. The recruiting pool for these early professional probation officers replicated the gender symmetry of police officers, in that men controlled both professions and excluded "outsiders," such as women and/or people of color (Martin and Jurik 1996). The gendered nature of the profession would change dramatically over the next century, in part, because probation work included a "softer" social work/rehabilitation thread (i.e., "women's work"), thus making women's presence on the job less threatening to the masculine domain of criminal justice occupations (Belknap 2001; Martin and Jurik 1996).

A review of the literature on gender and criminal justice professions suggests that the entrance of women into the probation profession was similar to their introduction into policing and prison work (Martin and Jurik 1996). Namely, the first female probation officers, like the first policewomen and female correctional guards, were restricted to working with women offenders and children-at-risk, which reflected populations and duties that male officers were not interested in. However, by 1974 women professionals in community corrections, such as probation and parole, were on more equal footing with their male counterparts, at least with respect to the duties and representation of line officers (Schoonmaker and Brooks 1975, as cited in Martin and Jurik 1996). "Cross-gender supervision" became a nationally recognized practice in probation and parole departments (Martin and Jurik 1996, 164). The proportion of men and women working as community corrections officers (probation and parole) today is evenly divided between the sexes (Goldhart and Macedonia 1992; Hunter 1992, as cited in Martin and Jurik 1996). It is interesting to note, however, that the sex offender unit to which I belonged was, and continues to this day to be, staffed primarily by female probation officers. Outsiders found it odd that women would disproportionately choose to work with sexually violent offenders, who are nearly always male. Still, many gender scholars would have predicted exactly this pattern: female practitioners and researchers often gravitate toward issues that principally affect their gender and/or children.

Purpose

The ultimate purpose and goal of probation has a turbulent history (Abadinsky 1991; McAnany, Thomson, and Fogel 1984). For instance, the original conceptualization of probation (lasting through the 1970s) was closely associated with the notion of curing offenders (MacKenzie and Souryal 1997). Any rehabilitative model of justice inevitably focuses primarily on the offenders, assessing the causes of their criminogenic behavior (e.g., drugs, alcohol, educational deficiencies, and mental illness) so that appropriate responses or "fixes" can be implemented. This theoretical model empowered probation officers with nearly unbridled discretion on how best to supervise individual clients and how best to respond to technical violations (O'Leary 1987). The next theoretical shift in criminological thinking, retributive justice or "just deserts," had only a minimal impact on the applied practice of probation, despite that fact that its philosophy had a lot of political appeal. Policymakers, legal analysts, and scholars were attracted to its ideals because it responded to the growing belief that nothing therapeutic worked to reform offenders and it addressed concerns about the individualized (disparate) way criminal sentences were meted out under the rehabilitation framework. Retributive models of probation suggested that proportionality ("let the punishment fit the crime") and a focus on the offense, not the offender, would be a preferred and more equitable approach to probation supervision (O' Leary 1987).

In reality, however, not much changed in the way probation officers did their jobs until the 1980s, an era characterized as the beginning of the "get-tough-on-crime" response to lawbreakers (Rothman 1983). The popularity of the crime-control movement directly impacted how probation functioned in this country. As a result, probation become more punitive and crime-control-oriented, which translated into intensive and restrictive supervision for convicted offenders, longer probation terms, and additional conditions and court mandates in probation contracts. Despite the undisputed influence that the crime-control model still has on today's probation practices, rehabilitation ideals remain and are evident in a myriad of factors (Ellsworth 1990). For example, attendance at a substance abuse program or anger management class or pursuing educational goals could be part of a probation contract. As such, most scholars agree that contemporary probation has two distinctive goals: crime control and rehabilitation of offenders (McShane and Krause 1993). Both of these objectives are evident in the operations of the sex offender unit where I once worked and later where I conducted my research. Specifically, frequent visits with a probation officer or surveillance team and unscheduled searches of the offender's residence or vehicle (crime-control goal) and mandatory attendance and progress in sex offender treatment (rehabilitation) are part of every sex offender's community supervision.

One of the sex offender probation clients I interviewed talked about his perception of probation's goal for him: "They don't wanna see me fail on this probation thing, they don't wanna send me back to jail, nobody here [referring to the probation department] wants to see me back in jail, they wanna keep me where I am, staying out of trouble, working and doing good, because the last time they put me back in jail I came out a total jerk. I feel very much that [mentions his female probation officer by name] wants me to do good, for everyone's sake. She helps me all she can, but she will slam me if I don't keep it right down the middle about what I need to do and what my priorities have got to be."

Probation Contracts

Although probationers live in the community, they remain under the jurisdiction of the court that sentenced them for their crime. Probation clients enter into a contractual agreement with the court and the department responsible for their supervision to not only remain law-abiding for the probationary period but to also comply with a host of standard and specialized conditions and restrictions on their behavior. The overarching goals and theories of probation (crime control and rehabilitation) are exemplified within both types of proba-tion conditions, while other punishment goals (e.g., retribution and restorative justice) are typified in other probation conditions, such as victim restitution and community service (MacKenzie and Souryal 1997). Another male sex of-fender on probation spoke openly about the conditions of his community-based supervision and how he says probation encourages desistance from crime: "I had to go to work-release as part of my probation, I also had lots of fines and fees and have to pay for my victim's therapy. I go to therapy too. I would do that anyway [attend therapy] because I know I need it. Probation's advantage is if you don't go, it's more of an external control because they force you to go and that is probably a good thing, especially in the beginning when offenders, I was too, can be combative about all the stuff they tell you to do." (This offender's claims about voluntarily seeking treatment are likely not accurate, as it is extraordinarily rare for sex offenders to enroll in treatment *before* they get in trouble with the law and are thus mandated to do so.)

Many probation mandates are fairly standard and, as such, are referred to as general conditions. Case in point, most jurisdictions require probationers to re-port in person to their officer, to be employed or be enrolled in school, to per-mit probation officers to visit (and search) their home and place of business, to refrain from moving or travel without prior permission, to pay monthly super-vision fees, to compensate victims for any personal harms or property damage, and to submit to drug and alcohol testing (McShane and Krause 1993). Sex of-fender probationers are required to comply with all the general requirements expected of any client on community supervision, in addition to a litany of other conditions designed specifically for them.

Additionally, probationers are often required to comply with special condi-tions that are tailored to their specific crime and the underlying conditions be-lieved to have contributed to offenders' criminal behavior. It is quite common for drug offenders or individuals convicted of drinking and driving to be or-dered into substance abuse counseling. Similarly, sex offender probationers are nearly always required to complete cognitive behavioral modification sex of-fender group therapy, with a focus on relapse prevention, prior to a successful termination of the court contract (Center for Sex Offender Management 2000, 2002a; Lane Council of Governments 2003; Meloy 2006; Stalans 2004). All of the sex offenders I interviewed and those that I once supervised as an officer were required to attend and successfully complete this same treatment proto-col. Despite its intensity (one to three times per week), duration (ranging from two to four years for successful completion) and cost (thousands of dollars), most of the probationers spoke positively about their experience with therapy.[2] Although the extant literature provides support for this type of rehabilitation effort, it is anecdotal evidence that suggests the efficacy of the specific pro-grams with which my department worked.

In addition to treatment mandates, supervising agents and probation departments believe that the use of specialized conditions, especially for criminal populations like sex offenders, is critically important because the standard set of probation conditions and typical "red flags," such as failure to report or indications of illegal drug use, alerting that trouble is brewing for an offender, are seldom present among sex offender probationers (Lane Council of Governments 2003). A common type of specialized condition among sex offender probation cases is to forbid unsupervised contact with any minors and to refuse any contact with victims. As one sex offender probationer describes: "See, I'm not allowed to be with my grandchildren or anybody of a certain age, under the age of eighteen. I had to change my church that I raised my children at because of this. I can't go where my kids and grandchildren go because of the 'no contact' condition. To avoid getting into any trouble, I agreed with them [probation] and the judge not to go to church there anymore so no one can say 'he was sitting next to them [his grandchildren] in church' or whatever."

Sex Offender Probation

Given the general fear surrounding sex crimes and sex offenders, it is likely that the public would be troubled to learn that most convicted sex offenders will indeed spend some (if not all) of their criminal sentence on probation or parole (Greenfeld 1997). Critics of sex offender community management are likely to demonstrate the potential dangerousness of this criminal justice policy by noting that the murderers in the high-profile cases of Polly Klass and Megan Kanka both were parolees when they abducted and killed their young victims.

Despite the statistical rarity of a sex offender murdering a victim or of a victim being abducted and sexually assaulted by a stranger, it is easy to see why regularly sentencing sex offenders to probation or allowing them to leave prison early to serve time on parole can strike fear in the hearts of citizens, especially those who base their knowledge on the media's presentation of sexual violence. The recognition of this public fear and the increasing use of community-based sanctions to monitor and control convicted sex offenders were instrumental in the creation of the Center for Sex Offender Management (CSOM), a collaborative effort of the Office of Justice Programs, the National Institute of Corrections, the State Justice Institute, the Center for Effective Public Policy, and the American Probation and Parole Association.[3] The center's primary goal is to increase public safety by reducing sexual victimization through the effective supervision and treatment of sex offenders who live in the community. To that end, CSOM is an excellent resource for the public, researchers, professionals dealing with sex offenders or anyone else looking for empirically based information on the risks and techniques associated with community supervision of convicted sex offenders.

Given the recognition by criminal justice professionals that these probation clients present unique challenges, the response to sex offenders is different than responses to other types of serious offenders (Center for Sex Offender Management 2002a; Lurgio, Jones, and Smith 1995; Meloy 2006; Stalans 2004). Probation and parole departments across the country are creating special units and/or providing additional training for officers who work with sex offenders. Most of these specialized sex offender community-based monitoring programs are modeled after the "containment approach" (English et al. 1996). There are three primary components to this approach, which are adopted in most jurisdictions where it is used (Stalans 2004). The first is the use of intensive supervision of sex offender probationers, which includes weekly or biweekly office visits to the probation officer, community surveillance of the offender, polygraph examinations (or other objective testing), and verification of other important information—all of which measures are crime-control-oriented. The next component of this type of sex offender supervision is successful progress and/or completion of a cognitive-behavioral and relapse-prevention group therapy. In other words, the goal of rehabilitation is believed essential. Finally, it is necessary to establish close ties between the probation department and treatment providers (Stalans 2004). The sex offender unit where I worked closely mirrored this intensive model of community supervision. Some offenders believed that the additional conditions imposed on their community supervision by the sex offender unit were excessive and antitherapeutic. As an officer, I once had a probationer criticize the practice of leaving our business cards, with the sex offender unit designation, as a notification that we stopped by their residence or place of employment unannounced. We did this to "keep the offenders on their toes" by leaving the impression of an omnipresent law-and-order force. The probationer told me that leaving the cards in a public setting (door jams, car windshields, or with roommates or employers) created additional stigma and ostracization, thus jeopardizing his success on probation and desistance from further crime.

Victim Prominence

One of the key ingredients to specialized sex offender probation is its victim-centered approach to community-based supervision, which prioritizes sex crime prevention and works to ensure that sex offender probation does not inadvertently create a "secondary victimization" whereby the system adds an additional layer of emotional harm to victims. For instance, probation and parole officers are taught to avoid retraumatizing victims by initiating contact with those who have asked not to be consulted about the offender's supervision or on any other issues such as restitution or no-victim-contact orders. Generally, it was the prosecuting attorney who advised us if the victim did not wish to be contacted by the probation department or by the offender's supervising officer. This situation seemed most common when the victim was a nonfamily member. In these instances, I relied on collateral information collected during the investigation and prosecution of the case to assess the specifics of the victimization, whether the victim was seeking restitution or other compensation, as well as the probationer's potential risk factors. For instance, a victim's statement may reveal that the offender provided her with alcohol while on a family visit to his home, showed her pornography, and then fondled her. This is important information for effective community supervision and avoidance of high-risk situations.

Probation officers are also advised to be receptive, responsive, and available to victims who wish to talk to an offender's probation officer. During my tenure in the unit, not a week would go by without receiving a phone call from a victim. Often these conversations were related to the status of a restitution payment or notification that the offender had violated a no-contact order with the victim (usually in the form of a letter or an attempt at phone contact). Other times, the caller wanted nothing more than to be heard or to be offered an opportunity to speak about the ways the victimization had affected her life and a forum to let me know how dangerous (or not) she believed the offender was. Also, victim advocates and clinicians working with sex offenders are important players in the collaborative approach to probation. The prominence of sex crime victims and the policy of victim protection forces officers and probation departments to consider the risks and needs of these victims. For example, prior to sentencing of a felony case, a probation officer may be asked by the judge to write a presentence investigation report, in part, to solicit the victim's wishes for an offender's sentencing, among other things. In these instances, the victim-impact statement becomes part of the permanent court record. As part of the offender's probation contract, sex offenders may be ordered to pay monies to victims to cover any relevant medical expenses and/or the cost of therapy for the victim. Additionally, courts often create probation contracts that stipulate "no victim contact" and/or "no contact with any minors," and convicted sex offenders can also be barred from establishments where minors are likely to be found, like schools, playgrounds, roller-rinks, parks, public pools, and so forth (Lane Council of Governments 2003).

Should Sex Offenders Be on Probation?

In general, sex offenders have much lower sexual recidivism rates than the public believes. For example, the Bureau of Justice Statistics reported that the sexual rearrest rate for sex offenders released from state prisons from across the country was 5 percent, for a three-year observation period (Langan, Schmitt, and Durose 2003).[4] Furthermore, sex offenders released from prison had lower rearrest rates than released armed robbers, kidnappers, and individuals incarcerated for serious assaults (Langan and Levin 2002).

A handful of studies specifically address the issue of recidivism of sex offenders on probation (Berliner et al. 1995; McGrath, Hoke, and Vojtisek 1998; Meloy 2005, 2006; Stalans, Seng, and Yarnold 2002). To varying degrees, these studies all demonstrate the efficacy of sex offender probation in that sex offender probationers have comparable or lower recidivism rates than other felons on probation or than sex offenders receiving jail or prison, instead of probation. For instance, the Berliner et al. (1995) study compared the recidivism rates of convicted sex offenders receiving a suspended jail sentence with those who received probation with mandatory treatment. Their results indicate that the sex offender probationers were less likely to be rearrested for a sex crime within a twenty-four-month follow-up period, compared with the sex offenders who served jail time only (as cited in Stalans 2004). Still, some sex offender probationers do violate the terms of their probation contract. One of the men I interviewed talked about breaking the rules of his community supervision and how he thinks even relatively minor rule infractions are taken very seriously when sex offenders commit them.

I had been on probation for nearly three years at the point this happened. I had an isolated incident where I smoked a marijuana joint with a woman who I use to date—she was a bad woman, not a bad women but a bad influence, she's a lot older than me, twenty-nine and I am nineteen and we smoked a joint together. And you know I came to my probation officer and the same day I had a drop [urine drug test], so I had a dirty drop [positive drug test]. The officer says because of my case, and this bothers me too because I am on probation for having sex with a girl who was only three years younger than me but she was a minor and I wasn't so I understand that part, but [mentions probation officer's name] says if I was in here for murder or burglary or arson and I had a dirty drop for marijuana we could talk it out or work out a deal for treatment or whatever. But because I have a sex case they have to take me to court.

This offender is describing officer or departmental discretion on how to respond to technical violations (rule infractions that do not amount to new criminal charges).

The state of Vermont investigated the impact of specialized sex offender supervision, similar to the containment approach, by comparing sex offender probationers sentenced to standard probation and individual therapy sessions with a second sample of convicted sex offenders sentenced to specialized probation and mandated group therapy that embraced a cognitive-behavioral modification focus. The probationers in the specialized probation and treatment group had much lower failure rates (i.e., any new arrest) than the men sentenced to standard probation and individual therapy (McGrath, Hoke, and Vojtisek 1998).

In yet another study, Stalans, Seng, and Yarnold investigated three counties in one midwestern state that utilized the containment approach (English et al. 1996) to sex offender probation by comparing sex offenders sentenced to specialized sex offender probation with sex offenders on standard probation in each of three counties. Coincidentally, one of the units evaluated by the Stalans's research team is the same department where I worked as a probation officer and later conducted my own research. Results indicated that in two of the three jurisdictions that were evaluated, recidivism rates were lower for some types of sex offenders supervised under the containment approach, compared with traditional probation supervision (Stalans, Seng, and Yarnold 2002). Collectively, these studies support the current use of sex offender probation as a sound public policy.

A few years ago, I investigated the performance and failure rate of a national sample of felony sex offender probationers, with an average follow-up period of thirty-six months, to determine if it was appropriate to place felony sex offenders on probation (Meloy 2005). In constructing this analysis, recidivism rates of felony sex offender probationers was studied and compared with the recidivism rate of felony sex offenders sent directly to prison. With a national sexual recidivism rate of 4.5 percent among this population and a general (nonsexual) recidivism rate of 12 percent, the evidence suggested that felony sex offender probationers failed less often than other types of serious criminals on probation (Langan and Cunniff 1992), and slightly less often than a national sample of sex offenders sentenced directly to prison (see Langan, Schmitt, and Durose 2003).

In an attempt to further elucidate the public safety impact of supervising these offenders in the community, I also investigated the failure rate of the sex offender probationers in the unit where I once worked as a (female) probation officer supervising (nearly all) male sex offenders (Meloy 2006). The quantitative results indicated that 20 of the 169 men (12 percent) in the sex offender unit committed an additional sexual crime (including failure to register as a sex offender) or sexual violation while on probation. In this study, sexual recidivism was defined and measured more broadly (i.e., official arrest data was augmented by polygraph results and by admissions to probation staff or therapists of sexual deviance) than the other probation studies previously mentioned, where only official arrest data was used to determine failure. Hence, it is quite probable that this sample of sex offenders did not fail more often than the samples in the other investigations, but that it used indicators that were more comprehensive in the calculation of failure. Given that 88 percent of the sample did not commit a new sex crime while on specialized probation, in concert with other outcome studies, the research suggests that the containment approach to sex offender management can be quite effective at controlling sex offenders.

My Sex Offender Unit

In 1996, the midwestern suburb where I worked as a probation officer became one of the first probation departments in the country to specialize in sex offender management with a self-declared mission of "no more victims." This department was designated as the hub to a collaborative effort between law enforcement, the courts, and the area's sex offender therapists, all charged with the mission to effectively and safely supervise sex offender probationers. Over the next several years, the department more fully adopted the containment approach to sex offender supervision (English et al. 1996), which was supported, in part, by earmarked state and federal funds.

To this day, the sex offender supervision unit has six dedicated probation and two surveillance officers. Each specialized caseload is limited to forty-five sex offenders per officer. As previously mentioned, women are (and have always been) overrepresented as line officers within the unit, despite the fact that the clientele is more than 90 percent male, with most of the victimizations occurring against women and children (specific breakdowns forthcoming). My female colleagues and I often thought it ironic that men, who exerted their power and control by sexually victimizing women and children, were spending their probation terms being "controlled" by other women. As a probation officer in this unit, I was responsible for a variety of tasks: conducting office appointments and field visits with clients; conferring with the surveillance team about their observations of and interactions with my clients; talking with therapists regarding an offender's treatment status; confirming employment and verifying the suitability of a client's job choice;[5] conducting frequent local and national criminal record checks; monitoring the client's compliance with stipulations to have no contact with his victim(s) and any other restrictions; making collateral contacts to family, friends, and victims; maintaining a schedule for all necessary tests, such as drug screens and polygraph examinations; collecting probation fees and restitution monies; filing status reports to the court; notifying the judge of any serious probation violations; preparing presentence investigation reports on probationers with new charges; and verifying compliance with the state mandate to submit to DNA/STD/HIV testing and to register with local law enforcement on the state's sex offender registry. Needless to say, officers in the sex offender unit, as well as probation officers in general, stay very busy and often find the tasks and responsibilities of the job onerous.

As noted earlier, my involvement with the department extended beyond my employment as an officer. Several years after leaving the court services division to complete my graduate studies, I returned as a researcher to empirically study men on sex offender probation (Meloy 2006). This experience provided the empirical grounding that allows me to speak in greater depth about the unit's philosophy, goals, offender and victim demographics, and efficacy.

My Clients: The Sex Offenders and Their Victims

The male probationers in this sex offender unit were convicted or plead guilty to an array of sex crimes. Consistent with most national probation data, the majority of the sex offender probationers in this unit were on probation for felonies (e.g., aggravated criminal assault, predatory criminal sexual assault, child pornography, and sexual exploitation of a child). However, the unit also supervises offenders who commit misdemeanor sex crimes such as public indecency, solicitation, criminal sexual abuse, and internet-related sex charges. The average probationer age was thirty-four, about three-quarters of the men were white, and the majority were not married. In addition, more than half of the probationers in the sex offender unit completed high school or attended college. This (higher) level of educational attainment is not customary in most criminal populations.

Similar to the extant victimization literature that suggests sex offenders rarely assault strangers (Bureau of Justice Statistics 2005), nearly all of the offenders in the probation unit knew their victims before committing their crimes. In fact, the vast majority of the men were friends or family members of their victims. My empirical investigation of the sex offender unit revealed victims as young as three years old and the eldest victim in her sixties. Probationer files revealed that the average victim age was fifteen years old. As I alluded to earlier, nearly 75 percent of these victims were female, and almost half of the victimizations (49 percent) involved a violation of trust of the victim-offender relationship. By this, I mean that the offender was a parent, relative, teacher, religious leader, or coach to the victim. For instance, one of the sex offenders in the probation unit molested a thirteen-year-old youth group member where the offender volunteered. He described the boy as coming from a "wild and mistreated family" and talks about the negative impact this has probably caused his victim. "I wish him the best and I know that I put scars on him which I would not want anyone ever to do to any kid. This kid was getting close to me, as a mentor or something, he was going through all sorts of things at home, family abuse, he was being hit, stepped on, spit on, and there were many similarities with my own abuse. He was hugging on me for support, like I was the big guy, and my emotions got all mixed up and it felt like there was something from him coming on to me. But as therapy has taught me, I had mixed up thinking. This kid was just reaching out to someone he trusted because he needed help." The probation contracts, supervisory and surveillance standards, and general and specific conditions of probation mirrored the fundamental facets of the containment approach (English et al. 1996), a technique that appears promising.

Managing a Man's World

I am often asked what it was like, as a woman, to be working with sexually aggressive and violent men. On a daily basis, I was sitting across a desk or visiting the homes of men who, on at least one occasion, had sexually victimized women and/or children. The answer is that it felt powerful. It was not the kind of power that drives people toward macho criminal justice positions. It was the power to use my authority and skills to help prevent these men from victimizing anyone else. The feeling of power came from my belief that what we were doing with these offenders would help stop sexual violence. As one offender nearing the end of his probation term told me:

This has all been a good thing for me. I didn't think I would ever say that. It's cost me a lot of money, a lot, and been real hard. Probation has been helpful though because it ensures that I'm heading down the right direction. They help keep me out of trouble and with my treatment; I now want to stay out of trouble. I pretty much was in trouble a lot before this. I don't want to hurt anyone else the way she must feel now [referring to his date rape victim]. I learned how bad this really hurt her from treatment and my p.o. [probation officer]. I wasn't no one to want to do treatment either. They had to put me in what they call "denial intervention" because I kept saying "I didn't do nothing to her" and threaten me with going back to jail because I didn't want treatment or all this probation stuff. It's hard to think about what you really did to somebody. That's why people lie and deny it. You know in your heart what you did, but you don't want to come to terms with the ugliness of who you are and what you did. That's why people deny. That's why I denied it. But it would have stayed in me and ate at me and made me angry and . . . that's why I am glad this is out and I understand why it happened and how I don't let it happen again. I wouldn't have got that if they just sent me to a cell to go crazy and get madder and madder and not work with me the way these people have.

Experts on sex offenders know to listen to these sorts of statements with a degree of skepticism, but this offender had little obvious incentive to lie or much to gain by speaking with me, and, according to his probation officer, he had completed all of his requirements and was already being discharged by the time we talked.

Sex offenders are known for their sophistication in manipulation and intimidation tactics. This is one of the reasons it has been deemed essential that therapists working with this population undergo specialized training. Similarly, extant literature suggests that criminal justice practitioners, especially judges and probation officers, be specifically trained on responding consistently and appropriately to violations of the probation contract and to the difficulties of working effectively with this population (Stalans et al. 2004). I will always perceive my first experience with offender manipulation and intimidation as inextricably related to my gender. I was the newest officer to join the sex offender unit. I was taking over the caseload from another female probation officer who was voluntarily transferring out of the unit to work in another capacity. Prior to her departure, she told the offenders my name (hence, revealing my gender) so they would know whom to contact in the event of an emergency. My first meeting with Sal made for a memorable first day on the job.[6] He was on probation for a conviction of aggravated sexual assault against a woman who lived in his apartment complex. Sal reported for his scheduled office appointment wearing unusually short cut-off denim pants. When he sat down in my office, it was readily apparent (which I concluded was exactly his intention) that he was not wearing any undergarments and that he was attempting to introduce me to more of himself than was even remotely appropriate. I managed to keep my composure while handling all of the business matters associated with our meeting, and concluded with a stern discussion of appropriate attire, probation officer–client boundaries, and the legal consequences if there were to be any further indiscretions. All of this transpired while never breaking eye contact with Sal. I was pleased that this was the first and last problem I had with this individual. A couple of years later (and following many additional months in therapy), he was successfully discharged from our program. I am left to speculate as to exactly what Sal hoped to accomplish this day, but the most likely scenarios have some relevance to my gender. Would he have dressed this way if his new officer was named Michael instead of Michelle? I sincerely doubt it.

My frequent meetings with offenders' clinicians, an integral component of the containment approach to supervising sex offenders in the community, provided not only insight into my clients' therapeutic performance but also their formal and informal statements about me, their supervising officer. Many times these sentiments, as shared between probationers as they gathered for their weekly group treatment sessions, were appropriate and related to my probation officer "style"—comments such as "she's tough but she cares about how you are doing." Other times, however, they were directed at my gender or appearance. "Oh, you got her as your officer? She tries too hard to be tough and act like she's a guy or something" or "The way she looks at me I think she's hot for me" or other unacceptable statements about my physique or targeted (female) body parts.

The therapists were quick to redirect these latter comments from probationers and use them as learning points or examples of appropriate and inappropriate statements, as evidence of their ability to make good decisions, as examples of mature or immature behavior and respect (or lack there of) of women, whether or not they were authority figures. These statements or conversations were shared with us as an indication of the offender's infancy in understanding the more complex issues of how to interact responsibly and respectfully with others (especially women) or as a warning to be especially careful with a particular offender. For instance, if he had mentioned a particular probation officer in a sexual context, in front of others no less, perhaps a one-on-one home visit is not the most prudent decision. Fortunately, over the course of several years, there were only a handful of occasions when gender-related safety concerns forced me to change my supervision style.

There are certainly other "war stories" that I could share about my tenure as a female probation officer working with sexually violent men, but for the most part, I found that establishing boundaries and expectations early on and interacting professionally and respectfully with offenders created a working environment that felt safe for me. It is my greatest hope that the intervention, supervision, and therapeutic resources provided by this unit, or other specialized sexual offender units, help make women and children safer by preventing these men from reoffending. I will always reflect on my years as a probation officer as encompassing some of the most valuable experiences of my professional life. I often tell my students who are struggling with decisions about what to do with their criminal justice degree to consider a career in probation. The job is demanding, operates at a hurried pace, is often undervalued and misunderstood by the public and, at times, even by other criminal justice professionals. But ultimately, it can be very rewarding.

Discussion Questions

1. Who is credited with being the first probation officer?
2. What is the most common criminal sanction given to convicted offenders?
3. What are the two primary goals and theoretical foundations of probation?
4. Discuss women's entrance into the probation profession and other criminal justice occupations and why women would be attracted to these traditionally male occupations.
5. Why might the public be hesitant to embrace the notion of convicted sex offenders being on probation or parole?

Notes

1. Currently, the House of Representatives and the United States Senate are considering federal versions of these sex offender bills.

2. However, probation still is far less costly than incarceration.

3. For additional information, visit http://www.csom.org.

4. Readers should be mindful that these figures are likely to be an underestimation of the true extent of sexual reoffending. Most studies use official data sources (arrest and reconvictions) to compile failure rates, and sex crimes are believed to be significantly underreported by victims, so there are undoubtedly sex crimes committed by these offenders that go undetected by law enforcement or probation officers.

5. I once had a sex offender probationer who was offered a second job, which he sought ostensibly to pay off his court and restitution fees, at a national toy store franchise. Even though the individual's victim had been an adult, not a child, this employment was not permitted.

6. To preserve confidentiality, offender names or other identifying information are not revealed, and pseudonyms are used. Although the descriptions are personal recollections of actual events, the names have been changed.

References

Abadinsky, H. 1991. *Probation and parole: Theory and practice.* Englewood Cliffs, N.J.: Prentice Hall.

Belknap, J. 2001. *The invisible women: Gender, crime and justice.* Belmont, Calif.: Wadsworth.

Berliner, L., D. Schram, L. Miller, and C. Milloy. 1995. A sentencing alternative for sex offenders: A study of decision making and recidivism. *Journal of Interpersonal Violence* 10:487–502.

Bureau of Justice Statistics. 2005. *Criminal Victimization, 2004.* Washington, D.C.: U.S. Department of Justice.

Center for Sex Offender Management. 2000. *The collaborative approach to sex offender management.* Available at http://www.csom.org/pubs/collaboration.html. Accessed on June 26, 2006.

———. 2002a. *Managing sex offenders in the community: A handbook to guide policymakers and practitioners through a planning and implementation process.* Available at http://www.csom.org/pubs/managehandbook.pdf. Accessed on June 26, 2006.

———. 2002b. *An overview of sex offender management.* Available at http://www.csom .org/pubs/csom_bro.pdf. Accessed on June 27, 2006.

Dressler, D. 1962. *Practice and theory of probation and parole.* New York: Columbia University Press.

Ellsworth, T. 1990. Identifying the actual and preferred goals of adult probation. *Federal Probation* 54:10–15.

English, K., S. Pullen, L. Jones, and J. Murphy. 1996. *Managing adult sex offenders: A containment approach.* Lexington, Ky.: American Probation and Parole Association.

Glaze, L., and S. Palla. 2005. *Probation and parole in the United States, 2004.* Washington, D.C.: U.S. Department of Justice.

Goldhart, J., and A. Macedonia. 1992. Organizing in Ohio: Community corrections workers form alliance to promote women's professional development. *Corrections Today* (August): 96–100.

Greenfeld, L. 1997. Sex offenses and offenders: An analysis of data on rape and sexual assault. Washington, D.C.: U.S. Department of Justice, Bureau of Justice Statistics.

Hunter, S. M. 1992. Women in corrections: A look at the road ahead. *Corrections Today* (August): 8–9.

Lane Council of Governments. 2003. *Managing sex offenders in the community: A national overview.* Washington, D.C.: U.S. Department of Justice, Office of Justice Programs.

Langan, P., and M. A. Cunniff. 1992. *Recidivism of felons on probation, 1986–1989.* Washington, D.C.: U.S. Department of Justice.

Langan, P., and D. Levin. 2002. *Recidivism of prisoners released in 1994.* Washington, D.C.: U.S. Department of Justice.

Langan, P., E. Schmitt, and M. Durose. 2003. *Recidivism of sex offenders released from prison in 1994.* Washington, D.C.: U.S. Department of Justice.

Lurgio, A., M. Jones, and B. E. Smith. 1995. Up to speed—child sexual abuse: Its causes, consequences, and implications for probation practice. *Federal Probation* 59:69–76.

MacKenzie, D., and C. Souryal. 1997. Probationer compliance with conditions of supervision. In *Correctional contexts,* edited by James Marquart and Jonathan Sorenson, 352–59. Los Angeles: Roxbury Publishing.

McAnany, P., D. Thomson, and D. Fogel. 1984. *Probation and justice: Reconsideration mission.* Cambridge, Mass.: Oelgeschlager, Gunn and Hain.

McGrath, R., S. Hoke, and J. E. Vojtisek. 1998. Cognitive-behavioral treatment for sex offenders: A treatment comparison and long-term follow-up study. *Criminal Justice and Behavior* 25:203–25.

McShane, M., and W. Krause. 1993. *Community corrections.* New York: Macmillan.

Martin, S., and N. Jurik. 1996. *Doing justice, doing gender: Women in law and criminal justice occupations.* Thousand Oaks, Calif.: Sage.

Meloy, M. 2005. The sex offender next door: An analysis of recidivism, risk factors, and deterrence of sex offenders on probation. *Criminal Justice Policy Review* 16:211–36.

———. 2006. *Sex offenses and the men who commit them: An assessment of sex offenders on probation.* Boston: Northeastern University Press.

O'Leary, V. 1987. Probation: A system in change. *Federal Probation* 51:8–11.

Petersilia, J. 1998a. *Community corrections: Probation, parole, and intermediate sanctions.* New York: Oxford University Press.

———. 1998b. Probation in the United States. *Perspectives* (Spring): 30–41.

Rothman, D. 1980. *Conscience and convenience: The asylum and its alternatives in progressive America.* Boston: Little, Brown.

————. 1983. Sentencing reforms in historical perspective. *Crime and Delinquency,* 29:631–47.

Schoonmaker, M., and J. Brooks. 1975. Women in probation and parole, 1974. *Crime and Delinquency,* 21:109–15.

Stalans, L. 2004. Adult sex offenders on community supervision: A review of recent strategies and treatment. *Criminal Justice and Behavior* 31:564–608.

Stalans , L., R. Juergens, M. Seng, and T. Lavery. 2004. Probation officers' and judges' discretionary sanctioning decisions about sex offenders: Differences between specialized and standard probation units. *Criminal Justice Review,* 29:23–45.

Stalans, L., M. Seng., and P. R. Yarnold. 2002. *Long-term impact evaluation of specialized sex offender probation programs in Lake, DuPage, and Winnebago Counties.* Chicago: Illinois Criminal Justice Information Authority.

Terry, K. 2006. *Sexual offenses and offenders.* Belmont, Calif.: Thomson-Wadsworth.

Chapter 10   Susan L. Miller, Kay B. Forest,
                                              and Nancy C. Jurik

Diversity in Blue

Lesbian and Gay Police Officers in a

Masculine Occupation

The struggle for social acceptance and equal rights for lesbian and gay Americans has been a long one. Recent battles over laws that would specifically prohibit hate crimes, the legality of same-sex marriages, the adoption and custody of children by gay and lesbian couples, and a wide range of state-level antigay and antilesbian initiatives have garnered massive public attention. The widely publicized debate over gays in the military also aroused intense sentiments both supportive of and opposed to the expansion of the rights for gays and lesbians in the workplace. Despite controversy and numerous setbacks, lesbians and gay men are now more visible to mainstream Americans, have "out" political leadership, and forcefully challenge old barriers (*Harvard Law Review* 1990; Marcus 1992).[1]

Social institutions have varied immensely in their acceptance of gays and lesbians. The criminal justice system is still dominated by a white, masculine, and heterosexual ethos (Messerschmidt 1993). As threats to dominant groups, people of color and/or women seeking police positions faced tremendous obstacles (Martin and Jurik 1996). Racist (Christopher et al. 1991; Leinen 1984) and sexist (Martin 1980, 1990; Pike 1991) attitudes and behavior remain a problem in many departments.[2] Employment of lesbians and gay males as police officers is especially threatening to an occupation that values "traditional masculinity and middle-class morality" (Shilts 1980).

This chapter explores how gay and lesbian police officers construct their identities within a traditionally masculine, heterosexually dominated police organizational environment. Through this exploratory study, we hope to generate hypotheses and theories that will be useful in future research efforts. In the first section, we discuss our conceptual framework, which posits the social construction of identities along gender, sexual orientation, and race, ethnic-ethnic lines. This "doing" of identity occurs within specific organizational and societal contexts. Work environments such as policing are gendered, sexualized, and racialized. Such environments shape gay/lesbian officers' construction of identities and shape their strategies for confronting potentially hostile work environments.

After discussing our framework, we turn to an analysis of survey data from gay and lesbian police officers. Our data are drawn from a series of open-ended questions designed to address gay and lesbian officers' perceptions of (1) stereotypes surrounding gender identity and sexual orientation, (2) the working environment, and (3) their strategies for coping with workplace barriers. The survey also explored the ways in which multiple identities of race, ethnicity, gender, and other dimensions contribute to officers' choices of the "best" strategies for doing their jobs and surviving a hostile organizational milieu.

The Social Construction of Gender and Sexuality in Work Organizations

We conceptualize gender and sexuality to be integrally connected parts of human identity. Along the lines of Candace West and Don Zimmerman (1987) and others (e.g., Connell 1987; Lorber and Farrell 1991; West and Fenstermaker 1993; Messerschmidt 1993; Martin & Jurik 1996), we view these identity components as ongoing social productions that emerge through social interaction. Moreover, individuals "do gender" and simultaneously "do sexuality" both with an awareness of dominant societal norms and in anticipation of the judgments of others (West and Zimmerman 1987, 127; West and Fenstermaker 1995; Omi and Winant 1994; Messerschmidt 1997). Thus, identities are elaborated in everyday social interactions framed by larger social structures (Giddens 1979, 1984).

Robert Connell writes that some images of gender—in particular, hegemonic masculinity and emphasized femininity—predominate over others. Hegemonic masculinity is most closely associated with the ideal mode of conduct for elite, white men in Western capitalist society. It is based on authority, aggressiveness, technical competence, and heterosexist desire for and domination over women (Connell 1993, 615). In contrast, emphasized femininity is defined by and subordinate to hegemonic masculinity. It is organized around themes of heterosexual receptivity to men, dependence, and motherhood; and is most readily associated with middle- and upper-class white women in Western societies. In this regard, predominant images of gender implicitly include other social dimensions, including race, ethnicity, class, sexuality, and physical ability/disability, to name a few.

Together gender, sexual orientation, and other dimensions of social difference serve as organizing features of work organizations (Britton 1997; Connell

1987; Martin and Jurik 1996). As such, work organizations are sites of the social production of difference. Joan Acker (1990) argues that organizational policies and interactions control, segregate, exclude, and construct hierarchies of workers. Qualifications for particular jobs are infused with conscious and unconscious images of the appropriate gender, race, ethnicity, class, and sexual orientation of the "winning" applicant. Individuals who deviate from the prescribed social type for their job and/or organization may confront formidable barriers to successful work performance. Rosabeth Moss Kanter identifies several such structural barriers.[3] Socially deviant workers are more visible than those of the dominant social type. Their performance is subject to intense scrutiny, and they must excel to be deemed competent. Members of the dominant social group may exclude deviant types, remind them of their difference, or stereotype them (Kanter 1977). Organizational practices and policies also may restrict the work assignments and organizational power allocated to deviant social types (Martin, 1980; Jurik 1985). Job expectations and performance evaluations often reflect the dominant social type; to succeed, deviant types must emulate the socially dominant category (Zimmer 1987).

Not surprisingly, norms of heterosexuality permeate most work organizations, especially those in the criminal justice system (Buhrke 1996; Cockburn, 1991; Messerschmidt 1993). Policing, in particular, "is defined culturally as an activity only 'masculine men' can accomplish" (Messerschmidt 1993, 175). This masculinity depends on the devaluation of all femininities as well as subordinated masculinities, including "gay masculinities" (Connell 1992). Historically, police work has been associated with images of working-class masculinity that emphasize physical strength and aggressiveness. Thus, the dominant ideal of police masculinity typically deviates from modern hegemonic masculinity, which emphasizes managerial and technical dominance. This hegemonic ideal is most closely associated with the behavior of elite white men (Jurik and Martin 2001; Messerschmidt 1993).

Police Organizational Culture

Since the rise of American crimefighting in the 1930s, police departments have been white, working-class male enclaves (Appier 1992, 1998; Martin and Jurik 1996; Miller 1999; Schulz 1995). White women were also present in this early history. In fact, the early police matron's movement was initiated during the social reform era of the nineteenth century. Early policewomen were associated with social service and crime prevention models of policing (Appier 1992). Yet their duties focused on the traditional female roles of service, nurturing, and protecting morals and virtues; as such, they did not threaten male police officers' terrain (Miller 1999; Schulz 1995).

In contrast to the police matron, the ideal male police officer emerged in the early decades of the twentieth century as the tough, fearless crimefighter, "the fierce warrior-robot, devoid of emotions. . . . Police*men* relied on technology, expertise in marksmanship, and their courage to bring criminals to justice" (Appier 1992; Miller 1999, 83, emphasis in the original). Over time, policing recruitment and selection practices effectively excluded "outsiders." These included physical requirements (to exclude women), written tests or educational requirements (to exclude blacks), and "background investigations and personal interviews [that] further screen out candidates who failed to express the 'correct' attitudes toward the meaning of masculinity, including an aura of toughness and aggressiveness" (David and Brannon 1976, quoted in Martin 1992, 286).

The relegation of white women officers to peripheral reform activities continued until the 1970s. At this time the Johnson administration urged police departments to increase hiring of racial minority, female, and college-educated officers for patrol, vice, and investigative divisions (Miller 1999). In succeeding years a growing number of gay men and lesbians also entered the policing ranks (Meers 1998; Miller 1999). As of 1992, ten departments directly recruited gay and lesbian officers: Boston, Minneapolis, Madison, Seattle, Portland (Oregon), Atlanta, Philadelphia, San Francisco, Los Angeles, and New York City (Leinen 1993, 11). Chicago has also initiated efforts to recruit officers in gay and lesbian communities.

Policing Sexualities: Chilly Climate Control

In combination, both reform and resistance can be understood as tensions in the social production of difference within police organizational culture, especially the construction of subordinate masculinities and emphasized femininity. As the number of "outsiders" increased within policing, the stable production of hegemonic masculinity was challenged and triggered the hostility of many traditional white male officers (Hunt 1990). The hiring of men of color became one of the first challenges to the all-white male work organization. As a group, men of color, especially African Americans, are still likely to be suspected of criminal activity by the police; and they are highly likely to be arrested and prosecuted (Coleman and Cressey 1999). Thus, their arrival on the police force contradicted a long-held antagonism between the hegemonic crimefighter and the subordinated criminal. Not surprisingly, policemen of color have struggled against exclusion, harassment, and limited advancement (Alex 1969; Buhrke 1996). In addition, reform professionalization strategies also increased the number of more highly educated officers from middle-class backgrounds (Jurik and Martin, 2001), a practice that challenged the working-class dimension of police culture. On both counts, "outsiders" have now made inroads into police organizations.

When women were integrated into patrol jobs, the traditional association of police work with masculinity was further threatened (Hunt 1984, 1990; Martin 1992). Women's presence has been met with covert and overt hostility. Policemen try to create differences between them and women officers by emphasizing women's "femininity" (Messerschmidt 1993, 182). Yet women are not treated uniformly. For example, white male officers might attempt to shield white women from the dangers of the job, whereas black women may not be accorded such protections (Martin 1994). Suspected lesbians may also be treated with less protection and increased hostilities (*Feminist Daily News Wire* 2000c; Martin and Jurik 1996). As a result, lesbians may feel pressured to demonstrate their conformity to ideals of emphasized femininity in order to avoid animosity (Schneider 1988).

Gender and sexual identities are closely intertwined in their production. In particular, an emphasis on sexuality serves as a significant component of gender subordination: "Enforced heterosexuality has been identified as a primary mechanism for subordinating women at home and at work" (Cockburn 1991; Rich 1980, 633). In part, because police departments regulate heterosexuality in society, they exude exceptionally strong norms of compulsory heterosexuality. Women police officers may endure questions about (or charges regarding) their sexual orientation. For example, according to a 1998 study by the National Center for Women and Policing, 80 percent of women police officers have been sexually harassed at work, including explicit lesbian-baiting and lewd commentary by male colleagues (*Feminist Daily News Wire* 1999, 2000c). Still other "women [officers] have been threatened with death, falsely accused of crimes like child abuse and drug violations, and alienated from colleagues" (*Christian Science Monitor* 1999).

Masculinity is further traditionally conferred on male officers through the policing of gay men, especially because police often view hate crimes committed against homosexuals as "harmless pranks or as an acceptable form of behavior" (Berrill 1992, 31). Gay-bashing by police symbolically confirms a police officer's heterosexual status. Again, this gendered aspect of policing permits the police to "construct a white, heterosexual, hegemonic masculinity through the authorized practice of controlling 'deviant' behavior of 'inferior' men," practices that leave little room for the legitimization of other sexualities (Messerschmidt 1993, 184).

In fact, until recently, being an openly gay or lesbian officer meant dismissal from the job (Doss 1990). The daily reality of conventional policing, as part of both a gendered and a sexualized institution, entails homo*sociality*—"men generating a closeness between men" for informing, socializing, and mentoring (Britton 1990; Cockburn 1991, 189). Any suggestion of traditionally "feminine" traits, such as gentleness or sensitivity, encourages colleagues to brand men as "sissies" or "faggots" (Blumenfeld 1992). Thus questioning a worker's sexual orientation is a common tactic for devaluing the actions of men workers who fail to conform to popular macho models; those who favor police reforms, or who support the inclusion of women officers may be denigrated and labeled "homosexuals" by defensive male coworkers (Martin and Jurik 1996). Closeted, gay men may likewise feel pressure to engage in conversational banter with coworkers about heterosexual conquests to avoid being ostracized or labeled sexually suspect (Messerschmidt 1993; Messner 1992; Remmington 1981). Because racial subordination is intertwined with gender and sexual subordination, problems in the workplace associated with being gay or lesbian may be intensified for men and women of color (Buhrke 1996; Rosabal 1996).

Overall, homosexual police officers—regardless of the race, ethnicity, or gender—are subordinated by the production of hegemonic masculinity (Connell 1987; Messerschmidt 1993). In this regard, lesbian and gay officers face barriers similar to those confronting racial-ethnic minorities and white women in policing; yet there are important differences (Buhrke 1996; Leinen 1993). Research suggests that homosexuals are the social group most disliked by police (Burke 1993). Such beliefs persist despite empirical evidence that lesbians and gay men perform police work as well as heterosexuals (Hiatt and Hargrave 1994). It is also still legal to deny employment on the basis of sexual orientation in most jurisdictions.[4]

With twenty-four states still criminalizing consensual same-sex sexual acts, gay and lesbian officers also occupy the ironic position of having to enforce penal codes that they themselves violate (Doss 1990; Leinen 1993). The hiring of lesbian and gay officers suggests to some that the "immoral behavior" of practicing homosexuals is condoned.[5] As a result, lesbians, gay men, and their allies in criminal justice fear for their jobs and sometimes even their lives (Buhrke 1996).

Workplace Strategies and Resistance: "Out" and "Closeted"

Gay and lesbian officers' adjustment to police or any other work is complicated by the issue of whether or not they will hide their sexual orientation (Schneider 1986; Taylor and Raeburn 1995; Woods 1993). As indicated earlier, some "closeted" gay and lesbian workers attempt to "pass" as heterosexual on the job (Burke 1994; Leinen 1993). Others may "come out" and openly define themselves as homosexual to varying degrees (Woods 1993). In fact, over the past twenty-five years, changes in police organizations have created some opportunities for gay and lesbian officers to work in "out" statuses in police departments. Recently, the formation of gay and lesbian police associations has challenged the compulsory heterosexuality of police organizations and police treatment of the gay and lesbian communities (Buhrke 1996; Burke 1993). These ongoing changes, in turn, inform the perceptions and strategies of gay/lesbian officers working within the police organizational context (Britton 1995; Lamphere 1993).

The decision to be "out," as well as other workplace strategies, is shaped not only by an individual's social location (e.g., gender, race, ethnicity) but also by situational factors, such a time on the job (Rosabal 1996). Organizational and community climates of support or hostility for gay/lesbian rights also shape individual and collective strategies for constructing sexual identity (Bernstein 1997; Buhrke 1996). For example, fears about coworker and supervisor hostilities, termination, loss of promotional opportunity, or denial of backup lead some officers to hide their sexual orientation (Buhrke 1996; Burke 1993; Leinen 1993). Tensions between the police and lesbian-gay communities encourage some officers to hide their occupation from gay/lesbian friends and acquaintances (Burke 1993). In either case, hiding consumes energy, creates stress, and can erode job productivity (Powers 1996). And being "out" is not necessarily freedom from workplace stress but may encourage further self-consciousness and pressures to overachieve (Meyer, Forest, and Miller 2004).

The arguments surrounding the "explicit" inclusion of homosexuals on the police force are complex. Opponents of gay and lesbian officers claim that respect for police would decrease and that department morale would be harmed. They claim that heterosexual officers might not assist homosexual officers in danger, and that unwanted sexual attention from gay officers might be forced on nongays (DeMila 1978; Shilts 1980). Proponents of gay male and lesbian hiring argue that sexual orientation is unrelated to competent job performance. They propose that once gay and lesbian officers prove their abilities, they will be accepted by their peers—as were white women and racial-ethnic minorities (Martin 1992)—and that police forces should reflect the diversity of the community (DeMila 1978; Shilts 1980). Some argue that gay and lesbian officers promote improved relations between police and the homosexual community, even though after decades of gay bashing and repression by police, many in the homosexual community view gay and lesbian officers as traitors (Buhrke 1993, 1996).

In the absence of protective federal legislation, some courts have ruled in favor of gay/lesbian employment rights (Buhrke 1996, 20). Despite continuing organizational pressures, these changes have provided an opening for workers to resist the pressures of hegemonic police masculinity or emphasized femininity. Some workers may consciously or unconsciously construct masculinities or femininities that oppose dominant ideals such as openly opposing macho, tough guy styles of policing, or opposing men's protection of women officers. Others may conform to dominant ideals or develop identities that are more covertly oppositional.

It should be noted as well that traditional masculinist police culture is not without its costs. Between 1990 and 1999, for example, the City of Los Angeles paid out $63.4 million for lawsuits involving excessive force, sexual assault, and domestic violence by male police officers (*Feminist Daily News Wire* 2000b). National and international studies of police brutality show similar patterns (*Feminist Daily News Wire* 2000a). As more police departments explore the benefits of community policing models, the inclusion of gay and lesbian police officers may represent more than a human rights effort; these nontraditional police officers may bring a range of roles and skills that can enhance the flexibility of policework without sacrificing its crimefighting mission.

The Present Study: Gay and Lesbian Policing in a Midwestern City

In 1992, the new police superintendent of the Midwestern Police Department promised "zero-tolerance" for insensitivity to and discrimination against lesbian and gay police officers; he also actively recruited gay men and lesbians (Griffin 1992). Within this supportive environment and with the culmination of almost a year of informal planning, the only two "out" homosexuals on the Midwestern police force—joined by two "closeted" police officers—formed a gay and lesbian police officers' association. The association's goals are to provide support for other gay and lesbian police officers, to develop a recruiting program for "out" gay and lesbian officers, to educate heterosexual officers, to dispel the fears of members of the gay and lesbian community about police officers, and to improve police-community relations. Although all four founding members were from the Midwestern Police Department, membership in the Lesbian and Gay Police Alliance (LGPA) is open to law enforcement officers across the state. The formation of this coalition parallels the efforts of lesbians and gay men in other police departments and in other occupations (Buhrke 1996; Burke, 1993; Taylor and Raeburn 1995).

This research first examines how police organizational climates inform workplace perceptions and experiences of gay and lesbian officers. Second, it describes how gay and lesbian officers produce policing identities and how they perceive that their multiple identifies affect job performance. Third, it discusses different strategies or levels of being "out" and how these strategies affect officers' perceptions of inclusion and exclusion, including multiple identities of gender, race, and ethnicity.

Methods

Data Collection

This study uses a sample of gay and lesbian police officers ($N = 17$) working in a large midwestern city that has twelve thousand police officers. To make contact with gay and lesbian officers, we approached the cofounder and current codirector of the Lesbian and Gay Police Alliance (LGPA) in the Midwestern Police Department with our ideas. She agreed to assist us in distributing the survey to all law enforcement members of the LGPA (N = 25). She also "vouched" for our support, objectivity, and sensitivity, which may have played a part in generating such strong cooperation from the members. Although there are currently fifty members of the LGPA, only twenty-five are police officers from the Midwestern Police Department; the remainder are from suburbs, other cities and towns in the state, as well as a few members from other midwestern states. Thus, the sample was not randomly selected; individuals volunteered to participate. All data were gathered through survey questions rather than by direct observation. The in-depth nature of the questionnaire resulted in respondents' offering a vast amount of material that would not have been gained if the survey was close-ended. To fully capture the extent of gay and lesbian officers' perceptions, beliefs, and experiences, we designed a twenty-two-page questionnaire consisting of primarily open-ended questions. Questions addressed officers' perceptions about stereotypes surrounding gender identity and sexual orientation, officers' working environment, and officers' strategies for coping with workplace barriers.[6]

There was ample space for responses, and the respondents were encouraged to provide as much detail as they wished. We provided the home phone number of one of the authors in case a respondent felt reluctant about participation and needed reassurance. We also asked the respondents to provide their phone numbers if they felt comfortable being contacted by us for clarification purposes. Five respondents did include their numbers and were contacted by one of the authors to provide further information on topics that were unclear or incomplete.[7]

Respondents answered the questions with very lengthy discussions. We also maintained contact with the gay male and lesbian cofounders of the LGPA, and they served as cross-check verification on information. We received seventeen completed surveys, giving us a 68 percent completion rate from the Midwestern Police Department members of the LGPA. The sexual orientation of eight officers in our sample is known at work. In order to assure confidentiality, self-administered questionnaires and postage-paid return envelopes were used, with the guarantee of respondent anonymity.[8] Despite the small sample size, given the relative rarity of gay and lesbian officers *willing* to discuss their sexual orientation and careers, the data are invaluable in contributing to our understanding of gay and lesbian police officers. Although there is an inevitable bias presented by using self-report surveys with sensitive populations, even when open-ended questions are constructed, we made every effort to minimize bias by cross-validating information with our (gay) contact officers, and telephoning respondents to probe for additional information when we were able to do so. Because our sample includes officers who have varying "out" and "closeted" statuses, as well as varying racial and ethnic identities, we can be reasonably sure that their responses capture the gamut of possibilities among this population.[9] The 68 percent response rate is sufficiently robust, given the sensitive and hidden population (Renzetti 1992).

Sample

Nine lesbian officers completed the questionnaire. Seven are white and two are Latina, and their ages range from twenty-five to forty-two. Two are single, and seven are engaged in long-term live-in relationships with their partners. Eight women indicated that they had some college education, and one had received a B.A. Together, they have had between two and thirteen years of experience on the Midwestern police force, and all except one has served in the capacity of patrol officer.

Eight gay male police officers also completed the questionnaire. Three are white, one is black, three are Latino, and one is Asian. Their ages range from thirty to forty. Two officers are single, and the remaining six are in long-term, live-in relationships with their partners. Four officers completed some college, two have an Associate's degree, one graduated from a four-year college, and another has completed a master's degree and is continuing with additional postgraduate study. All together, they have between one and twenty-six years of experience on the police force, and all served in the capacity of patrol officers (although two have achieved a rank above patrol officer positions). We discuss the degrees to which officers' sexual orientation was known in the police department in the findings section.

Findings

In this section, we discuss our analysis of gay and lesbian officers' open-ended survey responses. Our discussion focuses on (1) respondents' orientation to the job, including their perceived reception and experiences within the police organizational culture; (2) how gay and lesbian officers produce policing identities; and (3) how different job strategies or levels of being "out" affect officers' perceptions of inclusion and exclusion, across multiple identities of gender, race, and ethnicity.

Experiencing the Police Organizational Culture

Policing is traditionally both gendered and sexualized. As such, police culture typically embraces symbols of aggressive masculinity, such as toughness and physical strength, which are reinforced by practices that also confirm an officer's heterosexual status (Blumenfeld 1992; Burke 1994; Messerschmidt 1993). The latter can include dominating behaviors toward women and various forms of gay-bashing, such as ridicule and overt harassment. Yet the more recent inclusion of "outsiders" within policing has challenged this hegemonic masculine solidarity and generated tensions between traditional police officers and those who represent reform efforts. The organizational reforms mandating zero-tolerance of discrimination in this particular department have provided an avenue for officers to more openly challenge and question hegemonic masculinity and its links to police work.

Our sample responses indicate that most gay and lesbian officers experience what Kanter (1977) refers to as the increased visibility of minorities in work organizations; they are constantly scrutinized by others around them. In addition, the socially dominant group—in this case, heterosexuals—may try to establish boundaries between themselves and gay/lesbian officers through techniques of exclusion or verbal reminders of difference and subordinating stereotypes about their social category.

Every officer in the sample indicated that he or she had heard or been the target of anti-gay or -lesbian jokes or derogatory slang, and that they had seen anti-gay graffiti or cartoons around the station house, particularly in the locker room or on bulletin boards. Most of the "out" officers said that they had been excluded from "the grapevine" gossip, and they had not been invited to informal social activities, parties, or events. One "out" gay male officer explained, "Sometimes I'm excluded from social circles because some co-workers are uncomfortable about me being gay or are afraid of saying the wrong thing around me. Sometimes they treat me like I am sick" (Wayne). "Closeted" officers described their concern about how their current friendships and working relationships would suffer if their coworkers found out they were gay: "Many of the guys I like at work are ardent followers of Rush Limbaugh and make anti-gay comments on an almost daily basis. I would be ostracized" (Cody). "Closeted" officers also seemed to feel pressured to conform to models of hegemonic masculinity: "On the surface, it appears that most of my colleagues are either married or think that they are a gift to women. Most of that (straight) pressure is very uncomfortable because if I don't join in I would be viewed with suspicion" (Tim).

To demonstrate conformity to the dominant police culture, many officers utilized boundary maintenance activities: "And, as you well know, everyone wants to be accepted and if making fun of gay people gets you accepted, then you make fun of them" (Kelly). The frequency of such activities suggests that social-cultural diversity of any sort is not easily tolerated in most police departments (Leinen 1993; Martin and Jurik 1996); as one of our respondents said, "Anytime someone is different in any way, police officers tend to ridicule them" (Rosa). However, two gay male officers seemed to believe that once individual gay or lesbian officers became known and respected, other officers might become more aware and show tolerance: "Most speak from fear or lack of information. They say the things they say to conform to the larger group. If most knew about me, I think they would change their thinking after some soul-searching" (Gene). In analyzing the stereotypes held by their straight coworkers, respondents linked the police organization context to larger societal patterns: "Their homophobia forms a framework which negatively affects how they view everything gays or lesbians do or say. However, that's true for society as a whole. Police officers are products of our society and reflect society's ignorances [sic] and prejudices" (Wayne).

Lesbian officers were asked if they thought it was harder to break into the male world of policing, or into the heterosexual world of policing. All of the respondents felt it was more difficult to break into the male world, particularly when there are still older men on the force who remember when most police were men. All of the lesbian officers' responses suggested that, as one officer put it, "the good ol' boys' network still runs smoothly" (Jen). Another commented, "I feel it is much harder to break into the male world of policing. I think a lot of men become police officers for some sort of macho trip. The fact that women can then do the same job is a slap in the face. Misogyny is alive and well in our culture and the police culture is no different" (Michelle). Some lesbian officers felt a common bond with heterosexual women in combating sexism on the force: "It is the male world that most females have a problem with, whether gay or straight. This job in particular invites a macho-man attitude. It is a fact that men receive more privileges and receive a higher rating for the same job. A female on this job must do twice as much to prove herself" (Kelly).

Barriers to promotional opportunities have been a frequent problem for social minority groups in policing. We asked our sample of gay and lesbian officers if they felt that promotions were made using the same criteria as promotions of heterosexual officers, or if there would be any difference in the process because of sexual orientation. There was considerable variation in officers' perception about promotional opportunities and the best strategy for obtaining them. In fact, the officers in the Midwestern Police Department recommended a variety of strategies across the lines of rank, seniority, and gay versus "out" status. Half of the officers believed that being "out" could have a direct and negative effect on promotions. As one officer put it, "The 'don't ask, don't tell' policy works if you are seeking rank" (Tim). Another gay male officer, Jake, said, "You have to be married or perceived as marriage-able to be promoted. They believe you can't be led by a fag."

In contrast, about one-third of the officers believed that advancement opportunities might be enhanced for gay and lesbian officers in certain contexts, although they disagreed on the exact nature of the context in which opportunities were enhanced: "Advancement chances may be better because "out" gay/lesbian officers will be more visible and probably move up faster, so the Superintendent can say, 'look, I've promoted gays/lesbians' for visibility" (Annie). One gay male officer (Michael) said, "It may actually be better since I'm the only "out" gay in my district and I understand people are 'afraid' of me because I *am* out and do my job well. So, politically, for the department, promoting me may 'look good.'" Several respondents indicated that advancement opportunities would compare similarly with heterosexuals *only* if an officer was publicly known to be gay or lesbian, because then the department might face public pressure from the gay and lesbian community if the gay officer was not promoted simply because of her or his sexual orientation. However, the pattern that emerged from the responses suggests that the officers who believed that advancement chances were similar for gays and straights were primarily officers who had fewer years of experience as police officers, were assigned to desk duties, were *not* "out" to their coworkers, or had the longest amount of time on the force before coming "out." Thus this perception may be based on ignorance or lack of experience.

In their assessments of workplace interactions, these officers point to the ways that the relationships between hegemonic and subordinate masculinities are maintained within police culture. Widespread ridicule of "others" is used to solidify power relations among dominant heterosexual males (Kaufman 1998). In this context, being a "closeted" gay officer thus becomes the most subordinate masculinity, silenced by the threat implicit in homophobic humor and exclusion by the collective masculinity (Connell 1998). Paradoxically "out" gay and lesbian officers may have increased power owing to shifts in organizational hiring priorities; however, our data suggest that this "power" is relative and based more on speculation than reality. Also noteworthy is the fact that *all* of the lesbian officers saw the male world, and not compulsory heterosexuality as the greater barrier to advancement.

Overall, many of these lesbian and gay officers believed that their socially deviant statuses influenced assessments of their policing skills held by other officers. Such influence could work either negatively or positively for the gay or lesbian officer. Literature assessing the performance of "minority" social groups in the workplace consistently uses the performance of those in the majority social group as a baseline of comparison for new entrants (Zimmer 1987). The following section, however, reveals the extent to which there were considerable variations among gay and among lesbian officers in constructing their policing identities.

Performance Strengths and Pressures: Producing Policing Identities

Within our sample, officer sexual orientation and gender were closely intertwined salient features of the social construction of policing identities. Reflecting arguments made by Patricia Hill Collins (1991), who critiques *either/or* dichotomous thinking and calls for a *both/and* approach, officers in our sample viewed themselves and their job performance as both similar to and different from heterosexual officers. For some, these differences include unique abilities derived from the hard lessons of social marginalization.

Because not all of our sample was "out" on the job, the visibility issue is not the same as those connected with race, ethnicity, and gender minority statuses. In cases of "closeted" officers, visibility concerns have more to do with fear of coworker suspicions regarding their sexual orientation. Sexual suspicions are pervasive in police work, especially for women officers of any sexual orientation (Martin 1980). "If a female works with a female, then the other police officers may think they're both gay" (Kelly).

Lesbian officers reported that sexism as well as homophobia created barriers to their success in policing. They heard heterosexual officers make statements about the problems a lesbian officer might face when searching female suspects, including accusations of sexual harassment if the citizens were cognizant of the officer's lesbian identity. A few lesbian officers felt that, despite the sexism they must combat on the force, they could more easily gain acceptance as "out" lesbians than could "out" gay men. As Rosa, a "closeted" woman officer summarized, "the guys already assume you're gay if you are a woman who wants to be a police officer, so you should just focus on being the best officer you can be." Another lesbian officer said, "I know male cops who work with me willingly but [who] quite honestly state that if I was a gay man, they couldn't work with me. It still comes down to straight men being terrified of gay men" (Michelle). Two "out" gay men officers disagreed. They felt that "out" gay men were more easily accepted by straight male officers than were "out" lesbian officers. As Jake, a fully "out" gay officer suggests, "There's still the male bond; my police partner and I both talk about our dates in the same way, even though he is straight."

In contrast, most gay male officers believed that once their sexual orientation was known, they had or would have much difficulty proving that they were sufficiently tough for the job. In other words, their masculinity was questioned. One officer said that if his sexual orientation was known, he would have to "work twice as hard to be considered half as good" (Gene). Another officer explained that he had established his reputation as a tough cop before he revealed that he was gay. He said that stereotypes of effeminate gay men would negatively influence other officers' assessments of his policing abilities if the first piece of information they had about him was that he was gay. Still another officer argued that all officers, regardless of gender and sexual orientation had to establish "masculinity" on the job: "Not necessarily harder, but certainly necessary to prove [masculinity] nonetheless . . . but this may be true for *any* new cop, gay or straight, male or female" (Michael).

Thus, "proving masculinity" was a recurrent theme in our responses. Respondents perceived that there was little room for alternative or oppositional forms of masculinity. Yet one man, Jake, who conformed to some key aspects of hegemonic masculinity, felt that he had little problem in this regard: "I am quite big, athletic, and it is known that I will take no shit and can physically back that up." It may be that Jake's conformity to some dimensions of police hegemonic masculinity (i.e., his sheer size, physical strength, and aggressive qualities) offers some shield against challenges to his masculinity.

Despite concerns about gender and sexual identities on the job, the lesbian and gay officers in our sample believed that they were highly effective on the job; they also felt that they brought unique abilities to policing. In related research, studies on the integration of men of color and women into police work find that they perform similarly to, and as well as, white male officers (Alex 1969; Morash and Greene 1986). Some researchers argue further that, by virtue of their marginal or oppressed status in society, the pool of new entrants bring "special" talents and insights to police work that will improve services to victims and offenders, and promote better police-community relations (Alex 1969; Crites 1973).

Our respondents were asked whether they believe gay and lesbian officers use any different methods to accomplish policing goals (such as crime fighting, crime prevention and deterrence, maintaining order, and providing public safety and service). They emphasized that all police officers—regardless of sexual orientation—are taught the same methods at the academy; these methods are subsequently reinforced on street patrol. There was no disagreement about general policing goals. This uniformity in responses is consistent with the loyalty to the police occupation and subculture that so typically characterizes police officers (Skolnick 1994).

Yet greater visibility and boundary maintenance may also stimulate a heightened performance pressure to "prove" that gay and lesbian officers (the social minority) can do the job as well as social dominants—in this case, heterosexuals. Many officers described themselves as perfectionists or overachievers, stating that they worked harder on the job so that their performance would be above scrutiny, or so their effectiveness would not be challenged if their sexual orientation were to become known. "The gay cops I know are mostly more dedicated to the job. I think it's because they have to be above criticism" (Cody). "I think in a way [they are] even more effective because they are always aware of themselves. They don't tend to take things for granted. Always trying to do better so that their sexuality doesn't interfere with their performance as a police officer" (Kelly).

Although the above performance assessments represent the officers' own perception, all of the lesbian officers and seven of the eight gay male officers in our sample reported that they have received rewards, honors, or special recognition for their work in policing. Two officers (one male and one female) were valedictorians of their police academy classes. According to our contact on the force, it is fairly common for officers to receive Honorable Mentions (reflecting solid, good police work in making burglary or robbery arrests, for example), and Letters of Commendation. The officers in our sample, however, received more infrequently awarded honors, such as the Outstanding Community Service Award, various commendations for taking actions beyond the call of duty, Life Saving Award, and the Class Commander in Academy (meaning that the officers achieved the highest academic standing in their group). Such information lends additional credence to their overall performance assessments. It is not clear, however, that work performance strengths translate into formal work rewards, particularly for "out" gay males and lesbians (see Croteau and Lark 1995; Levine and Leonard 1984).

More explicit differences were raised when the gay and lesbian officers were asked if they bring any unique abilities, skills, and life experiences to the job of policing. Their perceptions of differences covered two categories: dealing with the general citizenry, and dealing specifically with gay and lesbian citizens. "I believe if gay or lesbian officers have a political consciousness and understand the dynamics of homophobia and bigotry, they can bring a certain sensitivity and patience to the job" (Michelle). "Being a 'minority' [*sic*] you see both sides of the coin. And if you work in the gay community, citizens will explain more to you than they would to a straight cop" (Jake).

Three of the officers in our sample were members of citizen-police liaisons within the gay and lesbian community, including groups focused on hate/bias-crime reporting, prior to joining the police force. In dealings with the general public, respondents believed that their own experiences of marginalization provide them with increased sensitivity and tolerance. They believed that, relative to most heterosexual officers, they were better able to transcend strict gender role dichotomies and to meet the needs of a diverse citizenry more effectively. "I believe that knowing how a society can push you aside and not care about you helps especially when dealing with lower income families and minorities, in general" (Jen). "As an 'out' gay cop I know first-hand the feeling of being oppressed and victimized. Not only will I do the job well, but it will be done compassionately (within reasonable limits). . . . I think by virtue of my personality and gayness I bring more efficacy to public relations as 'a cop who cares'" (Michael). As several gay male officers stated, "gay people who have come to terms with being gay are survivors—we have had to struggle against the norms and are stronger, more independent people because of it" (Wayne), and "We bring a rich life experience different in a host of ways from straight folks that enable us to deal with the public in our own unique way" (Charlie).

Even as lesbian and gay officers bring unique strengths to policing, they may also have to adjust their workplace behaviors to compensate for homophobic tensions and a persistent degree of exclusion by heterosexual coworkers (Powers 1996). We asked our respondents if their sexual orientation inhibits their job performance. Noting that heterosexual officers also made statements that suggest the danger of both lesbian and gay officers being around children, one lesbian officer remarked, "Heterosexual people are of the opinion that gay people are sick, loose, and have no morals (even though most pedophiles are heterosexual)" (Kelly). Gay male police officers echoed some of these concerns: "I'm cautious about being alone with kids for fear of misconduct accusations by malicious co-workers" (Jake). And as Michael says, "Fear of contracting AIDS is very real in the police community and gay officers are sometimes treated as though we're all plague carriers."

Officers utilized a variety of strategies for survival in the police organization. The opportunities and selection of these alternatives are often intertwined with rank, seniority, gender, and racial-ethnic dimensions of policing identities. Organizational and community climates also serve to shape differing opportunities for, and choices of, strategies in doing policework. Perhaps the greatest variations can be seen in the constructions of "out" versus "closeted" identities. In the following section, the constraints of police hegemonic masculinity on the expression of alternative sexualities become most evident.

Survival Strategies and Resistance

The choice of "out" or "closeted" status in the department is not a mutually exclusive dichotomy. Being "closeted" or "out" is more of a continuum of openness with considerable variability from one individual to the next. All of the lesbian officers in our sample said that their sexual orientation was known to other gay or lesbian officers, but that they were more protective of this information with heterosexual officers on the force. Two lesbian officers indicated that their sexual orientation has been complete public information on the police force since the beginning of their careers (at the training academy). Three other officers indicated that their sexual orientation is known to only some people for the past two or three years; these are also the three women who have served the longest as police officers, spending at least half of their careers closeted. It may be that they already had established their reputations as competent officers prior to coming "out" as lesbians. For the remaining four officers, two have not come "out," but believe some coworkers are beginning to suspect (one of these officers indicated that she would like to come "out," but does not want to implicate her lover, who is a very "closeted" police officer not in our sample). The other two officers are only "out" to their police patrol partners.

Interesting racial-ethnic differences are also present. The two women of color in our lesbian sample are the most "closeted" to other members of the force, yet they did disclose their sexual orientation to their police partners, who are also women of color and/or lesbian. These officers' reticence to disclose their sexual orientation to any other officer may reflect their triple-minority status on the force: Latina, woman, and lesbian (Rosabal 1996). These multiple disadvantaged statuses may also help explain why the lesbian officers were able to disclose to their police partners, who also had marginalized statuses in the department and therefore might be seen as more trustworthy than the dominant members of the force.

Similar to the lesbian officers, all the gay males acknowledged that their sexual orientation is known to a few other gay or lesbian officers, but it is not necessarily common knowledge in the department at large. In fact, only four of the eight officers indicated their sexual orientation is widely or completely known at work. One of the officers came "out" on his résumé when he applied for the job; one of the other gay officers came "out" after eleven years; another came "out" the first year of his career; and another has been "out" for several years after serving on the force for nine years as a married heterosexual officer.

Again, interesting racial differences emerge. All of the white gay men are completely "out" at work, while four of the five men of color are closeted. The only gay man of color whose sexual orientation is public knowledge was also married to a female police officer for many of his early years on the force (and they had children together). These patterns appear to illustrate the hegemonic protections of race and gender. For those who retain protection in either racial status (i.e., white) or former and *demonstrated* heterosexuality, sexual orientation may be less dangerous to acceptance in police culture.

We asked all gay and lesbian officers who were *not* "out" to other officers to discuss the risks that surround disclosure of sexual orientation and describe the current climate or working environment (with regard to sexual orientation) they experience. Overwhelmingly, the "closeted" officers stated that the biggest fears that prevent them from coming "out" involve safety and trust issues. Safety issues included the possibilities of being physically or verbally abused, as well as fear that backup would be slow. Half of the officers agreed with Ryan that "you could get killed because [of] lack of back-up if the other officers knew of your sexual orientation." Trust issues included the reactions of coworkers, who would withdraw support and friendship, and the fear that their moral authority in the eyes of the community would diminish. As one fully "closeted" gay male stated, ". . . the weight of any judgment calls or discretionary decisions I made would be diminished by people who disagreed because they would think: 'He's just a fag'" (Cody). Another commented, "The guys would treat me differently, especially in the locker room. My current friendships would be detrimentally affected because friends would feel pressure to conform to other officers who have a problem with gays" (Gene).

The psychological costs of a "false front" are extraordinarily high in a job that is already very stressful (Goffman 1963; Powers 1996). These costs include the belief that "if police officers think they've discovered a secret someone is trying to hide, they can be very cruel—they perceive it as a weakness if you're trying to hide it" (Michelle). All of the closeted officers described the stress of hiding part of their identity and of hiding their significant relationships. The "closeted" lesbian officers were especially fearful of losing the respect of coworkers once their sexual orientation became known, particularly if the coworkers felt that the "closeted" officers had lied to them (see Rosabal 1996). Respondents envied the heterosexual officers who never experienced the burden of having to pretend their private lives did not exist or had no impact on their public lives. Yet the risks of social and professional ostracism seemed too high.

In spite of these fears of revelation, however, the benefits reported by "out" officers, as well as the benefits of being "out" projected by "closeted" officers are many: "I am able to talk about my personal life openly" (Paula). "I can be myself" (Jen). As has been found in other research (Burke 1993; Leinen 1993), "out" respondents were pleased to reduce the disjuncture between their work selves and private selves: "I could stop bringing a 'fake date'—like my cousin—to work-sponsored dinners, dances, or parties. . . . The further you advance, the more separate you become unless you have a partner of the opposite sex and therefore 'fit in' with the brass" (Lisa). "Freedom to be me. Freedom to talk about my social life, to flirt with guys I meet on the job—just like the straight men flirt with women, the chance to educate co-workers about what being gay is about" (Wayne). "I can talk about my lover. I am no longer invisible. I can receive and make phone calls. I can share my life as they [straights] do" (Ben). Being "out" was also believed to reduce work-related stress: "You can relax; you are not always worrying about saying something that would give you away as a lesbian" (Annie). "Being 'out' would let me relax and stop hiding who I am. When the subject of significant others comes up, I'm tired of referring to 'he' instead of 'she'" (Rosa).

Although research suggests that the motivations for coming "out" in recent years are often more personal than political (Taylor and Raeburn 1995), several respondents went beyond the personal advantages to discuss the political importance of coming "out" on their job:

"Benefits include helping other gays or lesbians (cops or citizens). I am looked up to for guidance" (Jake). "They called me to handle the victim of an anti-gay attack because they knew I was gay. That made my very short (so far) career worthwhile . . . and the victim called brass the following day to thank them for sending me" (Michael). Despite these advantages, the racial differences and varying seniority among more "out" versus "closeted" officers suggests the complexity surrounding the decision to come "out" of the closet.

Not surprisingly, there was some tension between "out" and "closeted" officers, particularly when identity ambivalence may encourage "closeted" officers to attempt to "normalize" behavior to reduce visibility (Burke 1994, 198).

The following response speaks clearly to the continuing pressures for some to reproduce hegemonic masculinity and emphasized femininity as a survival strategy: "The 'closeted' gay male officers try to act more macho and tougher and turn me off as a person. "Closeted" lesbians try to act more (hyper) feminine and it's very false looking. These stereotypical appearances hurt all gay officers and make it harder to come 'out'" (Annie).

Although difference in the construction of "out" and "closeted" identities may create tensions both within and among gay and lesbian officer groups, our respondents perceive that the lesbian and gay officer coalition and their department's zero-tolerance policy have improved the climate for them within the police force. These organizational-level changes provide gay and lesbian officers with additional avenues for confronting harassment and other workplace barriers. One-third of the officers indicated that, since the new police superintendent's appointment and his publicized "zero-tolerance" policy toward gay and lesbian discrimination, they believed their concerns would be taken more seriously by supervisors, even though homophobic attitudes might remain unchanged. If the climate continues to improve, more officers may feel comfortable with coming "out" to a greater degree.

Despite these perceived improvements, situational context and harassers' status within the department still shaped the decision to report or not to report an incident: "It depends on who was doing the harassing. . . . If it was an officer who already has a reputation for being a 'dog,' the other officers would probably be supportive of you. However, if the harasser was a well-liked officer, it could alienate other officers from you" (Michelle). The fear of retaliation also influences reporting decisions: "If you reported harassment from co-workers to supervisors, the harassment would stop but then you'd get no back up" (Ryan).

Discussion

In this chapter, using a sample of "out" and "closeted" gay and lesbian police officers, we explored officers' perceptions about how their sexual orientation affects their success in a hypermasculine subculture and occupation. Overall, our findings indicate that these officers sense patterns of social exclusion as well as overt sexist and antigay behavior within the police organization. At the same time, the data also support a profile of our respondents as loyal to the police profession, committed to many traditional police goals, and striving to be recognized as competent officers within the organization. Finally, these officers support a caring and humane approach to policing and see themselves as particularly qualified to work within marginalized communities because of their greater perceived ability to connect with citizens. Department policies of zero-tolerance for discrimination based on sexual orientation may have provided gay and lesbian officers with an organizational "space" from which to challenge the hegemonic link between heterosexism, masculinity, and effective police work.

Earlier research found that some women police officers deemphasized their femininity while employing stereotypic masculine traits such verbal and physical aggressiveness as way of gaining acceptance in a traditionally male occupation (Berg and Budnick 1986; Gross 1981). Some lesbians in our sample believed that they were able to "do gender" in the masculine tradition of policing without threatening heterosexual male officers to the extent that heterosexual women do (Burke 1994). Paradoxically their sexual orientation may offer a "waiver" from social pressures to enact emphasized femininity to reproduce traditional masculinist police culture. To avoid association with subordinate forms of masculinity, some gay male officers overemphasized their toughness and strength to facilitate acceptance into a profession that values and expects such "macho" attributes (Meyer, Forest, and Miller 2004). Relative to gay male accounts, lesbian officers' comments focused as much on their experience of gender-related as on sexual orientation–related barriers. *These experiences were conditioned by their degree of "outness."*

Gay and lesbian officers also described efforts to reshape their roles as police officers. This transformation includes a heightened sensitivity to the needs of those citizens who are most disenfranchised from society—and who often feel most alienated from police officers. Although observational data are needed to confirm these perceptual findings, these "subjective claims" are supported by officers' reports of informal and official departmental recognition for "going the extra step" and for being able to establish a more mutually respectful rapport with community members. Of course, our sample may not be representative of all gay and lesbian police officers. Moreover, too much emphasis on the heightened sensitivity and tolerance of gay and lesbian officers as a group can ignore the range of diversity of work orientation and other characteristics within groups of gay and lesbian officers. Such imagery may become just one more stereotype or essentializing discourse to restrict individual gay and lesbian officers' behavior. The limitations raised by survey data also tempers the generalizability of our findings.

Despite the barriers of homophobia and the accompanying visibility, boundary maintenance, and stereotyping that tempered full acceptance, the gay and lesbian officers in our sample struggled to balance job demands with sexual orientation. The data suggest that "being out" removes some of the pressure of having to participate in a compulsory heterosexualized department culture. Closeted officers appear to not feel as free, although being "out" appears to benefit lesbian more than gay officers. Moreover, self-imposed compensatory overachievement may further dilute the advantages of being open. In short, remaining "closeted" supports—however unintentionally—the social dominance of the traditional model of police masculinity, a construction that requires the silence of alternative sexualities to survive (Messerschmidt 1993).

Skin color privilege—being white—also shapes acceptance into the hegemonic traditions of the police world. White, heterosexual men are simply granted more legitimacy—and thus power—both within the departmental structure as evidenced by promotions to higher ranks (Martin 1994; Pike 1991) and by society at large (Messerschmidt 1993). For men of color whose homosexuality becomes known, this recognition might jeopardize their already tenuous alliances with the predominately white straight police force. Our data confirms this possibility: the "out" officers typically possess statuses that accord them legitimacy through other personal characteristics, such as skin color or gender privilege.

Several of the "out" gay and lesbian respondents in our study believed that their promotion opportunities were equal to or better than those of heterosexual officers. They attribute this possibility to the current political climate and leadership that is striving to embrace a more diverse police force. At the same time, these officers acknowledge that advancement is also linked to test performance. Yet if promotion of gay and lesbian officers is perceived to be tied to sexual orientation, not competence, this raises concerns that there may be a backlash against gay and lesbian officer progress. In related research on race, gender, and policing, Martin (1994, 388) found that white officers (particularly males) felt victimized by affirmative action programs if the promoted officers scored lower on exams, even when the exams are found to provide "advantages or disabilities in ways that are both gendered and racially biased."

Given the progress of gay and lesbian officers in the Midwestern Police Department and elsewhere around the country, it is important to assess continued efforts by administrators to ensure equal treatment and advancement opportunities for "out" officers. For example, Martin (1994, 388) contends that despite the visibility of recent affirmative action polices, the continuity of "old boy networks" and informal sponsorship across traditional white, heterosexual, male lines goes unnoticed.

Overall, our study reveals considerable diversity among lesbian and among gay male officers even given our small sample. Despite the variation across individuals of different gender, race, ethnicity, rank, seniority, and "out" versus "closeted" status, we also observe important, recurrent themes. Officers in our sample are loyal to many norms and goals of traditional policing subculture (such as crime fighting, crime prevention and deterrence, maintaining order, and providing public safety and service). Yet the majority of officers' responses also suggest that the inclusion of lesbians and gay men on the police force may bring new flexibility to the character of policing, particularly because their own experience in marginalized groups may facilitate greater ease in responding to the needs of other oppressed groups. At a time when improved community relations seems to be the direction of new policing policy (Alpert and Dunham

1986; Miller 1999), admirable qualities in officers are no longer aloofness and toughness, but qualities that express a more humane dimension (Jurik and Martin 2000; Manning 1984). As Bem (1974, see also 1993) argued two decades ago, rigid sex-role differentiation may have outlived its utility in a society in which human flexibility is increasingly associated with higher standards of psychological health, not to mention professional performance.

Although these findings are preliminary, given our small sample size, they indicate directions for future research. As Collins (1990) suggests, we need to look at a larger "matrix of domination," both within and across a variety of organizations, including intersections of race, gender, class, and sexual orientation. Martin (1994, 397) suggests that domination pervades "three levels at which people experience and resist it: the individual; the group or community; and social system." Following this guideline, future research could include these three dimensions. For instance, interviews with community members (both gay and straight) could explore if increased contact with gay and lesbian police officers decreases homophobia and intolerance as well as how gay and lesbian officers identify themselves as such to citizens.

Research could also address the process, and problems, of coming "out" in the course of one's career. It would also be important to explore the reasons why some gay and lesbian officers left the police force to determine if these factors are related to a homophobic environment, overt discrimination or even violence, or the emotional costs of maintaining a false front. This kind of research could also explore the resiliency of officers working with multiple identities and the strategies they use to negotiate and secure their position within the police subculture. Research could also analyze the correlations between stress and medical leave in "out" and "closeted" officers. In addition, gay men and lesbians are not the only individuals breaking out of gendered and sexualized social behaviors; further study could investigate other influences of a "modernized" policing approach, including the effects of greater contact with gay and lesbian colleagues on *heterosexual* officers (both patrol and supervisors).

Parallel research could explore the career and promotion paths of "closeted" and "out" officers vis-à-vis heterosexual officers to determine any difference in the amount of time it takes to attain higher positions, controlling for performance evaluations, rank and years on force, and so forth. It may be that as police departments grow more diverse, the promotion process will reflect a receptivity to "different" officers, following the "Good Cop Syndrome," as named by a chief inspector of the Metropolitan Police Force in England. This "syndrome" means that as long as "odd" individuals are seen as effective officers by others, they will be accepted and even respected (Burke 1993). A more policy-related suggestion is to encourage departments to place "out" officers with higher rank in training positions so that the newest recruits are cognizant of difference among respected leaders from their first exposure to the police environment in the training academy.

On the one hand, findings from this study suggest the potential benefit gained if lesbians and gays endeavor to be more "out" in order to create increased visibility for the heterogeneity of gays as a group, thus challenging stereotypes. On the other hand, given the current stigma, stereotypes, discrimination, and possible violent consequences of being "out," gays and lesbians may be understandably reluctant to put themselves in a vulnerable position. The personal costs, real and perceived, of being "out" may be too dear. Yet the consequence of silence can be far-reaching: "Each time homosexuals deny their sexual orientation they hurt themselves slightly, which has a cumulative effect on their energies and vitality" (Wells and Kline 1986, 192). Clearly, given the high levels of fear associated with crime and police officers' professional responsibilities, what should be most salient is the quality and effectiveness of one's policing, and not one's sexual orientation. In fact, the lesbian and gay police officers in this sample describe themselves as possessing the very qualities that increasing numbers of police departments are striving to establish as exemplary of first-rate officers to improve community-police relations. Being "out" can be very powerful and may interrupt the stronghold of hegemonic masculinity for *all* members of the police force through the contradiction of existing stereotypes by honest daily examples of the competency of gay and lesbian police officers. This visibility rests on the receptivity of a police subculture, however, that continues to embrace enduring images of tough, macho, hypermasculine officers.

Discussion Questions

1. What are the strategies that lesbian and gay police officers use to navigate their work environment?
2. How might occupational pressures escalate for gay and lesbian police officers of color?
3. What strengths do lesbian and gay officers bring to policing?
4. How do gay and lesbian officers challenge traditional perceptions of masculinity and femininity about police work?
5. What can be done to change the hostile work environment for "nontraditional" officers?

Acknowledgments

Reprinted with permission from *Men and Masculinities,* 2003 5(4): 355–385. We would like to thank Carol Walters and Rita Potter for their research assistance, a particular sergeant on the Midwestern Police Department for her boundless support, the members and friends of the Midwestern Lesbian and Gay Police Alliance for their participation in our research, David Luckenbill for his helpful comments, and the very insightful comments from *Men and Masculinities* reviewers.

Notes

1. The concept of "out" or "being out" means that the respondent has both personally acknowledged his or her own sexual orientation and that this status is known by others. "Closeted" refers to those respondents who identify themselves as lesbian or gay but do not disclose this status to others.

2. Diversity on the police force—though supported by some—is viewed as undesirable by many, and elusive by most: women constitute less than 10 percent of sworn police officers, and minority (primarily black) women make up 4 percent of all officers; minority women account for 16 percent of all minority personnel, whereas white women constitute only 7 percent of white police personnel (Martin 1995, 395).

3. We are aware of the criticisms of Kanter's structural theory of organizational disadvantage, in that she fails to recognize that dominant social groups such as white males are not disadvantaged when they occupy the position of proportional minority in organizations. The perceptual disadvantages that Kanter describes so well accrue differentially to societally oppressed groups such as women, persons of color, and gay and lesbian workers (Williams 1989; Zimmer 1988). Despite these problems, we find Kanter's discussion of perceptual barriers to be useful for describing the experiences of gay and lesbian police officers.

4. In their rejection of hiring gays and lesbians as police officers in 1979, the International Association of Chiefs of Police stated that ". . . every policeman should conduct his private life so that the public . . . regard(s) him as an example of stability, fidelity, and morality" (IACP 1979). Leinen (1993, 8) counters, "The inference, of course, is that gays are not stable, trustworthy, or morally principled."

5. Difficulties for gay and lesbian police officers also stem from police policy precedents. To encourage community support, police administrators must "establish and maintain high standards of professional and personal conduct for officers under their command," and one potential area for scrutiny is the "life style choices" of officers, including a range of behaviors from fitness, drug use, and financial status to sexual orientation or conduct (Doss 1990, 194–96). Sexual behavior that is criminal, such as sex on duty, sexual harassment, sexual assaults, sex with a suspect or prisoner, or any other similar behavior, would be illegal for any officer, regardless of sexual orientation. Although there has been some success in challenging regulations using rights such as privacy, due process of law, equal protection, and the freedom of association, the U.S. Supreme Court has not yet struck down as unconstitutional police department regulations stipulating "conduct unbecoming an officer" (Doss 1990). See also, Annotation, "Sexual Misconduct or Irregularity as Amounting to 'Conduct Unbecoming an Officer,' Justifying Officer's Demotion or Removal or Suspension From Duty," 9 A.L.R. 4th 614 (1981) and 9 A.L.R. 4th 41 (F. Supp. 1988). In 1986, the Supreme Court held in *Bowers*

v. Hardwick that homosexual behavior is not a constitutionally protected fundamental right and that homosexuals do not fall under a protected "suspect" class. Following the *Bowers* precedent, an Ohio court ruled that dismissal on the grounds of homosexuality was acceptable for military and law enforcement personnel (Doss 1990, 197). Subsequent court rulings have reinforced the assumption that a police officer's sexual orientation exerts a negative impact on the ability to perform effectively, the police department's morale, and the community reputation (Doss 1990). Suspensions, dismissals and other sanctions have also been imposed on officers who engaged in sexual impropriety (such as cohabitation, adultery, use of prostitutes), though no evidence was used to demonstrate that these activities—occurring off-duty—had any effect on officers' effectiveness or public service while on the job. As evidenced by the recent efforts to actively recruit lesbian and gay male officers, however, some departments have relaxed or changed policies deemed unrelated to job performance.

6. For our purposes for this chapter, the analysis focused on the following items on the survey: *work environment:* extent of homophobia in their working environment, experience of bias against the respondents, fear and consequences of being "out," strategies used to maximize inclusion into subculture, the link between sexism experienced by women on the force and sexuality, and the construction of masculinity among men and how that may be exacerbated for gay men; *performance:* strengths and unique abilities brought to the job, pressures, job skills, consequences of heightened visibility, perceptions of the promotion process and how "out" status may affect it; and *strategies of survival and resistance:* convergence of gender, race, ethnicity, and sexuality; decisions about who to be "out" to; risks related to disclosure; personal costs of false fronts; benefits of being "out"; and tensions between "out" and "closeted" officers.

7. The survey is available on request from the authors. The questions cover the following: *demographics:* relationship and family information, *general occupational facts:* work experience, years on force, trajectory of assignment and promotions, why did officer select this career, awards or honors received, special job duties—such as gangs, drugs, juveniles; *social support* network information across a range of issues: family, friends, children, and under what circumstance they came "out" to these people and their reactions (initial and current), and any consequences; *career experiences:* "out" status, anticipated problems, when did officer come "out" and the circumstances, responses, effects on others' assessments of officers' policing performance, benefits and risks of being "out"; *job-related:* examining gender v. sexuality—who is advantaged and disadvantaged and why, work expectations, comparison of opportunities between heterosexual and homosexual officers, consequences of being "out" in how other officers treat the respondents, homophobic environment, assignments avoided because of sexuality or reactions of others, how to validate reputation; *harassment:* experiences, actions taken, consequences of actions taken, community bias against gay officers and reactions, responding to stereotypes and ignorance; *differences and similarities:* comparison of uniqueness v. sameness between heterosexual officers and homosexual officers, perception of effectiveness; *social life:* inclusion and exclusion into informal police culture, other social aspects; *general:* examining masculinity construction and sexism and how they intersect, sexuality within police profession, supportive responses to them after coming "out."

8. Although the cofounders and "out" officers were willing to reveal their identities, we choose to use pseudonyms for all of the officers and their department so that potential homophobic backlash would not jeopardize their work environment.

9. Our race/ethnicity analysis is limited to exploring patterns in the data, given the small sample.

References

Acker, Joan. 1990. Hierarchies, jobs, bodies: A theory of gendered organizations. *Gender and Society* 4:139–58.

Alex, N. 1969. *Black in blue: A study of the Negro policeman.* New York: Appleton-Century-Crofts.

Alpert, Geoffrey P., and Roger G. Dunham. 1986. Community policing. *Journal of Police Science and Administration* 14:212–22.

Amott, Teresa L., and Julie A. Matthaei. 1991. R*ace, gender and work: A multicultural economic history of women in the United States.* Boston: South End Press.

Appier, J. 1992. Preventive justice: The campaign for women police, 1910–1940. *Women and Criminal Justice* 4:3–36.

———. 1998. *Police women: The sexual politics of law enforcement in the LAPD.* Philadelphia: Temple University Press.

Bem, Sandra L. 1974. The measurement of psychological androgyny. *Journal of Consulting and Clinical Psychology* 42(2):155–62.

———. 1993. *The lenses of gender: Transforming the debate on sexual inequality.* New Haven, Conn.: Yale University Press.

Berg, B., and K. Budnick. 1986. Defeminization of women in law enforcement: A new twist on the traditional police personality. *Journal of Police Science and Administration* 14:314–19.

Bernstein, Mary. 1997. Celebration and suppression: The strategic uses of identity by the lesbian and gay movement. *American Journal of Sociology* 103(3):531–65.

Berrill, Kevin T. 1992. Anti-gay violence and victimization in the United States: An overview. In *Hate crimes: Confronting violence against lesbians and gay men,* ed. Gregory Herek and Kevin Berrill, 19–45. Newbury Park, Calif.: Sage.

Blumenfeld, Warren J. 1992. *Homophobia: How we all pay the price.* Boston: Beacon Press.

Bowers v. Hardwick. 1986. 478 U.S. 186, 92 L.Ed. 2nd 140.

Britton, Dana M. 1990. Homophobia and Homosociality: An Analysis of Boundary Maintenance. *Sociological Quarterly.* 31(3):423–39.

———. 1995. "Don't Ask, Don't Tell, Don't Pursue": Military Policy and the Construction of Heterosexual Masculinity. *Journal of Homosexuality.* 30(1):1–21.

———. 1997. Gendered Organizational Logic: Policy and Practice in Men's and Women's Prisons. *Gender and Society* 11:796–818.

Buhrke, Robin A. 1996. *A matter of justice: Lesbians and gay men in law enforcement.* New York: Routledge.

Burke, Marc E. 1993. Coming out of the blue: British police officers talk about their lives "on the job" as lesbians, gays, and bisexuals. London: Cassell.

————. 1994. Homosexuality as deviance: The case of the gay police officer. *British Journal of Criminology* 34:192–203.

Christian Science Monitor. 1999. Women face "blue wall" of resistance, August 18 (Internet).

Christopher, Warren, J. A. Arguelles, R. Anderson, W. R. Barnes, L. F. Estrada, Mickey Kantor, R. M. Mosk, A. S. Ordin, J. B. Slaughter, and R. E. Tranquada. 1991. *Report of the independent commission of the Los Angeles Police Department.*

Cockburn, Cynthia. 1985. *Machinery of dominance: Women, men and technical know-how.* London: Pluto Press.

————. 1991. *In the way of women: Men's resistance to sex equality in organizations.* Ithaca, N.Y.: ILR Press.

Coleman, T. W., and D. R. Cressey. 1999. *Social Problems.* 7th ed. New York: Longman Publishers.

Collins, Patricia Hill. 1990. *Black feminist thought: Knowledge, consciousness and the politics of empowerment.* New York: Routledge.

Comstock, Gary D. 1991. The police as perpetrators of anti-gay/lesbian violence. In *Violence against lesbians and gay men,* ed. Gary D. Comstock, 152–62. New York: Columbia University Press.

Connell, Robert W. 1987. *Gender and power.* Stanford, Calif.: Stanford University Press.

————. 1992. *Gender and Power.* Palo Alto, Calif.: Stanford University Press.

————. 1993a. The big picture: Masculinities in recent history. *Theory and Society* 22:597–623.

————. 1993b. Masculinities and globalization. *Men and Masculinities* 1:3–23.

Crites, L. 1973. Women in law enforcement, *Management and Information Services,* 5.

Croteau, J. M., and J. S. Lark. 1995. On being lesbian, gay or bisexual in student affairs: A national survey of experiences on the job. *NASPA Journal* 32:189–97.

David, D. and R. Brannon. 1976. *The forty-nine percent majority: The male sex role.* Reading, Mass.: Addison/Wesley.

DeMila, S. 1978. Homosexuals as police officers? *New York Times.* February 10.

Doss, M. T., Jr. 1990. Police management: Sexual misconduct and the right to privacy. *Journal of Police Science and Administration* 17(3):194–204.

Feminist Daily News Wire. 1999. Purported male deputies reveal hostilities in online forum. April 8 (Internet).

————. 2000a. Scandal highlights need for gender-balanced force/*60 Minutes* reports police family violence scandal. February 29 (Internet).

————. 2000b. Gender differences in police brutality lawsuits: Men cost more. September 18 (Internet).

————. 2000c. Judge speaks out in case of harassed lesbian police officer. September 29 (Internet).

Giddens, Anthony. 1976. *New rules of sociological method.* London: Hutchinson.

————. 1979. *Central problems in social theory.* London: Macmillan.

————. 1984. *The constitution of society.* Cambridge: Polity Press.

Goffman, Erving. 1963. *Stigma: Notes on the management of spoiled identity*. New York: Simon and Schuster.

———. 1976. Gender display. *Studies in the Anthropology of Visual Communication* 3:69–77.

Griffin, J. L. 1992. Rodriguez says he won't allow police insensitivity toward gays. *Chicago Tribune*. May 21, sect. 2.

Gross, S. 1981. Socialization in law enforcement: The female police recruit. In *Final report*. Miami: Southeast Institute of Criminal Justice.

Harvard Law Review, ed. 1990. *Sexual orientation and the law*. Cambridge, Mass.: Harvard University Press.

Hiatt, D., and G. E. Hargrave. 1994. Psychological assessment of gay and lesbian law enforcement applicants. *Journal of Personality Assessment* 63:80–88.

Hunt, Jennifer. 1984. The development of rapport through negotiation of gender in field work among police. *Human Organization* 43:283–96.

———. 1990. The logic of sexism among police. *Women and Criminal Justice* 1:3–30.

Hurtado, Aileen. 1989. Relating to privilege: Seduction and rejection in the subordination of white women and women of color. *Signs: A Journal of Women in Culture and Society* 14:833–55.

IACP (International Association of Chiefs of Police). 1979. Gay police. *New Jersey Record*. August 12.

Jenness, Valerie. 1995. Social movement growth, domain expansion, and framing processes: The gay/lesbian movement and violence against gays and lesbians as a social problem. *Social Problems* 42:145–70.

Jones, D. C. Carlson, N. Bloys, and M. Wood. 1990. Sex roles and friendship patterns. *Sex Roles* 23(3–4):133–45.

Jurik, Nancy. 1985. An officer and a lady: Organizational barriers to women working as correctional officers in men's prisons. *Social Problems* 32(4):375–88.

———. 1988. Striking a balance: Female correctional officers, gender role stereotypes, and male prisoners. *Sociological Inquiry* 58(3):291–304.

Jurik, Nancy C., and Susan E. Martin. 2001. Femininities, masculinities and organizational conflict: Women in policing and corrections occupations. In *Women, Crime, and Justice: Contemporary Perspectives*, ed. Lynne Goodstein and Claire Renzetti, 264–81. Los Angeles: Roxbury.

Kanter, Rosabeth Moss. 1977. *Men and women of the corporation*. New York: Basic Books.

Kaufman, Michael. 1998. The construction of masculinity and the triad of men's violence. In *Men's Lives*, ed. Michael S. Kimmel and Michael A. Messner, 4–16. 5th ed. Boston: Allyn and Bacon.

Lamphere, L., P. Zavella, R. Gonzales, and P. Evans. 1993. *Sunbelt working mothers: Reconciling family and factory*. Ithaca, N.Y.: Cornell University Press.

Leinen, Stephen. 1984. *Black police, white society*. New York: New York University Press.

———. 1993. *Gay cops*. New Brunswick, N.J.: Rutgers University Press.

Levine, M. P., and R. Leonard. 1984. Discrimination against lesbians in the work force. *Signs: A Journal of Women in Culture and Society* 9:700–710.

Lorber, J., and S. A. Farrell. 1991. Preface in *The social construction of gender*, edited by Judith Lorber and Susan A. Farrell, 1–5. London: Sage.

Manning, Peter K. 1984. Community-based policing. *American Journal of Police* 3:205–27.

Marcus, Eric. 1992. *Making history: The struggle for gay and lesbian equal rights, 1945–1990.* New York: Harper Collins.

Martin, Susan E. 1980. *Breaking and entering: Policewomen on patrol.* Berkeley: University of California Press.

———. 1990. *On the move: The status of women in policing.* Washington, D.C.: Police Foundation.

———. 1992. The changing status of women officers: Gender and power in police work. In *The changing roles of women in the criminal justice system: Offenders, victims, and professionals,* ed. Imogene L. Moyer. 2nd ed. Prospect Heights, Ill.: Waveland.

———. 1994. "Outsider within" the station house: The impact of race and gender on black women police. *Social Problems* 41:383–400.

———. 1995. The interactive effects of race and sex on women police officers. In *The criminal justice system and women: Offenders, victims, and workers,* ed. Barbara Raffel Price and Natalie J.Sokoloff, 383–97. New York: McGraw-Hill.

Martin, Susan E., and Nancy C. Jurik. 1996. *Doing justice, doing gender: Women in criminal justice occupations.* Newbury Park, Calif.: Sage.

Messerschmidt, James. 1993. *Masculinities and crime: Critique and reconceptualization of theory.* Lanham, Md.: Rowman and Littlefield.

———. 1997. *Crime as structured action: Gender, race, class, and crime in the making.* Thousand Oaks, Calif.: Sage.

Meers, Eric. 1998. Good cop, gay cop. *The Advocate* 3 (March):26–33.

Messner, Michael A. 1992. *Power at play: Sports and the problem of masculinity.* Boston: Beacon Press.

Meyer, Kristen, Kay B. Forest, and Susan L. Miller. 2004. "Officer Friendly" and "Tough Cops": Gay and lesbian police officers. *Journal of Homosexuality* 47 (1):17–37.

Miller, Susan L. 1999. *Gender and community policing: Walking the talk.* Boston, Mass.: Northeastern University Press.

Milton, Catherine. 1972. *Women in policing.* Washington, D.C.: Police Foundation.

Morash, M., and J. Greene. 1986. Evaluating women on patrol: A critique of contemporary wisdom. *Evaluation Review* 10:230–55.

Oberweis, Trish, and Michael Musheno. 1999. Policing identities: Cop decisionmaking and the constitution of citizens. *Law and Social Inquiry* 24(4):897–923.

Omi, M., and H. Winant. 1994. *Racial formation in the United States: From the 1960s to the 1990s.* 2nd ed. N.Y.: Routledge.

Pharr, Suzanne. 1988. *Homophobia: A weapon of sexism.* Little Rock, Ark.: Chardon.

Pike, Diane L. 1991. Women in police academy training: Some aspects of organizational response. In *The changing roles of women in the criminal justice system: Offenders, victims, and professionals,* ed. Imogene Moyer, 261–80. 2nd ed. Prospect Heights, Ill.: Waveland.

Powers, Bob. 1996. The impact of gay, lesbian, and bisexual workplace issues on productivity. *Journal of Gay and Lesbian Social Services* 4(4): 79–90.

Remmington, Patricia W. 1981. *Policing: The occupation and the introduction of female officers.* Washington, D.C.: University Press of America.

Renzetti, Claire M. 1992. *Violent betrayal: Partner abuse in lesbian relationships.* Newbury Park, Calif.: Sage.

Reskin, Barbara, and Patricia Roos. 1990. *Job queues, gender queues: Explaining women's inroads into male occupations.* Philadelphia: Temple University Press.

Rich, Adrienne. 1980. Compulsory heterosexuality and lesbian existence. *Signs* 5:631–60.

Rosabal, Gina S. 1996. Multicultural existence in the workplace: Including how I thrive as a Latina lesbian feminist. *Journal of Gay and Lesbian Social Services* 4(4):17–28.

Schneider, Beth E. 1986. Coming out at work: Bridging the private/public gap. *Work and Occupations* 13:463–87.

———. 1988. Invisible and independent: Lesbians' experiences in the workplace. In *Women working,* ed. A. Stromberg and S. Harkess, 273–96. Palo Alto, Calif.: Mayfield Publishing.

Schulz, D. M. 1995. From social worker to crime fighter: Women in United States municipal policing. New York: Praeger.

Shilts, Randy. 1980. Gay police. *Police Magazine* (January): 32–33.

Skolnick, Jerome H. 1994. *Justice without trial: Law enforcement in democratic society.* 3rd. ed. New York: Macmillan.

Smith, George W. 1988. Policing the gay community: An inquiry into textually-mediated social relations. *International Journal of the Sociology of Law* 16(2): 163–83.

Taylor, Verta, and Nicole C. Raeburn. 1995. Identity politics as high-risk activism: Career consequences for lesbians, gay, and bisexual sociologists. *Social Problems* 42(2): 252–73.

Weeks, Jeffrey. 1991. *Against nature: Essays on history, sexuality, and identity.* London: Rivers Oram Press.

Wells, J. W. and W. B. Kline. 1986. Self-disclosure of homosexual orientation. *Journal of Social Psychology* 127:191–97.

West, Candace, and Don H. Zimmerman. 1987. Doing gender. *Gender and Society* 1:125–51.

West, C., and S. Fenstermaker. 1993. Power, in-equality and the accomplishment of gender: An ethnomethodological view. In *Theory on gender/feminism,* ed. by P. England. New York: Aldine.

———. 1995. Doing difference. *Gender and Society* 9:8–37.

Williams, Christine. 1989. Gender differences at work: Women and men in nontraditional occupations. Berkeley: University of California Press.

Wilson, Nanci K. 1982. Women in the criminal justice professions: An analysis of status conflict. In *Judge, lawyer, victim, thief,* ed. Nicole H. Rafter and Elizabeth A. Stanko, 359–74. Stoughton, Mass.: Northeastern University Press.

Woods, James. 1993. *The corporate closet: The professional lives of gay men in America.* New York: Free Press.

Zimmer, Lynn. 1987. How women reshape the prison guard role. *Gender and Society* 1(4): 415–31.

———. 1988. Tokenism and women in the workplace: The limits of gender neutral theory. *Social Problems* 35:64–77.

Chapter 11   Dana M. Britton and Andrea L. Button

"This Isn't about Us"

Benefits of dog training programs in a women's prison

My first experience was with a dog that I had had for about nine months, and she was graduating as a guide dog. . . . And up until then I think I wondered. You know that you're doing a good thing, and you know that you're giving somebody their independence back . . . but then we went to a graduation ceremony. It actually made it easier, because it put back into focus why we do this. Sitting through that graduation, watching dogs be placed with their people, it was like . . . this is why we leave with broken hearts. This is why we do this. This isn't about us.

— Kansas inmate dog trainer

By most accounts, rehabilitation is no longer a primary goal of the American criminal justice system. Prisons now focus on confinement, aiming to hold more and more prisoners for sentences that have grown increasingly lengthy. We now incarcerate more of our citizens, per capita, than any other nation in the world and the incarceration binge shows few signs of slowing. Taking all of this at face value, we might assume that the American public is increasingly willing to embrace "get tough" policies, that they see little hope for the reform of those caught up in an ever-widening net of social control. Yet even as anti-crime hysteria reaches its peak, we see evidence of contradictory trends. The American public, it appears, has not entirely given up on the promise of reform. Sixty-nine percent of Americans surveyed agree that we should decrease crime by "attacking the social and economic problems that lead to crime" compared with only 29 percent who believe that the solution is "more prisons, police and judges." (Gallup Organization 2003). And 72 percent believe that the criminal justice system "should try to rehabilitate criminals, not just punish them" (Pew Research Center for People and the Press 2003). Clearly the public's view of the correct balance between rehabilitation and punishment is more conflicted than a one-dimensional analysis might suggest.

Criminal justice policies reflect this ambivalence. "Supermax" prisons, in which inmates are locked down for twenty-three hours a day and where rehabilitation is definitely *not* on the agenda, are increasingly common. But at the same time we still find prison administrators who embrace initiatives like drug treatment, in-prison nurseries, and "restorative justice" programs in an effort to change the lives of prisoners. At least some prison officers also see their jobs as an avenue for creating change, as in the case of this officer in a women's prison, interviewed by Britton (2003): "What's interesting to me is working with the people I guess at the lowest part of their lives. And trying to somehow make things a little better or just be something positive in their lives." Though not all officers or administrators feel this way, again it is too simplistic to say that American prisons have given up the prospect of rehabilitation. More accurately, although we might say that a custody ethic is now in the ascendance, there is a reform discourse that coexists uneasily alongside it in the minds of the public and in the views and practices of those who manage the criminal justice system.

This chapter focuses on the issue of reform in the context of a type of prison program that has proliferated in recent years, one in which inmates train animals, usually dogs, that are eventually returned to the community as pets or as service animals. There are no comprehensive data on the existence of these programs, but anecdotal accounts tell us that they now operate in at least thirty-six U.S. states, Canada, Australia, New Zealand, and Italy. There has as yet been little systematic research on the benefits or disadvantages of these programs, however. Here we report the results of interviews with twenty women inmates who are involved in two different dog training programs in Kansas prisons. In particular, we examine the benefits that these women perceive they gain from their participation, as well as their understanding of the way their work affects the community.

Animal Training Programs in Correctional Settings

The study of human-animal interaction (HAI) is a fairly recent development and to date most research has been done with populations outside prison walls (Furst 2006). Even so, studies have now clearly established that interacting with animals can produce a wide array of physiological and psychological benefits. HAI has been shown to improve survival rates among cardiac and AIDS patients (Arkow 1998; Friedman et al. 1980; Friedman and Thomas 1995; Gorczyca, Fine, and Spain 2000; National Institutes of Health 1988); decrease blood pressure and cholesterol (Anderson, Reid, and Jennings, 1992); lower stress (Eddy, Hart, and Boltz 1988; Serpell 1991); increase mental activity among Alzheimer's patients (Batson et al. 1998; Edwards and Beck 2002); and play a beneficial role in child development (Filiatre, Millot, and Montanger 1983; Melson 2003).

There is evidence of animals being used in custodial institutions in the United States as early as 1919. During World War II, German prisoners in American POW camps adopted rabbits, crows, and even a bear cub (Koop 1988; Strimple 2003). The first formal animal therapy program in a U.S. prison began—by accident—in 1975, when patients at the Lima State Hospital in Ohio adopted an injured wild sparrow. Staff noticed an immediate change in the behavior of inmates on the ward and later approved an animal therapy program. After a yearlong study, they discovered that inmates on the ward with animals required 50 percent less medication and had reduced violence and fewer suicide attempts when compared with inmates on a similar ward who did not have access to animals (Furst 2006; Harkrader, Burke, and Owen 2004; Lee 1987).

The first modern program to use dogs in a prison setting began in 1981 at the Purdy Treatment Center for Women, in Gig Harbor, Washington. In this program women learned to train and groom dogs taken from a local animal shelter; the first trainer was a former inmate. As a result of the inmates' work many more dogs became adoptable and were hence saved from being euthanized; others were sent for advanced training to work as assistance animals. Administrators also noted immediate positive effects in the inmates, whom they perceived to become more cooperative and more willing to accept responsibility (Furst 2006; Hines 1998). At about the same time, yet another program paired shelter dogs with men inmates at a Virginia prison, who were then allowed to adopt the dogs on release. A study of this program (Moneymaker and Strimple 1991) found that men who participated had fewer disciplinary offenses and reported significantly less psychological stress (Furst 2006).

These early positive results undoubtedly fueled the recent growth of prison animal training programs. In the only comprehensive survey of prison administrators on this topic, Furst (2006) documents the existence of 159 separate programs; most have been established since 2000. There are at least seven distinct designs across the states, ranging from visitation, in which community members bring animals to prisons to socialize with the inmates, to wildlife rehabilitation, in which inmates care for wounded animals that are eventually returned to the wild. The most common design is the community service or "second chance" model, in which shelter dogs are socialized and trained by inmates and then made available for adoption by community members. The second-most common model involves inmates in the early socialization and/or training of assistance dogs (Furst 2006). Both of these latter designs are operating at the prisons we studied.

Administrators have clearly been attracted to these programs by their potential for producing change in inmates and in institutional climates. There are pragmatic financial reasons as well; in a time of tight state budgets and declining institutional resources such programs are appealing because they are relatively inexpensive and promise to achieve the elusive administrative goal of keeping inmates busy. Most prison animal programs involve a connection with a nonprofit agency that provides the animals and/or trains the inmates and also rely on donations of food, medical attention, and supplies from local humane societies or from companies like Science Diet, Iams, and WalMart (Furst 2006). In some states inmates volunteer their labor; in others the only cost to the state is the standard rate for inmate work—in Kansas this amounts to between $0.45 and $1.05 per day. Administrators are also attracted to such programs by their potential to improve community relations. Seeing inmates interacting with animals and giving back to the community by saving the lives of dogs who would otherwise be euthanized or providing service animals for the disabled may serve as a powerful counterweight to the prevailing stereotypes of criminals as irredeemable monsters deserving of the harshest possible punishment. In an age in which the public is increasingly isolated from prisoners and the prisons that hold them, this may be one of the few such opportunities available.

The Current Study: Context and Methods

In this chapter we focus on the potential of prison animal training programs to produce change, drawing on interviews we conducted with thirty-eight inmates in Kansas prisons. Though the larger project involves interviews with both men and women inmates, here we focus on the twenty women we interviewed. We do so partly as a way of highlighting gender-based inequalities in the American prison system. As others have amply documented, women now make up a rapidly increasing part of the American prison population. Though still only 7 percent of the total, the rate of increase in women's incarceration has recently been dramatic and rapid; women's incarceration rate increased 300 percent between 1984 and 2004 (from a rate of 16 per 100,000 to a rate of 64 per 100,000), twice the 150 percent rate of increase for men (from 370 to 920 per 100,000) (Harrison and Beck 2006).

Women inmates, and women's prisons, have always been afterthoughts in a correctional system designed primarily for men, however. When women began to be housed separately from men in early American prisons, they were often held in basements, attics, or cellars; even the scant disciplinary and rehabilitative regimens designed for men were not imposed on the women convicts, who instead sewed and mended for men inmates and prison staff (Britton 2003;

Rafter 1990). Though women are now housed in separate institutions, these facilities continue to be low priorities for correctional officials. Programs available to women often draw on gendered stereotypes, with work assignments more likely to involve sewing or clerical tasks. In many states women inmates have in fact filed lawsuits in order to gain access to the same training and work opportunities available to men inmates. In a continuation of this pattern, though the modern model for inmate animal training programs arguably began in a women's prison, women today have less access to such programs than men (Furst 2006). It thus seems worthwhile to examine the effects of dog training programs in a women's institution as a way of exploring the specific benefits that accrue to women from their participation.

In Kansas, animal training programs currently exist in six of the eight state prisons, including the state's only prison for women. This institution actually operates two programs. Inmates classified as medium or maximum custody are eligible for the "blue ribbon" dog program, in which animals from a local shelter slated to be euthanized are sent to the prison for obedience training. If the dogs pass an obedience test given by a local trainer, they are placed on a "do not destroy" list and returned to the Humane Society for adoption. Almost all eventually find homes. Training dogs is the sole prison work assignment for these women, and they receive the standard inmate pay rate. Those in minimum security provide service dog training in a partnership with Kansas Specialty Dog Services (KSDS). All of the women who train these dogs have jobs in the community or inside the institution, and the training is done on a volunteer basis during nonwork hours. Both programs are almost entirely supported by volunteers in the community and private and corporate donations.

During the summer of 2005 we conducted formal interviews with twenty inmate participants and two staff members at the state women's prison and spoke informally to a number of other administrators and staff. We interviewed staff and inmates on-site at the facility. These interviews took the form of semistructured conversations; with the permission of our respondents we recorded these interviews and transcribed them verbatim for analysis. Analysis of the data was accomplished by reading over the transcripts multiple times to identify recurring themes. We coded these themes with the assistance of a qualitative data analysis program (NUD*IST 6, QSR International). In this chapter we focus on those themes that emerged from the data that invoke the notions of personal change, institutional change, and the notion of giving back to the community.

Personal Changes

Many inmates who participate in the program report that they have been profoundly changed by the experience. Part of this comes from the difference the dogs make in women's day-to-day existence. Adjustment to life in prison is always difficult; women are separated from friends, family, and loved ones, and the geographic isolation of most women's prisons means that women are often housed at much greater distances from their families than men. The result is loneliness and, for many women, depression. Just as in the world outside prison walls, however, interacting with dogs seems to help to mediate the stresses of prison life. This is certainly true for these program participants:

I had dogs and horses on the outside, but here they give me the love and comfort to make it through this time. When I came in, I was taking antidepressants, and the more I worked with the dog that first year, I just started backing off. They give us so much more than we give them. I feel it in my heart.

. . .

And have you had somebody that really sort of turned themselves around because they wanted to do this? Yeah, several young kids . . . even older people. Like, this one lady, she just came from the mental health pod over there, and she's really, really gotten herself together. She was diagnosed as schizophrenic, but the dog . . . she loves it. Her parents are finally starting to come see her again, they're really so proud of her with the dog and stuff.

This evidence is only anecdotal, but it certainly supports other research that has found the presence of animals can relieve depression and lessen the use of psychotropic drugs (Lee 1987). The second case is an especially dramatic example. This effect alone could be particularly valuable in the prison context, in which women are three times as likely to be prescribed such drugs as men (Beck and Maruschak 2001).

Although some of this effect is undoubtedly the result of the unconditional love the animals provide, it probably also derives in part from the fact that caring for an animal imposes routines and schedules. For many women, the dogs literally force them to interact with the outside world. Their experiences bear this out:

I think that sometimes with these women who are depressed or what they call bipolar, if you've got a dog, you've got that responsibility, and there's no way . . . the dog still has to go to the bathroom, you still have to get up and go to training, you still have to take the dog to play, which gets you outside, when some of these women just want to lay in bed. I think it's positive in that way, I've seen that happen, and I think that's real positive.

. . .

How do you think this place would have been for you without [this program]? It would be a lot more cold, dismal. . . . There are days when . . . it's what I call the "jailhouse blues" days . . . where you just don't want to get up. But when you have a dog, you don't have a choice, and it makes you get going [starts crying]. That's what helps to save you, to keep you going.

This woman was not the only inmate to talk about the dog program in terms of having been "saved" by it or of its having helped her to deal with depression. Interestingly, though men we interviewed also spoke of emotional changes they experienced, almost all talked about the ways the dogs helped them to deal with their anger, or taught them patience. This may well speak to a gendered effect of human-animal interaction; at the very least it suggests that men and women speak of their experiences in gendered terms.

Institutional Changes

The second way women perceive that the program creates changes is at the level of the institution itself. Dogs have the effect of "normalizing" the prison environment. As one staff member puts it, having the dogs in the institution "makes it less of a sterile environment, and more of an actual human environment." This observation is mirrored by program participants: "You feel a little bit more normal. . . . it's like when you come home and your dog's all happy to see you. . . . For me, it's . . . and [for] a lot of people, it's a settling down thing. When we bring the dog into the alcove where everybody's sitting, and we let them go . . . they go from person to person to get love. Stressful things can be going on and a dog can kind of smooth those over, at least for awhile, and maybe make things a little less volatile, when they do resume." Although many might object that prisons are not intended to be "normal" environments, no administrator or officer wants to work in a setting in which verbal and physical altercations are commonplace. This observation is not unique to the women's institution we studied; both men and women speak of the dogs as calming prison environments.

Part of this calming effect is probably a result of the social control exerted by the program. Inmates who participate in the dog training program must have attained "level three" status in the prison's behavioral hierarchy. This is the most privileged level an inmate can reach; doing so takes at least eight months of good behavior. As this woman observes, the prospect of losing the dog is a powerful disincentive to misbehavior: "Now we're getting a lot [of people in the program] . . .young kids . . . you'd be amazed. We get them working with the dog, and it gives them something to work for. Because if you lose your level, or if you get in trouble, you lose your dog. You have to be a level three, and you can't get in trouble. If you do, you lose your dog, everything. And really a lot of people behave for it, especially a lot of young kids, because they don't want to lose their dogs." We did indeed hear many women speak with considerable trepidation about the prospect of losing their dogs owing to a disciplinary infraction. From an administrative perspective, participation in the program is a clearly a powerful carrot that helps to encourage good behavior.

There is evidence that this effect extends even to inmates who are not dog handlers. Though some inmates do not like dogs or want to be in close quarters with them, according to the women we interviewed, the vast majority do. Though there were only five dogs being trained at the women's prison when we were there, sixty-seven women participate in the "Pooches and Pals" club that supports the dog program. These women carry out fundraisers and support the program in indirect ways; most will never become dog handlers. As this woman observes:

It's an incentive. . . . At some point I would say that the majority of the women here want some kind of interaction with the dogs. Pooches and Pals has a lot of members, it's not just the dog teams. There are people that do poop detail, and they don't even have a dog! That to me is very amazing [all laugh]. We have a sheet, a poop sheet, that you have to fill in your name, and on that day you go around to all the containers, and you empty them out and you take them to the trash. A lot of them, that's their only interaction with the dogs, other than playing with them once in a while.

In this way the calming effect of the dog program can extend more broadly to the institution as a whole, by providing incentives for good behavior among those who enjoy the presence of the dogs. This was true in the men's institution we studied as well; a staff member there told us that entire housing units became attached to "their" dogs.

Another way dogs change the institution is by improving relationships between staff members and inmates. As much research (Britton 2003; Kauffman 1988) has demonstrated, prison culture is often characterized by a sort of "us versus them" mentality, one in which neither officers or inmates trust each other. Yet we also know that social control in the prison could not be accomplished without a certain amount of verbal give and take between staff and inmates—normative social control in the prison is literally the product of a negotiated order. The inmates to whom we spoke see the dogs as a sort of bridge between the mutually antagonistic beliefs of officers and inmates. This woman notes the ability of the dog to change the context of interactions: "The dogs are kind of a mediator between staff and inmates. They build rapport between the staff. They're just more open to you, 'cause they talk to the dog. . . . it's kind of like when you have your kids . . . people might talk to you more . . . they're a conversation piece."

A staff member echoes this sentiment. Her perceptions of the benefits of the program are worth quoting at length:

I like the relationship that it helps build between the staff and the inmates. We have many staff-friendly dog people, and I really like the fact that there is something that we can talk about other than rules, parole plans, stuff like that. That really, I think, bridges a gap. There's a common variable there, it's no longer just an inmate and a staff [member], there's a dog there. [Officers will say] "Hey, let me pet the dog," and there's that bonding. One of the officers, he's real strict for the rules, and if you cross him, you're going to get addressed. But, when it comes to dealing with dogs, he might get the dog and walk it around the perimeter, and he's got a uniform on, [but he's] trying to help the inmates out. So, there's something that wouldn't happen if it wasn't for the dog, pretty strict officers going above and beyond with an inmate. The inmates watch him, they think, "Well, this guy ain't so bad, he's willing to do that."

As this staff member's comments indicate, the effect of the dogs' presence works both ways, softening an officer's otherwise authoritarian stance and at the same time altering inmates' perceptions of him. The dogs apparently create a sort of neutral ground between staff and inmates, becoming a "conversation piece" that facilitates interaction. We heard of several staff members at this particular prison who had in fact adopted animals raised there (at least one officer had adopted two). Though certainly the "us versus them" atmosphere in this prison has not magically disappeared, there is little doubt that the presence of the dogs has helped many women to relate better to the staff, as well as vice versa. A former administrator at this prison, responsible for having started the dog program, was in fact the subject of genuinely affectionate comments by several of the women inmates who remembered her.

Giving Back

The most common theme in our interviews invokes the notion of giving back to the community. Seventeen of the twenty-two women we interviewed mentioned this as an important benefit of their participation of the program (the same was true of the majority of the men we interviewed). For women in the "blue ribbon" program, in which shelter dogs are trained and then put up for adoption, the primary mechanism for giving back to the community comes from helping dogs that would otherwise undoubtedly be euthanized:

My opinion is that this is the best job to have while you're here, 'cause you just love something that loves you back. And, I know that it benefits the dogs, 'cause they'll come where they're not eating, they're very skittish . . . some of them are very standoffish . . . and you just gradually, as weeks go by, just see them really flourish into a wonderful dog. My understanding is that they get adopted pretty quickly when they go back to the shelter, so I'm sure that it saves a lot of dogs' lives. . . .Some of these dogs, you can tell the ones that have been abused, and it's wonderful to see them come out of that. We had one little dog down there, that little dog would just pee all over everything when you would come close to it . . . and now she's just all happy to see everybody. I don't think she even remembers the time of being scared like that.

It is in fact the case that these dogs have an extremely high adoption rate; we heard stories from program staff of people literally waiting in line to adopt dogs trained at the facility. This account also hints at another potential benefit of the program that may be particularly powerful in women's prisons. Women in prison are much more likely than men to have been physically or sexually abused. Though none of the women we interviewed made this connection explicitly, it seems logical that working with abused animals could give these women one way to begin to work through such issues in their own lives.

It is the women training assistance dogs for whom the connection to the community is most powerful, however. These inmates train dogs who pull wheelchairs, serve as "bracing" dogs for those with mobility problems, work as therapy animals, and do a wide array of other jobs for people with disabilities. For these inmates the connection to the community is particularly salient. As these women observe:

With one of my service dogs, I got to meet the lady, and it was very emotional. We became pen pals, and she visits me regularly now, and I see [the dog] working. I don't think I've ever been so humbled, or a part of something that makes you feel so human. Because when you come here, sometimes it feels not human. You feel very desensitized. These guys make you feel human, and working for those people makes you feel like you're giving them something.

. . .

I think that there is nothing more wonderful in a prison system, then to have people understand what this means to us, and what it means to the people. We give them a whole other way of living once they get a dog. What we have done is to give them everything that we can, so that they can give them such a better life when they leave here, and a better quality of life, too.

The dog the first woman trained works with a woman who has multiple sclerosis and is in a wheelchair much of the time. Through their work in the program both of these inmates now see themselves as contributing to their communities in a tangible way. As another woman puts it: "I feel like I'm utilizing my time and not warehousing it, you know?" This opportunity for meaningful work is rarely offered by prison labor, much of which involves institutional maintenance or other "make work" tasks. Such jobs may be particularly common in women's prisons (Britton 2003), whose smaller populations mean that they are rarely economies of scale in the same way that men's institutions are.

As this woman's comment indicates, however, the provision of feedback is important if women are to understand their contributions. This may be understandably difficult to accomplish for prison inmates. At the men's institution we studied, this occurs through a regular graduation ceremony in the prison itself, in which inmate trainers and recipients of the dogs meet face to face (Britton and Button 2006). There is no such ritual in the women's prison, though some women in the program have been able to leave the prison to attend ceremonies off site. This is always a powerful experience, as this account illustrates:

The first graduation I went to [sighs, begins to cry], there will never be a place that I will go, and be in a room with so many people that did not care that I was an inmate, and that appreciated me for everything that I had done. There was not a person in there that did not come up and hug you, that didn't tell you what a good job you did, that they appreciate everything that you do. One graduation a girl came up to me . . . and she said that every time she looked into her dog's beautiful brown eyes, she knew that she had somebody to go on this journey with her [crying]. Until the girl got [the dog] she hadn't been walking, she had been using a wheelchair that whole time—and she walked up the aisle during the graduation. To see those kinds of things, no matter what I go through here, whether it's a staff person fussing with me about the dog, or an inmate or whatever, it makes it all worthwhile.

All of the inmates—men and women—we interviewed who had been to graduation ceremonies spoke of them in this way. Unlike the men, the women we interviewed are less likely to attend graduations, owing to the fact that the ceremonies are held off-site and state budget cuts have reduced the number of staff available to take women outside the institution. This is unfortunate, because participation in graduations is a win-win proposition. The inmates benefit by feeling appreciation for their work and seeing its tangible results. Yet there is also a gain here for community members, who in this day and age have precious few opportunities to interact with inmates in a positive context. This lack undoubtedly helps to make the walls between prison and the "free world" so impermeable, even for inmates released from captivity.

Conclusion

The weight of the evidence now makes it clear that interacting with animals has a wide variety of positive effects on our physical and mental health. There is little reason to think that such benefits would not extend to those who live behind prison walls. As our interviews demonstrate, dog programs have the potential to improve the lives of individual inmates by decreasing stress and perhaps even reducing the severity of mental illness. They "normalize" institutional environments and lower barriers between inmates and staff, and perhaps most important, provide prison inmates a tangible way to give back to their communities. Communities themselves also gain by receiving dogs adoptable as pets or useful as service animals—all for little to no investment of public funds.

Such programs also have the potential to cause problems in institutions of course. In the men's prison we heard an account of at least one fight having broken out because an inmate had been accused of abusing a dog by "overcorrecting" him (pulling too hard on his leash to correct his behavior). In still another instance a dog was used to bring contraband into the prison, and authorities responded by barring dogs from the visiting room.[1] Neither of these occurred at the women's prison. It is also possible that dogs could be abused, though our educated guess is that this occurrence is less likely in prison, where dog trainers are watched around the clock by staff and other inmates, than in the "free world." It is probably the case that dog training programs impose no more than the usual adjustment difficulties that go with any new prison program, and institutions will develop new rules as necessary to deal with these.

One final difficulty may be created by community members, some of whom will undoubtedly resist any attempt to improve the lives of prison inmates. In fact, a newspaper article in a Kansas paper about the women's prison dog program did elicit an angry letter from a family member of a crime victim who was outraged that convicted criminals are able to train dogs and benefit from doing so. This same objection could be made against any prison program, however. As we note at the outset, such resistance should not be taken solely at face value. The American people are clearly conflicted about the prospect of rehabilitation, with "get tough" sentiments coexisting with an ethic that admits the possibility of reform. Programs like the one we studied offer one promising mechanism through which this potential might be realized. The changes it fosters ultimately go both ways, however, as this woman inmate realizes. We give her the last word: "It's not going to be hard to [give this dog up], because I knew when I got him what this was for. I have been preparing for it this whole time, for him to go. I know the kind of dog that he is. He is going to give somebody . . . freedom from themselves. I know that sounds kind of weird, but we're locked up inside a fence, those people are locked up in their own bodies. I am glad that I can give them some freedom to live."

Discussion Questions

1. Evidence demonstrates interaction with animals can improve the physical, emotional, and mental lives of individuals. Should animal training programs become available in more correctional settings? Why or why not?
2. In what ways might such programs produce change in their participants? Do these benefits extend outside the institutions? Does what you have read here convince you that these programs make a difference? For whom?
3. State budgets are increasingly tight, and funding priorities always require that if some program receives additional funds, others will lose. Though these programs are generally *not* supported by state funds, do they seem a worthwhile investment of public money?

4. Prisons are some of the most deeply gendered organizations in American society. Do you see evidence here that prison dog programs might have different effects in men's versus women's institutions? Is there any reason to believe they might benefit women more than men (or vice versa)? What inequalities between men's and women's prisons do you find in this chapter?
5. If you were a prison administrator, how would you defend the existence of these programs? Imagine you were confronted with an angry letter like the one described above. How might you respond?

Acknowledgments

The authors would like to thank Keven Pellant and Linda Hull-Viera for their assistance in facilitating this project, and though we cannot do so by name, we also offer our sincere gratitude to the women we interviewed.

Note

1. Yet another potential institutional problem emerged in February 2006, when an inmate in a Kansas men's prison who participated in a dog training program was smuggled out of the prison in a dog crate by the administrator of that program. The administrator and the inmate were captured after a short time; both are now in prison. Though this escape perhaps testifies to the ingenuity of inmates who would prefer to be elsewhere, it does not imply that these programs pose more of an institutional risk than any other. The warden of the prison where this escape took place has in fact expressed his continuing commitment to its dog training program.

References

Anderson, William P., Christopher M. Reid, and G. L. Jennings. 1992. Pet ownership and risk factors for cardiovascular disease. *Medical Journal of Australia* 157:298–301.

Arkow, Phil. 1998. *Pet therapy: A study and resource guide for the use of companion animals in selected therapies.* 8th ed. Colorado Springs: The Humane Society of the Pikes Peak Region.

Batson, Kathryn, Barbara McCabe, Mara Baun, and Carol Wilson. 1998. The effect of a therapy dog on socialization and physiological indicators of stress in persons diagnosed with Alzheimer's disease. In Cindy Wilson and Dennis Turner, eds., *Companion animals in human health,* 203–15. Thousand Oaks, Calif.: Sage.

Beck, Allen J., and Laura M. Maruschak. 2001. Mental health treatment in state prisons, 2000. *Bureau of Justice Statistics*. U.S. Department of Justice. http://www.ojp.usdoj .gov/bjs/pub/pdf/mhtsp00.pdf. Accessed June 19, 2006.

Britton, Dana M. 2003. *At work in the iron cage: The prison as gendered organization*. New York: New York University Press.

Britton, Dana M., and Andrea L. Button. 2006. Prison pups: Assessing the effects of dog training programs in correctional facilities. *Journal of Family Social Work*. 9(4):79–95.

Chesney-Lind, Meda. 1996. Sentencing women to prison: Equality without justice. In Martin D. Schwartz and Dragan Milovanovic, eds., *Race, class and gender in criminology: The intersection*. New York: Garland Press.

Eddy, J., L. Hart, and R. P. Boltz. 1988. The effects of service dogs on social acknowledgements of people in wheelchairs. *Journal of Psychology* 122:39–44.

Edwards, N. E. and A. M. Beck. 2002. Animal-assisted therapy and nutrition in Alzheimer's disease. *Western Journal of Nursing Research* 24(6): 697–712.

Filiatre, J. C., J. L. Millot, and H. Montagner. 1983. New findings on communication behaviour between the young child and his pet dog. In *The human-pet relationship: International symposium on the occasion of the 80th birthday of Nobel prize winner Prof. Dr. Konrad Lorenz*, 50–57. Vienna: Institute for Interdisciplinary Research on the Human-Pet Relationship.

Friedman, E., A. H. Katcher, J. J. Lynch, and S. A. Thomas. 1980. Animal companions and one-year survival of patients after discharge from a coronary care unit. *Public Health Reports* 95: 307–12.

Friedman, E., and S. A. Thomas. 1995. Pet ownership, social support, and one-year survival after acute myocardial infarction in the cardiac arrhythmia suppression trial (CAST). *American Journal of Cardiology* 76: 1213–17.

Furst, Gennifer. 2006. Prison-based animal programs: A national survey. *Prison Journal* 86: 407–30.

Gallup Organization. 2003. The Gallup poll. *http://www.albany.edu/sourcebook/pdf/ t228.pdf*. Accessed June 19, 2006.

Gorczyca, K., A. Fine, and C. Spain. 2000. History, theory, and development of human-animal support services for people with AIDS and other chronic/terminal illnesses. In Aubrey Fine, ed., *Handbook on animal-assisted therapy: Theoretical foundations and guidelines for practice*, 253–302. San Diego: Academic Press.

Harkrader, Todd, Tod W. Burke, and Stephen S. Owen. 2004. Pound puppies: The rehabilitative uses of dogs in a correctional facility. *Corrections Today* 66:74–79.

Harrison, Paige M., and Allen J. Beck. 2006. Prison and jail inmates at midyear 2005. U.S. Department of Justice, Bureau of Justice Statistics. http://www.ojp.usdoj.gov/ bjs/pub/pdf/pjim05.pdf. Accessed June 16, 2006.

Hines, Linda M. 1998. Overview of animals in correctional facilities. In Delta Society, ed., *Animals in institutions*. Renton, Wash.: Delta Society.

Kauffman, Kelsey. 1988. *Prison officers and their world*. Cambridge, Mass.: Harvard University Press.

Koop, Allen V. 1988. *Stark decency: German prisoners of war in a New England village*. Hanover, N.H.: University Press of New England.

Lee, D. 1987. Companion animals in institutions. In Phil Arkow, ed., *The loving bond: Companion animals in the helping professions,* 23–46. Saratoga, Calif.: R & E Publishing.

Melson, Gail F. 2003. Child development and the human-companion animal bond. *American Behavioral Scientist* 47:31–39.

Moneymaker, James M., and Earl Strimple. 1991. Animals and inmates: A sharing companionship behind bars. *Journal of Offender Rehabilitation* 16:133–52.

National Institutes of Health. 1988. *Health benefits of pets: Summary of working group.* Washington, D.C.: U.S. Department of Health and Human Services.

Pew Research Center for People and the Press. 2003. The 2004 political landscape: Evenly divided and increasingly polarized. *http://*www.albany.edu/sourcebook/pdf/t246.pdf. Accessed June 19, 2006.

Rafter, Nicole Hahn. 1990. *Partial justice: Women, prisons, and social control.* 2nd ed. New Brunswick, N.J.: Transaction Publishers.

Serpell, James. 1991. Beneficial effects of pet ownership on some aspects of human health and behaviour. *Journal of the Royal Society of Medicine* 84:717–20.

Strimple, Earl O. 2003. A history of prison inmate–animal interaction programs. *American Behavioral Scientist* 47(1): 70–78.

Criminal Justice, Gender, and Diversity

A Call for Passion and Public Criminology

Why should those thinking of working in the criminal justice system think about diversity? Because, simply put, "crime" has become an established code word for race in American political life. Likewise, "getting tough on crime" has come to mean placing more and more African Americans and other people of color, both female and male, in prison—creating what some have called a "new apartheid" in the United States (Davis, Estes, and Schiraldi 1996). Correctional supervision, especially detention and imprisonment, seems increasingly to have replaced other historic systems of racial control (slavery, Jim Crow laws, ghettoization) as ways of keeping women and men of color in their "place" (Schiraldi, Kuyper, and Hewitt 1996).

Although this might sound extreme, consider the evidence. Over the past three decades, the United States has launched a social policy some call "mass incarceration," and the impact of this new penalism is clearly racialized. Roughly one out of three African American men between the ages of twenty and twenty-nine are under some form of correctional supervision, and one in eight were in either jail or prison in 2004 (Mauer 2005: 1). African American men now stand a 32 percent chance of spending some time in prison, and Latinos are increasingly likely to be criminalized as well, standing a 17 percent chance of serving time in prison (Mauer 2005: 1).

In a related trend, some of us (Bloom, Chesney-Lind, and Owen 1994) have noted that the war on drugs has also become an undeclared war on women. The overall number of women in prison in the United States has quintupled since 1980—a trend explained largely by the implementation of gender blind, "get tough" policies on drug and other offenders. This new national zeal for imprisoning women has taken a special toll on women of color. Current data show that African American women account for "almost half (48 percent)" of all the women we incarcerate (Johnson 2003: 34). Mauer and Huling's earlier research adds an important perspective here. They noted that the imprisonment of African American women for drug offenses grew by more than 828 percent between 1986 and 1991, while that of white women grew by 241 percent, Hispanic women by 328 percent, and black men by 429 percent (Mauer and Huling 1995).

More than a century ago, W.E.B. DuBois saw clearly how the prison system reinforced other systems of racial control and oppression. Commenting on the dismal failure of "reconstruction," he concluded: "Despite compromise, war, and struggle, the Negro is not free. In well-nigh the whole rural South the black farmers are peons, bound by law and custom to an economic slavery from which the only escape is death or the penitentiary" (cited in Johnson 2003: 284). DuBois's comments are prescient, as race, gender, poverty, prison, and death actually feature prominently in this volume, which explores exactly how these three factors are intimately involved in the current criminal justice system.

As the articles in this volume stress, those who work within the criminal justice system, as researchers, as practitioners, and as teachers owe a special obligation to speak the truth about the effects of current crime policies. We also have a responsibility to chart the way forward for a country that has the dubious distinction of having the world's highest incarceration rate (Mauer 2005: 1), as well as being one of the only developed nations to still rely on what is coming to be seen as an increasingly aberrant and disturbing death penalty (Amnesty International 2007).

A specific focus on diversity is vital if the US criminal justice system is to regain its legitimacy. This will not be easy, because it must be understood that the current conservative takeover of American political life owes much to the racist framing of the "crime problem" and "criminals" (see Chesney-Lind 2006). This likely began with Barry Goldwater's 1964 unsuccessful presidential campaign, which repeatedly used phrases like "civil disorder" and "violence in the streets" in a "covertly racist campaign" to attack the civil rights movement (Chambliss 1999: 14). Both Richard Nixon and Ronald Reagan refined the approach as the crime problem became a centerpiece of the Republican party's efforts to wrest electoral control of southern states away from the Democratic party. Nixon's emphasis on "law and order" and Reagan's "war on drugs" where both built on "white fear of black street crime" (Chambliss 1999: 19).

Over time, crime policy became a staple in the Republican attacks on Democratic rivals. When Reagan's former vice-president, George Bush, Sr., ran for office, he successfully used the Willie Horton incident (where an African American man on a prison furlough raped and murdered a woman) in his decisive defeat of Michael Dukakis in 1988 (Chambliss 1999). The Bush campaign also made much of the fact that Dukakis opposed the death penalty, even in the case of someone who had "raped and murdered his wife." This question, raised in the second debate was a crucial moment in the 1988 campaign, and Bush used it to effectively label Dukakis as a "liberal" (CNN 2000: 1).

Bill Clinton, a Democrat, learned the lesson well. No Republican was going to "out-tough" him on crime. While running for president in 1992, then-Governor Clinton interrupted his New Hampshire campaign to return to Arkansas and preside over the execution of Rickey Ray Rector, a black man sentenced to death by an all-white jury for killing a police officer. After the shooting, Rector tried to commit suicide but succeeded only in inflicting serious brain damage on himself, thereby becoming so mentally retarded he did not understand he was being executed. In fact, he saved a piece of pie from his last meal because he thought he was coming back to his cell (Sherrill 2000: 1). Clinton's presidency established a sad precedent for succeeding waves of Democratic politicians; simply mimic the Republican strategy of toughness on crime or risk political suicide.

That said, the Republican ownership of the crime issue is indisputable. In fact, George W. Bush would gain the presidency as a direct result of backlash criminal justice policies, because felony disenfranchisement of largely African American voters in Florida was crucial to his political strategy in that state (Lantigua, 2001). In his second election campaign, though, another feature would be added to the Republican mix: an appeal to "moral values." Included in the "moral values" agenda, designed to attract right-wing Christians, is the rolling back of the gains of the women's movement of the last century, including the recriminalization of abortion and the denial of civil rights to gay and lesbian Americans. Bush's nominee to the Supreme Court, John Roberts, has even questioned "whether encouraging homemakers to become lawyers contributes to the public good" (Goldstein, Smith, and Becker 2005). This provides even more reason to consider meanings of diversity beyond race: including gender and sexual orientation, topics that also received attention in this volume.

The consequences of conservative framing of the crime problem are irrefutable and painful to those of us who actually deal with its very real consequences, including as has been noted, a very racialized mass incarceration. As many scholars have remarked, the increased reliance on what is often called "law and order" strategies to control crime and delinquency run deep within the American culture, economy (Garland 2001), and its race relations, and, in fact, rest within the larger shift in the United States from a "welfare state" to a "penal state" (Wacquant 2001). Along with this shift, of course, comes public attitudes about the crime issue and criminals that reinforce prison as a viable "solution" to the many social problems associated with this nation's long struggle with racial justice and income inequality.

Needless to say, many of us have grown up in this conservative political environment, and because of this fail to see any alternatives to the crime problem beyond more reliance on punishment and prisons. This generalization is partic-ularly true of those drawn to criminal justice majors. Consider the figures that Jo Belknap and Hillary Potter reported: that the criminal justice students at five universities and colleges scored a 33.2 on a scale measuring "empathy" (com-pared with 51.7 for majors in other fields); this was described as "remarkably low" by the researchers who gathered the data. They went on to say that the criminal justice students were "more punitive in their attitudes toward crime, criminals, and the criminal justice system" (Courtright, Mackey, and Packard 2005: 140).

This book has suggested that we thoughtfully consider how to talk with and ultimately teach these students who, after all, will *be* the criminal justice system of the new millennia. We have three tasks, according to Susan Miller, who pulled this work together: we need to help students to appreciate the role of "research" in our field, we have to talk to them about our actual colleagues in the field (not the pasteboard caricatures seen on television and in the mo-vies), and then we have to talk to them about the kinds of issues and situations they will confront doing the work they hope to do. Finally, I share Belknap and Potter's hope that we can imbue our students with a "passion" for justice, not punishment.

Talking about "research" increasingly involves a thoughtful consideration of how one "does" research. For many authors in this volume, this means en-gaging in a set of questions about epistemology (the theory of knowledge) used by the researcher, an awareness that the researcher and her/his characteristics affect the gathering of knowledge, as well as the choice of methodology. Femi-nist researchers like Shana Maier and Brian Monahan approach the research experience with a keen eye toward feminist epistemological and methodologi-cal issues. All are aware that particularly in the area of criminal justice, one must negotiate across vast differences in terms of race, class, gender, and sex-ual orientation. Being thoughtful about how one focuses on "being real" and "listening" allows one to negotiate across divides that seem impossibly huge. Yet, that is just what one must do, not only to do "research" about crime and the criminal justice system, but more important, if one is to work effectively in the system.

This is very definitely seen in the accounts of those who now work in the system. Consider the voices of Daniel Atkins and Eliza Patten whose conversa-tion we get to listen in on. Both discuss the bone-deep exhaustion that is asso-ciated with "lawyering for the poor." In a moment of incredible candor, Atkins likens his work to "being drafted into a professional sports league minus the lu-crative bonuses." Elsewhere he muses that "in more than fifteen years I had yet to lift a single client out of poverty." His colleague Eliza discusses the ways in which she connects with her clients, often in gendered ways, because she, a mother, can so easily connect with their challenges; this is a clear example of what both call "affective lawyering" which, in contrast to "instrumental law-yering" focuses on client empowerment and rapport building rather than the in-strumental approach that "rations" resources, narrows the scope of representa-tion, and focuses on "controlling" the lawyer-client relationship and on "winning." As they both note, they feel that while affective lawyering takes time, it also improves the chance of winning; moreover, it makes it far easier to establish a trusting relationship with a client who is, they believe, rightly dis-trustful of the "system."

The role of poverty in the lives of those we work with in the criminal justice system also comes out in two other essays that consider the death penalty. Jill McCorkel opens her essay with an eloquent statement from a young man whom she was trying to help avoid the death penalty. He talked about his life being "filled with such violence" that the shooting he engaged in was almost inevitable. In her moving account of her work with Abdullah Tanzil Hameen, she explains that initially she never thought of her work as part of her academic criminology; it was "strictly activist" in content, after all. Gradually, though, through readings of current sociologists, like Michael Burawoy, who presses sociologists to consider a "public sociology" that "aims to enrich public debate about moral and political issues by infusing them with sociological theory and research" (Burawoy 2004: 1603), McCorkel realized that her work needed to be documented and disseminated.

McCorkel decided that "sociologists have every reason to put themselves on the front lines of legal and political battles *especially* when the stakes are life and death." In her work with Hameen, she sought to help him prepare a narra-tive that could be presented to the Delaware Pardons Board. She clearly en-gaged the project with a passion, and in her work with Hameen we all travel from a narrative that constructs him as a cold-blooded killer to a young man ex-tremely fearful of being killed and who, in the hyperviolent world of drug deal-ing, misread a particular situation with tragic consequences. Like soldiers in a battle zone, such "mistakes" happen, and it is clear to us all reading his words, that Hameen found himself in the criminal equivalent of a free-fire zone. This is not to excuse the murder, but it is to put it in an important context that we can all understand. After that voyage, hardest of all was to read the words, "Abdul-lah Tanzil Hameen was executed on May 25, 2001."

Another perspective, and one decidedly less grim, is provided by two re-searchers, Saundra Westervelt and Kimberly Cook, who share thoughts about their work with those who *have* been exonerated from the death penalty. They note that this is not an insubstantial sum: since 1973, more than 122 men and one woman have been exonerated "based on substantial evidence of their ac-tual innocence." They were able to engage in conversations with sixteen of these individuals about the challenges they faced coming out of such an ex-tremely stressful and horrific circumstance. Here, again, the role of poverty in our system of criminal justice rears its ugly head, as we hear of defense attorneys who come to court so drunk they "threw up in the judge's chambers." We hear of a woman so horrifically scared after being condemned to death that she mistakes the date of her execution, and then we hear the stories of others exiting from such a hellhole only to discover that many people still regarded them as guilty, despite having been exonerated. How do they survive not only the "frightful trauma" and the death of many of their dreams? Said Delbert Tibbs, one of those exonerated, "you have to make medicine out of poison."

Westervelt and Cook also think carefully about the role of their feminist research methods in their work with men, noting that their attention to the "ethic of care" extended to their relationship with each other as well as their relationships with the exonerees. They stay in touch, they continue to have affection and concern for those they interviewed, and they attend celebrations.

The importance of being resilient and relying on feminist as well as conventional insights also comes out quite powerfully in Susan Caringella and Drew Humphries's account of working in the academy. They offer important information about the challenges as well as the opportunities afforded those who seek an academic life, and do a fine job of laying out the often hidden realities of the choice. One of the issues they touch on illuminates the ways in which a job that appears so attractive in a number of respects has hidden pitfalls, particularly for women and people of color (see Chesney-Lind, Okamoto, and Irwin 2006).

Take parenthood: when men become academics, they do not face the often painful childrearing and childbearing choices that women confront. Mason and Golden examined the childbearing patterns of individuals who received their doctorates between 1978 and 1984 and continued working in academia. They found that "overall, male professors were much more likely to marry and have a family than female professors. Only 44 percent of all the tenured women in the study were married and had children within 12 years of earning their Ph.D.'s. But 70 percent of tenured men married and became fathers during that time period" (Mason and Golden, cited in Wilson 2003). Why? To those of us who know the academy, the answer is crystal clear, and it is a decidedly feminist issue—the academic career, complete with its lengthy training period and tenuring process, is a decidedly male-model career (one that assumes a wife to assist with the heavy burdens of family life). Apparently, few males want to sign up for this role, so it is academic women, not men, who face the Hobson's choice between career and children. This is about gender and work, but the pressures are worse in academia than in other workplaces (Wilson 2003).

What about other challenges facing women who must contend with not only gender bias but also racism? Decidedly upbeat despite the challenging work they face are the insights provided by Angela Moore Parmley and Jocelyn Fontaine. As African American women they have faced daunting challenges attending graduate school, and then working in a system that, as noted earlier, criminalizes so many of their race. Their response is to vigorously encourage the participation of African Americans in the criminal justice system so as to challenge the racism within that system as well as the racism that often characterizes the research literature in criminology. Here they cite an academic literature (Young and Sutton 1991) that contends that the contribution of African American criminologists is often systematically ignored, reminding us again that even in the "market place of ideas" solid research can be systematically marginalized while other work is celebrated.

How can we know this? Bowker (1988) did us all a terrific favor in his paper titled "Publishing Feminist Research: A Personal Note from Lee Bowker." Bowker, whose publications number in the hundreds, made his name in many areas of criminology. But when he began doing work on wife abuse, he suddenly noticed problems with the peer-review process that had never dogged him previously. In a table, he noted that when he submitted nonfeminist articles and book manuscripts, his acceptance rate was 85 percent. However, when he submitted what he labeled "feminist" publications, his acceptance rate fell to 54 percent. In reviews of his feminist work, he further noted that he was assumed to be female, and his work was generally rejected for poor methodology. He quipped, "From my experience with gatekeeper journals, I think I have found the answer to the question, 'What is the correct methodology for carrying out feminist research?' It is 'Whatever methodology you didn't use.'" (Bowker 1988: 171). He even caught one editor shopping for a negative review through a slip-up in the editor's communication with him.

Speaking of feminist men, Walter DeKeseredy's biographical essay on his intellectual and political evolution as a criminologist reminds us that dealing with male violence against women is a project to which men bring a special responsibility as well as keen insights derived from having been raised as a man. Given his own history of having been raised by a mother who had been gang raped, as well as his own experience of having been bullied as a boy, he was well aware of the problem of male violence. These experiences directed him to seek out the sources of this male violence *in men*.

As he notes, given the clear research evidence that whereas studies of the characteristics of "victimized" women is largely fruitless, a focus on the characteristics of men who are violent has identified "key risk factors such as men's adherence to the ideology of familial patriarchy (e.g., male domination and control in intimate settings)." Walter's work has repeatedly exemplified the important perspectives that progressive men can bring to the issue of crime and justice; moreover, his intellectual voyage also exemplifies the role that critical criminology has increasingly played in supporting and nurturing scholars who focus on intersectionality and diversity.

Walter talked about his efforts to "escape" the "man box," but that is clearly not on the minds of all men. In fact, hegemonic masculinity is precisely what makes the lives of lesbian or gay police officers so difficult in a field that has come to epitomize hypermasculinity. Documenting that "gay bashing" is often seen as a way to firmly establish heterosexual status, Susan Miller, Kay Forest, and Nancy Jurik, the authors of the chapter on "Diversity in Blue," then chronicle the stress on those gay and lesbian officers who are "out" in the force, as well as the pain suffered by those who feel that they cannot tell their coworkers of their sexual orientation. The article focuses on the tensions between these two groups, but it also documents increasing "progress" in a midwestern department that is working to end discrimination against gays and lesbians, particularly the fact that these officers will bring new flexibility to the character of policing because of their own experiences of marginalization and discrimination.

Another woman facing a daunting and challenging task, that of serving as a probation officer in a sex offender supervision unit, Michelle Meloy, noted that it is very important that professional women be involved in crafting responses to male sexual violence. Her challenge, every day when she was in probation, was to "use my skills to prevent these men from victimizing anybody else."

The final chapter in the volume takes a look at the prison proper, but instead of the grim accounting of the pains of imprisonment that the readers of most articles on prison life might be led to expect, Dana Britton and Andrea Button take us in a quite different direction. Focusing on the benefits of a dog training program in a women's prison, Britton and Button document the dramatic impact of bringing dogs into the prison environment, both in the inmates as well as the staff of the prison. Noting that the American public is actually considerably less punitive than our elected leaders, the authors then take a look at this innovative prison program as an example of "restorative" justice, or a program that seeks to reform prison inmates rather than just punishing them. The authors note that there are at least thirty-six states that currently use inmates to train animals, usually dogs, to be returned to the community either as pets or service animals.

Having established the popularity of these programs, the authors then explore the surprising impacts that this work brings to an institution that embraces the program. Notably, the institution sees an immediate, and dramatic drop in the medication required by inmates in the program (50 percent), as many were taking these to deal with loneliness and depression. Dogs, especially dogs with a history of abuse, also help the women, many of whom have their own abuse trauma, to deal with and heal from their painful histories. Finally, the dogs serve as a bridge between the staff and the inmates, breaking down barriers and also normalizing prison life. In this study, in fact, the authors found the staff adopting the dogs the inmates worked with on a number of occasions. Said one woman in the program, "I'm utilizing my time, not warehousing it."

If America is to get past its own love affair with what one author has, in fact, called the "warehouse prison" (Irwin 2005), we need to find a way to talk about the realities, and the costs (both financial and opportunity costs) of the current incarceration binge. First, we have to recognize that today's college students, and particularly those in criminal justice programs, many of whom are from working-class backgrounds, are paying for the prison boom by paying higher tuition (and taking on larger and larger student loans) than was the case in years past (Hickey 2002). In fact, in most states, the money to fund corrections, the fastest-growing item in state budgets, came directly out of higher education (because lower-education and social welfare are often seen as fixed costs) (Gangi, Shiraldi, and Zeidenberg 1998). Second, we need to encourage those working in the actual system as either academics or practitioners to engage in the type of research and publishing that powerfully document the realities of the current system as well as challenging the media hype around crime that tends to fuel the punitive approach to crime prevention and intervention.

To do this, we need to get beyond the traditional way of doing criminology, as the articles in this book ably demonstrate. Specifically, we have to query our field's traditional bias toward quantitative methods. While I am a great fan of quantitative data, when they are simply presented and appropriate to the subject at hand, more sophisticated methods are generally not accessible to even able and engaged policymakers. Moreover, in my view, these methods are often "overkill" for the quality of the data used. Finally, they encourage us to stay off the streets, in front of our computers, doing what John Hagedorn has called "courthouse criminology" (Hagedorn 1990: 244) or worse. To change people's minds about crime will require that we do more than run regressions. We need to tell them, in simple terms, what incarceration is costing them, and we need to reach their hearts as well as their pocketbooks. Here, qualitative methods of the sort used in this book will get us the data we need. We also need to broaden the definition of "research" and "publishing" to include the sort of public sociology or perhaps public criminology (Flavin 2006) that speaks to broader public audiences.

Those of us who work or hope to in the field of criminal justice and criminology have a huge job ahead of us. We must challenge the crime myths that are played out in the media every day. We must find a way to oppose a policy of criminalizing poverty, and we must name the racism, and sexism, that informs current popular thinking about crime and victimization. We must document the economic consequences of the war on crime that will further bankrupt the United Stats economy, already drained from the mindless spending on the Cold War of previous decades. Finally, we must shamelessly seek arenas to talk sense about crime—in our own communities, as well as across the country.

As to how we should go about such work, I am reminded of one of my favorite Bertold Brecht quotes, which ably captures the sort of work we should be doing. "One must have the courage to write the truth when the truth is everywhere opposed; the keenness to recognize it, although it is everywhere concealed; the skill to manipulate it as a weapon; the judgment to select in whose hands it will be effective; and the cunning to spread the truth among such persons" (Brecht 1996). Fortunately, this is not impossible, and the works collected here document that quite powerfully.

References

Amnesty International 2007. United States of America: The experiment that failed. A Reflection of 30 Years of Executions. *AMR*. http://web.amnesty.org/library/Index/ENGAMs10112007. Accessed January 16, 2007.

Bloom, Barbara, Meda Chesney-Lind, and Barbara Owen. 1994. *Women in Prison in California: Hidden Victims of the War on Drugs*. San Francisco: Center on Juvenile and Criminal Justice.

Brecht, Bertolt. 1996. *Galileo*. Edited and with an introduction by Eric Bentley. English translation by Charles Laughton. New York, NY: Grove Press.

Bowker, L. 1988. "On the relationahip between wife beating and child abuse." In *Feminist perspectives on wife abuse*, ed. K. Yllo and M. Bograd, 158–75. Thousand Oaks, Calif.: Sage.

Burawoy, Michael. 2004. "Public Sociologies: Contradictions, Dilemmas and Possibilities." *Social Forces* 82(4) (June): 1603–18.

Chambliss, W. 1999. *Power, Politics and Crime*. Boulder, Colo.: Westview Press.

Chesney-Lind, Meda. 2006. "Patriarchy, Crime and Justice: Feminist Criminology in an Era of Backlash. *Feminist Criminology* 1(1): 6–26.

Chesney-Lind, Meda, Scott Okamoto, and Katherine Irwin. 2006. "Thoughts on Feminist Mentoring: Experiences of Faculty Members from Two Generations in the Academy." *Critical Criminology* 14:1–21.

CNN.com. 2000. "1988 Presidential Debates." Debate History. http://www.cnn.com/ELECTION/2000/debates/history.story/1988.html.

Courtright, K. E., D. A. Mackey, and S. H. Packard. 2005. "Empathy among College Students and Criminal Justice Majors." *Journal of Criminal Justice Education* 16 (1):125-44.

Davis, Christopher, Richard Estes, and Vincent Schiraldi. 1996. *"Three Strikes": The New Apartheid*. San Francisco: Center on Juvenile and Criminal Justice.

Donziger, Steven, ed. 1996. *The Real War on Crime*. New York: Harper Perennial.

Flavin, Jeanne. 2006. "Public Criminology: How Do We Publish While Others Perish." *DivisoNews*. (ASC Division on Women and Crime) 22:000.

Gangi, Robert, Vincent Schiraldi, and Jason Zeidenberg. 1998. *New York State of Mind? Higher Education vs. Prison Funding in the Empire State, 1988–1998*. Washington D.C.: Justice Policy Institute.

Garland, David. 2001. *The Culture of Control: Crime and Social Order in Contemporary Society*. Chicago: University of Chicago Press.

Goldstein, A., J. Smith, and J. Becker. 2005. "Roberts Resisted Women's Rights." *Washington Post,* August 19.

Hagedorn, John. 1990. "Back in the Field Again: Gang Research in the Nineties." In Ron Huff, ed., *Gangs in America.* 2nd ed., 240–59. Newbury Park, Calif.: Sage.

Hickey, Jenni. 2002. "Breaking the Bank to Go to College." Insight on the News. *News and Society.* September 9.

Irwin, John. 2005. *The Warehouse Prison: Disposal of the New Dangerous Class.* Los Angeles: Roxbury.

Johnson, Paula C. 2003. *Inner Lives: Voices of African American Women in Prison.* New York: New York University Press.

Lantigua, J. 2001. "How the GOP Gamed the System in Florida." *Nation,* April 30, 1–8.

Mauer, Marc. 2005. "Facts about Prisoners and Prison." *Sentencing Project* (October).

Mauer, Marc, and Tracy Huling. 1995. *Young Black Americans and the Criminal Justice System: Five Years Later.* Washington, D.C.: Sentencing Project.

Schiraldi, Vincent, Sue Kuyper, and Sharon Hewitt. 1996. *Young African Americans and the Criminal Justice System in California: Five Years Later.* San Francisco: Center on Juvenile and Criminal Justice.

Sherrill, Robert. 2001. "Death Trip: The American Way of Execution." *Nation,* January 8. http://www.thenation.com/doc/20010108/sherrill.

Wacquant, Loic. 2001. "Deadly Symbiosis: When Ghetto and Prison Meet and Mesh." *Punishment and Society* 3:95–134.

Wilson, R. 2003. "How Babies Alter Careers for Academics." *Chronicle of Higher Education.* http://chronicle.com/weekly/v50/i15/15a00101.htm. December 5.

Young, V., and A. T. Sulton. 1991. Excluded: The Current Status of African-American Scholars in the Field of Criminology and Justice. *Journal of Research in Crime and Delinquency* 28:101–16.

Contributors' Biographies

Daniel Atkins is a lawyer with Community Legal Aid Society, Inc. ("CLASI"), a nonprofit law firm in Delaware that represents people who are poor, disabled, or elderly. Dan serves as both co-deputy director for CLASI, and as legal advocacy director for CLASI's Disabilities Law Program. He is also an adjunct professor at Widener University School of Law, where he teaches courses in poverty law and disability law. Dan has been a public interest lawyer for sixteen years.

Joanne Belknap received a Ph.D. in criminal justice and criminology from Michigan State University in 1986. She is a professor of sociology and women and gender studies at the University of Colorado. Belknap has numerous scholarly publications, most of which involve female offenders and violence against women and girls. She recently published the third edition of her book *The Invisible Woman: Gender, Crime, and Justice* in 2007. She has also secured almost a million dollars in grant money to conduct research on women, girls, and crime (as a principal or coprincipal investigator). Recent and forthcoming empirical publications are about college campus fraternity rapes, the court processing of woman battering cases, delinquent girls transferred to adult court, a gender comparison of delinquent girls' and boys' trauma histories, and focus groups with delinquent girls and those who work with them in Ohio and Colorado. She has served on state advisory boards for female offenders and women in prison, on U.S. Attorney General Janet Reno's Violence against Women Committee, and gave expert testimony to the Christopher Commission investigating the Rodney King police brutality incident in Los Angeles. Belknap is the recipient of the 1997 Distinguished Scholar of the Division on Women and Crime national award of the American Society of Criminology and won the Student-Nominated University of Colorado Teaching Award in 2001 for her class "Violence against Women and Girls." She is a former chair of the Division on Women and Crime of the American Society of Criminology. Finally, Belknap is the 2004 recipient of the Boulder Faculty Assembly Teaching Award, the most prestigious teaching award at the University of Colorado, and the 2004 Inconvenient Woman Award from the American Society of Criminology for speaking out on behalf of college women reporting rapes by football players.

Dana M. Britton is associate professor of sociology at Kansas State University. Her research interests are in the areas of gender, work, social control, and social history. She is the author of *At Work in the Iron Cage: The Prison as*

Gendered Organization (2003) and is the current editor of the journal *Gender and Society.*

Andrea L. Button is a graduate student in sociology at Kansas State University. Her research interests include gender, social control, religion, and social movements. She is currently working on her thesis, which focuses on mechanisms of control and resistance in prison dog training programs.

Susan Caringella is a professor in the department of sociology, in the department of gender, and in the department of women's studies program at Western Michigan University. Her work has been recognized with national, state, and university honors, such as the American Society of Criminology's Division on Women and Crime Senior Scholar Award, and the Division on Critical Criminology (where she was founding chair) Lifetime Achievement Award. She is deputy editor for the *Journal of Women and Criminal Justice* and on the editorial boards of the *Journal of Violence against Women, Feminist Criminology,* and Lexington's series on critical criminology. Her most recent book, *Addressing Rape in Law and Practice,* is forthcoming from Columbia University Press.

Meda Chesney-Lind is professor of women's studies at the University of Hawaii at Manoa. Nationally recognized for her work on women and crime, her books include *Girls, Delinquency and Juvenile Justice* (1992); *The Female Offender: Girls, Women and Crime* (2004); *Female Gangs in America; Invisible Punishment* (1999); and *Girls, Women and Crime* (2004).

Kimberly J. Cook is professor of sociology and chair of the department of sociology and criminal justice at the University of North Carolina, Wilmington. Cook earned her Ph.D. in sociology from the University of New Hampshire and has conducted research on abortion, capital punishment, shelter services for battered women, and restorative justice. Her publications include *Divided Passions: Public Opinions on Abortion and the Death Penalty* (1998), "Doing Difference and Accountability in Restorative Justice Conferences" in *Theoretical Criminology* (2006); and (with Denise Donnelly, Debra Van Ausdale, and Lara Foley) "White Privilege, Color Blindness and Services to Battered Women," in *Violence against Women* (2005).

Walter S. DeKeseredy is professor of criminology, justice, and policy studies at the University of Ontario Institute of Technology. Included in the *Canadian Who's Who* (published by University of Toronto Press), DeKeseredy has published more than sixty refereed journal articles and scores of book chapters on woman abuse, crime in public housing, and criminological theory. He is also the author of *Woman Abuse in Dating Relationships: The Role of*

Male Peer Support (1988) and *Women, Crime and the Canadian Criminal Justice System* (2000); with Barbara Perry, coeditor of *Advancing Critical Criminology: Theory and Application* (2006); with Ron Hinch, coauthor of *Woman Abuse: Sociological Perspectives* (1991); with Desmond Ellis, coauthor of the second edition of *The Wrong Stuff: An Introduction to the Sociological Study of Deviance* (1996); with Martin Schwartz, coauthor of *Contemporary Criminology, Sexual Assault on the College Campus: The Role of Male Peer Support* (1996), and *Woman Abuse on Campus: Results from the Canadian National Survey* (1998); with Linda MacLeod, *Woman Abuse: A Sociological Story* (1997); with Shahid Alvi and Desmond Ellis, *Contemporary Social Problems in North American Society* (2000); with Shahid Alvi, Martin Schwartz, and E. Andreas Tomaszewski, *Under Siege: Poverty and Crime in a Public Housing Community* (2003); and with Desmond Ellis and Shahid Alvi, *Deviance and Crime: Theory, Research and Policy* (2005). In 2004, he jointly (with Martin D. Schwartz) received the Distinguished Scholar Award from the American Society of Criminology's (ASC) Division on Women and Crime, and in 1995, he received the Critical Criminologist of the Year Award from the ASC's Division on Critical Criminology. In 1993, he received Carleton University's Research Achievement Award. Funded by the National Institute of Justice, DeKeseredy is currently writing papers and coauthoring a book for Rutgers University Press based on his exploratory study of sexual assault during and after separation/divorce in three rural Ohio communities. DeKeseredy is also the recent corecipient of a Social Science and Humanities Research Council of Canada grant to study hate crime on a Canadian university campus.

Jocelyn Fontaine is a Ph.D. student in American University's department of justice, law, and society. She is a research assistant at the National Institute of Justice, working in the Violence and Victimization Research Division on projects related to violence against women and female criminality. Her other research interests include racial residential segregation, police legitimacy, and criminal justice policy, generally. She received her master of science degree in justice, law, and society from American University and her bachelor of arts degree in sociology from Villanova University.

Kay B. Forest is associate professor and chair of the department of sociology at Northern Illinois University. Her areas of teaching and research include gender and sexuality studies, family diversity, and stress and coping processes. She is currently exploring the effects of civil war, natural disaster, and dislocation on poor women and their families in Sri Lanka.

Drew Humphries is professor of criminology and founder of the graduate program in criminal justice at Rutgers University–Camden in New Jersey. With an all-female faculty, Humphries likes to say, "We hire on merit." She received her doctorate of criminology from the University of California, Berkeley, where she was one of the founding editors of *Crime and Social Justice* and was involved in the early development of radical and feminist criminology. She has published on topics ranging from the political economy of crime, critical criminology, and sentence reform, to legislative changes in the areas of abortion and birth control. Her more recent scholarship focuses on women, feminism, and critical theory as exemplified in *Crack Mothers: Women, Pregnancy and the Media* (1999) and *Women, Violence, and the Media* (2008), coedited with Susan Caringella, longtime friend and collaborator. Humphries's contributions have been recognized in a number of ways, but she is especially honored to have received the Distinguished Scholar Award from Division of Women and Crime of the American Society of Criminology. She has also served in leadership roles in the American Society of Criminology, the Society for the Study of Social Problems, and the American Sociological Association. Throughout her career, she has remained politically active, especially with prison rights organizations, which includes current work with the families of men and women incarcerated as a result of the war on drugs.

Nancy C. Jurik is professor and director of graduate programs in the School of Justice and Social Inquiry at Arizona State University. She teaches courses on women and work, entrepreneurialism and society, and economic justice. Her publications focus on gender, work organizations, economic development, and small business. She has published *Bootstrap Dreams: U.S. Microenterprise Development in an Era of Welfare Reform* (2005); *Doing Justice, Doing Gender: Women in Legal and Criminal Justice Occupations,* 2nd ed. (2006), and numerous articles on gender and work issues. She is a past-president of the Society for the Study of Social Problems.

Shana L. Maier, B.S. in criminal justice, Saint Joseph's University; M.S. in criminal justice, Saint Joseph's University; and Ph.D. in sociology, University of Delaware, is an assistant professor in the department of criminal justice at Widener University, Chester, Pennsylvania. Her research interests include violence against women, the treatment of victims by the criminal justice and legal systems, the transformation of rape crisis centers, and the experiences and struggles of rape advocates. Maier has published articles appearing in *Violence against Women, International Review of Victimology,* and *Women's Health and Urban Life.* She recently coauthored a book chapter, "Women on the Bench: The Voices and Experiences of Female Judges," in Claire M. Renzetti, Lynne Goodstein, and Susan L. Miller, eds., *Rethinking Gender, Crime, and Justice* (2006). Maier is a member of the American Society of Criminology and the Society for the Study of Social Problems.

Jill McCorkel is assistant professor of sociology at Villanova University. Her research examines recent changes to the structure of punishment in women's prisons, as well as the collateral consequences of mass incarceration for impoverished urban neighborhoods. Her research on these topics has appeared in numerous scholarly journals and edited collections, and her book on women's prisons, *Unruly Subjects: Gender, Punishment, and the Self,* is forthcoming.

Michelle L. Meloy is an assistant professor in the department of sociology, anthropology, and criminal justice at Rutgers University–Camden. She received her Ph.D. in criminology from the University of Delaware. She is the author of *Sex Crimes and the Men Who Commit Them* (2006) and numerous other works on sexual violence and gender and crime. Her research areas include intimate partner violence, sex crimes and offenders, victimology and victim's issues, and criminal justice policy.

Susan L. Miller received her Ph.D. in criminology from the University of Maryland and is professor in the department of sociology and criminal justice at the University of Delaware. Her research examines gender and criminal justice policy issues, victimology, and intimate partner violence. Her books include *Crime Control and Women: Feminist Implications of Criminal Justice Policy* (1998); *Gender and Community Policing: Walking the Talk* (1999); *Victims as Offenders: The Paradox of Women's Violence in Relationships* (2005); and several other coauthored books. Her current research explores restorative justice practices for victims of severe violence.

Brian A. Monahan, B.A. in criminal justice, Radford University; M.S. in sociology, Virginia Commonwealth University; Ph.D. in sociology, University of Delaware is assistant professor in the department of sociology at Iowa State University. His areas of interest include criminology, deviance, and social problems. Monahan's current research explores how certain categories of offenders initiate, organize, and carry out their offenses. A secondary area of research interest is the role of the media in constructing meanings about crime, social problems, and other social issues. Monahan is the coauthor of articles appearing in the *Journal of Contemporary Ethnography* and the *FBI Law Enforcement Bulletin.* He is a member of the American Sociological Society, the Midwest Sociological Society, and American Society of Criminology, and the Society for the Study of Social Problems.

Angela Moore Parmley is chief of the Violence and Victimization Research Division, Office of Research and Evaluation, National Institute of Justice (NIJ), U.S. Department of Justice. She oversees cooperative agreements, grants, contracts, demonstration projects, and intramural research in the areas of domestic and sexual violence, child maltreatment, elder abuse, situational crime prevention, victimization, and crime and justice regarding American Indians and Alaska Natives. She also directs NIJ's Violence against Women and Family Violence Research and Evaluation Program, located within the division. In addition to her supervisory functions, Moore Parmley conducts research in the areas of domestic/intimate partner violence, intimate partner homicide, and police response to domestic violence. She is also an adjunct faculty member at the University of Maryland, University College. Prior to joining NIJ, Moore Parmley taught at the University of Maryland, College Park, and worked in human resources at the Federal Bureau of Prisons in New York City. She received her Ph.D. in criminology from the University of Maryland and her B.S. and M.P.A. degrees from Pennsylvania State University.

Eliza Patten graduated from New York University School of Law in 2001 and then worked for three and a half years at CLASI, first as a Skadden Fellow and then as a staff attorney, representing clients in dependency and neglect proceedings and working at the state level to reform the foster-care system. Eliza previously worked with Susan L. Miller and Dan Atkins on a law review article, "Striving for Justice with the Violence against Women Act and Civil Tort Actions," published in the *Wisconsin Women's Law Journal,* and then published a law review article of her own, "The Subordination of Subsidized Guardianship in Child Welfare Proceedings," in the *New York University Review of Law and Social Change.* More recently, Eliza spent a year teaching legal research and writing at Stanford Law School. She now resides in Berkeley, California, with her husband and two children.

Hillary Potter is assistant professor of sociology at the University of Colorado. Her research centers on racial, ethnic, gendered, and classed issues as they relate to crime causation, the commission of crime, and the crime-processing system. Some of the research projects she has recently conducted have focused on domestic violence, capital punishment, and Hurricane Katrina. Dr. Potter is the author of the forthcoming book *Battle Cries: Understanding and Confronting Intimate Partner Abuse against African American Women* and the editor of the forthcoming book *Racing the Storm: Racial Implications and Lessons Learned from Hurricane Katrina.*

Claire M. Renzetti is professor of sociology at the University of Dayton. She is editor of the international, interdisciplinary journal *Violence against Women,* coeditor of the Interpersonal Violence book series for Oxford University Press, and editor of the Gender, Crime and Law book series for Northeastern University Press. She has authored or edited sixteen books, as well as numerous book chapters and articles in professional journals. Her current research focuses on the violent victimization experiences of economically marginalized women living in public housing developments. Renzetti has held elected and appointed positions on the governing bodies of several national professional organizations and is past-president of the Society for the Study of Social Problems.

Saundra D. Westervelt is associate professor of sociology at the University of North Carolina at Greensboro. Her early work examined the development of a new criminal defense strategy based on victimization, culminating in her first book, *Shifting the Blame: How Victimization Became a Criminal Defense* (1998). Since then, her work has focused on the wrongful conviction of the innocent. In 2001, she published *Wrongly Convicted: Perspectives on Failed Justice* (with John Humphrey), the first edited book in the United States to bring together original essays by the leading legal scholars and social scientists in the field. For three years, she and Kimberly Cook have been engaged in an examination of the consequences of a wrongful capital conviction for death row exonerees through in-depth personal interviews.